Research on the Education of Our Nation's Teachers

D1470710

Teacher Education Yearbook

Volume 5   *Founded 1991*

Editors

David M. Byrd, *University of Rhode Island*

D. John McIntyre, *Southern Illinois University at Carbondale*

Editorial Advisory Board

Research on the Education of Our Nation's Teachers

Teacher Education Yearbook V

Editors

David M. Byrd
D. John McIntyre

CORWIN PRESS, INC.
A Sage Publications Company
Thousand Oaks, California

For information, address to:

Corwin Press Inc.
2455 Teller Road
Thousand Oaks, California 91320
E-mail: order@corwin.sagepub.com

SAGE Publications Ltd.
6 Bonhill Street
London EC2A 4PU
United Kingdom

SAGE Publications India Pvt. Ltd.
M-32 Market
Greater Kailash I
New Delhi 110 048 India

Printed in the United States of America

Library of Congress Cataloging-in-Publication Data

ISSN: 1078-2265
ISBN: 0-8039-6512-5 (hardcover)
ISBN: 0-8039-6513-3 (paperback)

97 98 99 00 01 02 03 10 9 8 7 6 5 4 3 2 1

Editorial Assistant:	Kristen L. Green
Production Editor:	Diana Axelsen
Production Assistant:	Denise Santoyo
Typesetter/Designer:	Marion Warren
Indexer:	Mary Mortensen
Cover Designer:	Marcia R. Finlayson
Print Buyer:	Anna Chin

Contents

Foreword

Margaret Ishler

Margaret Ishler is chairperson of the Department of Curriculum and Instruction and President of the Association of Teacher Educators, 1996 to 1997.

Having been a teacher educator for the past 23 years, I view the topic of this book—The Education of Our Nation's Teachers—as vital to the welfare of our country. We teachers and teacher educators are a major force in shaping our country's destiny. The developing minds of our country are entrusted to us and, depending on our knowledge, pedagogical skills, and commitment, we help Americans learn citizenship and evolve as a democratic society. Therefore, examination of teacher education needs to be an ongoing critical, generative effort.

As president of the Association of Teacher Educators (ATE), I have sat through many meetings and attended many conferences where I heard speeches—some uplifting, some informative, some disturbing—about teacher education. The most disturbing occasions were those meetings in which teacher education was not mentioned during discussions that examined educational reform and direction. The omission of any reference to teacher education attested to the public's lack of understanding concerning teacher education's impact on the nation's teachers.

Equally disturbing are the negative voices you and I have heard in the media from education critics who influence the nation's legislators and public opinion concerning the irrelevancy of teacher education. As was discussed in the recent ATE report on *Quality Standards and Enhancement of Teacher Education* (Roth & Murphy, 1996), numerous national figures such as former Secretary of Education William Bennett; Lynne Chaney, former Chair of the National Endowment for the Humanities; and Michael Fullan have made statements to the effect that university-sponsored teacher education may be unnecessary. Even the National Board for Professional Teaching Standards does not identify formalized study in teacher education as necessary to national board certification.

Equally disturbing is the increasing competition between colleges and inservice agencies providing a narrow conception of teaching focused on practice in contrast to a more social, theoretical, intellectual approach that builds on the professional knowledge base. Nightmare tales are emerging about degree programs being offered within a time span of a few weeks or several months. These programs shortchange our teachers' preparations and knowledge base. These programs of lesser quality that ignore the theoretical, research, and pedagogical content dimensions of teachers' knowledge to provide "quick pedagogical fixes" for people who want to fill our nation's classrooms do a disservice to potential teachers and master's candidates. As teacher shortages continue to increase over the next five years, more and more people will be entering K to 12 classrooms without the professional education they need to meet the challenges of our classrooms.

This concern does not suggest that quality in teacher education is equivalent only to university-sponsored teacher education preparation. Credentialing of teachers through completion of undergraduate programs in teacher education does not guarantee quality. Quality alternative routes must continue to be developed that are built on the current knowledge base and identified needs of today and tomorrow's teachers.

This edition of the Teacher Education Yearbook examines teacher education through four focuses—content, process, curriculum, and communication. The authors present insightful perspectives based on their research and practice. I take the liberty here to share my views on teacher education organized around these four focuses. The four focus areas raise key questions:

1. Context: How does context influence teacher education?
2. Processes: What processes must be considered in the knowledge base of teachers?
3. Curriculum: What is the essential knowledge that should be included in all teacher education curriculum?
4. Communication: What are teachers saying through their voices developed by teacher education?

In response to these questions, I offer twelve recommendations for teacher education informed by my research, teaching experiences and professional activities through ATE and the National Council for the Accreditation of Teachers (NCATE):

Context Influences?

1. The rising tide of intolerance and of radical supremacist groups; the problems of crime, poverty, and isolation within our nation and our own communities; and the deterioration of our moral and civic fiber at all levels of modern life necessitate that teacher education emphasize the development of strong values. Teachers need to construct democratic classrooms and nurture democratic ideals of social justice, equity, community, responsibility, and respect for diversity. Teachers need to have a sense of striving to create the ideal community, while preparing students for democratic citizenship.

2. Another context to consider is the profession itself. Teacher education should build a sense of professionalism, of belonging to a vast group of more than 2.5 million teachers who influence our country's welfare. The teaching profession should encourage professional ethics and professional practice.

3. The changing demographics within our country is a context influence that necessitates our teachers learning how to incorporate a multicultural focus into the classroom

4. The context of teacher education itself presents problems and opportunities such as the university's reluctance to be a partner in teacher education while the professional development school model has most or all of teacher education school based. Although balance needs to be maintained to keep teacher education from returning to its former "normal school status," the education of teachers needs to be conducted largely in a school-based setting within a district that has undertaken systemic educational reform. Teacher education needs to be continued throughout the inservice years, especially through the induction years, with both the school and the university taking responsibility for the development of the teacher.

Process Knowledge for Teachers?

5. Important process knowledge is learning how to individualize instruction. Teacher education should help the teacher learn how to individualize instruction to meet the needs of the diverse learners in our classrooms, including students at risk, special needs students, gifted and talented students, and students from diverse cultural and linguistic backgrounds.

6. Teacher education needs to prepare teachers to use varied approaches to assessment and to build on the information gathered from assessment measures to further guide students' learning. Teachers need to learn the strengths and limitations of authentic assessment and the power of developing self-assessment in students.

7. Teacher education needs to prepare teachers to help students build their critical thinking skills. Debate and critical discussion need to be encouraged in the classrooms, along with problem solving. Teachers must be able to model critical thinking and informed decision making—essential skills for democratic living.

Teacher Education Curriculum?

8. Teacher education curriculum should be built on a professional knowledge base formed by theory, current research (see the second edition of the *Handbook of Research on Teacher Education;* Sikula, 1996), and pedagogy generic as well as related to content and the wisdom of practice.

9. Teacher education curriculum needs to encourage a solid preparation in general knowledge through liberal studies and later specialization in a subject area. Teachers needs a breadth of knowledge in many areas to integrate the curriculum and to enrich learning experiences beyond the requested curriculum.

10. Teacher education curriculum needs to include current information on learning, covering learning theories and cognitive science research in such areas as schematic theory, scaffolding, cognitive structuring, multiple intelligence, misconceptions, and expertise research. These theories and research need to be studied to see how they are influencing our understanding of the constructivist approach to learning.

Communication—Teacher Voices?

11. In the area of communication, teacher education should help teachers develop a sense of responsibility as advocates for children, for better schools, and for the maintenance of public education. John Goodlad stated in *Teachers for Our Nation's Schools* that it is the responsibility of teachers to exercise stewardship of the public schools and to teach in a nurturing way to connect with students' lives. Teachers need to be encouraged to take an advocacy role to keep before the public the plight of children in inferior schools. As fewer taxpayers have children of school age, the teaching force of the nation needs to advocate more strongly on behalf of children and public schools.

12. Building a sense of community participation through parent and business partnerships, and social service agencies' linkages is another important direction teacher education needs to instill in teachers. Through close communication with the community, teachers can build partnerships that are more responsive to community needs. This partnering should be present in the teacher education program as well.

These 12 recommendations that I see as essential for the education of our nation's teachers do not cover all the dimensions necessary for quality teacher education, but they do represent some key responses to questions raised by the four organizational areas of this book—context, processes, curriculum, and communication. These recommendations are already characteristics of many of our excellent teacher education programs throughout the country. The major message being conveyed here is that teachers need university-supported teacher education along with practice in the field. Our teachers are confronted with increasingly complex problems and need the professional knowledge base to aid their teaching. After all, our nation's children deserve the best education from the best prepared teachers in the field.

May the following chapters increase your understanding of needs and issues, and may we continue to work together in ATE for quality teacher education.

Introduction:
Educating Our Nation's Teachers

D. John McIntyre

David M. Byrd

D. John McIntyre is Professor and Director of Professional Education Experiences at Southern Illinois University at Carbondale. He is past president of the Association of Teacher Educators and has received ATE's award for Distinguished Research in Teacher Education. He has nearly 100 publications in the area of teacher education. He is a graduate of Otterbein College, the Ohio State University, and Syracuse University.

David M. Byrd is Associate Professor and Director of the Office of Teacher Education at the University of Rhode Island. He has a long-term professional and research interest in the preparation of teachers, preservice through inservice. He is a graduate of the doctoral program in teacher education at Syracuse University. He has authored or coauthored nearly 30 articles in professional journals.

One of the most recent goals added to the original Goals 2000 program focuses on the professional development of teachers. This addition supports the emerging view that educational reform and increased student learning are tightly linked to the continued professional development of teachers. Professional development, however, does not occur in a vacuum. We must ask ourselves, how does research inform our attempts to educate our future and current teaching force?

Sprinthall, Reiman, and Thies-Sprinthall (1996) stated that the elements for effective teacher development are seriously flawed. They point out that beginning teachers are expected to teach a full load, are often assigned the worst classes, and are observed infrequently by their building administrator. They cited a study by Griffin (1986) that identifies the elements for an effective teacher education program that spans preservice and inservice teachers. Griffin asserted that a program must be embedded in and sensitive to a school context, and be purposeful and articulated, participatory and collaborative, knowledge based, ongoing, developmental, and analytic and reflective.

Sprinthall, Reiman, and Thies-Sprinthall (1996) identified three broad models that have been used in the delivery of professional development programs. The *direct model* approach is, obviously, direct. In this model, a supervisor meets with a student teacher or practicing teacher and identifies the teacher's strengths and weaknesses, and then provides examples of how the teacher can improve his or her performance. The teacher is given very little opportunity to reflect on her or his performance or to develop strategies based on these reflections to improve his or her own practice.

Research supporting the effectiveness of this model is scarce. Feiman (1979), Zeichner (1983), and Richardson (1994) have criticized the direct model for not encouraging teachers to become more active and reflective in analyzing their own teacher behavior and for not being more active in developing strategies for modifying their classroom practice.

The *expert model* uses a core of knowledge and experience that expert teachers have garnered throughout their careers. This model forms the structure for many inservice programs, including short-term and long-term workshops. The premise for the model is that both novice and experienced teachers need expert advice to improve their classroom practice.

Researchers have complained that the expert model is often too prescriptive and singular in its approach to be effective. Stallings and Krasavage (1986) pointed out that, over time, there appears to be a gradual erosion of the effects of this model in practice. In too many situations, the expert presented his or her knowledge through a series of workshops but offered very little classroom follow-up to assist classroom teachers in implementing strategies.

The third model is the *interactive model*, which seeks to include the teacher as an active participant in the professional development process. Thus, a more collaborative approach to professional development is encouraged between the teacher and the teacher educator. In addition, the interactive model encourages the teachers to be reflective about their practice and their role in the profession.

Many collaborative professional development programs are in their infancy. Book (1996) discovered that these programs have been somewhat effective in encouraging teachers and teacher educators to examine their traditional roles and to forge a more collaborative role of teacher educator. Data are still lacking, however, regarding the success of these programs in preparing more effective teachers.

The purpose of this yearbook is to provide educators with research and guidelines for improving the education of preservice and inservice teachers. Although it is possible to see the various aforementioned professional development models within the various chapters, especially interactive models, it also important to note the emergence of multicultural education and diversity as a factor in the education of teachers. One fourth of the chapters in the yearbook focus on multicultural education and its role in educating teachers. Thus, it is clear that the changing demographics of our nation's classrooms must be considered in future programs.

The authors of this yearbook help inform us about current research on the education of our nation's teachers. We hope that the information within these chapters provokes insight and sparks debate about the current state of the continuum of professional development.

References

Book, C. (1996). Professional development schools. In J. Sikula (Ed.), *Handbook of research on teacher education* (2nd ed., pp. 194-212). New York: Macmillan.

Feiman, S. (1979). Technique and inquiry in teacher education: A curricular case study. *Curriculum Inquiry, 9*(1), 63-79.

Griffin, G. (1986). Clinical teacher education. In J. Hoffman & S. Edwards (Eds.), *Reality and reform in clinical teacher education* (pp. 1-24). New York: Random House.

Richardson, V. (1994). *Teacher change and staff development process: A case of reading instruction.* New York: Teacher College Press.

Sprinthall, N., Reiman, A., & Thies-Sprinthall, L. (1996). Teacher professional development. In J. Sikula (Ed.), *Handbook of research on teacher education* (2nd ed., pp. 666-703). New York: Macmillan.

Stallings, J., & Krasavage, E. (1986). Program improvement and student achievement in a four-year Madeline Hunter follow-through project. *Elementary School Journal, 87*(2), 117-138.

Zeichner, K. (1983). Alternative paradigms of teacher education. *Journal of Teacher Education, 34*(3), 3-9.

CONTEXT:
OVERVIEW AND FRAMEWORK

Thomas Weible

John E. White

Thomas Weible is Professor in the Department of Curriculum and Instruction at the University of Maryland at College Park and Director of the Office of School/ University Cooperative Programs, which facilitates partnerships between all colleges on the UMCP campus and Maryland's schools. His research and publications focus on teacher certification.

John E. White is Associate Professor of Education and Chair of the Austin Teacher Program of Austin College in Sherman, Texas. He spends much of his professional time working in school-university partnerships, and in developing authentic experience-based teacher education activities. He has held numerous leadership roles within ATE, including chairing the 1997 Annual Meeting.

Preparing individuals to meet the challenges and opportunities of tomorrow's classrooms presents a formidable task for teacher preparation programs. Our rapidly changing world will undoubtedly place demands on the teaching workforce that we have yet to anticipate. The knowledge explosion combined with ever-sophisticated technology will force teacher educators to continuously assess the quality of their programs and the effectiveness of the classroom teachers they produce. We are all aware of the reports, commissions, and collaborations of the past two decades that have proposed numerous recommendations for school reform and teacher preparation programs. Many of the approximately 1,200 institutions that prepare teachers have made significant program changes. A growing body of research regarding the knowledge bases for teaching, human development, and effective clinical experiences for preservice teachers has also contributed to this agenda. Although this is encouraging, we must ponder whether we will be able to keep pace with forces that will create increasingly complex demands on the teaching workforce. Change in teacher education, historically, has been difficult because of what Schwartz (1996) identifies as the many stakeholders:

> There are a myriad of stakeholders with interests in teacher education, among them university professors, school administrators, inservice teachers, state credential boards, local school boards, state boards of education, professional accreditation associations, regional accrediting entities, community leaders, role specialists, reformers, legislators, and local businessmen. Teacher education is a complex production with many voices. (p. 5)

Teacher educators will have to develop a greater expertise in communicating and negotiating with this varied array of stakeholders if they are to successfully navigate the ship of programmatic change. Equally important will be the challenge of preparing teachers who can accept and influence change.

In the second edition of the *Handbook of Research on Teacher Education,* Barone, Berliner, Blanchard, Casanova, and McGowan proposed that teacher education should be built around the unifying image of the "strong professional" (1996, p. 1111). Graduates of such a program would be reflective thinkers capable of effectively articulating their judgments about what constitutes best practice and how to operationalize this in their classrooms. The strong professional will also need the political savvy to attain the support needed to implement educationally sound programs.

Using the framework of the strong professional to guide our thinking, we attempted to provide greater detail to this concept from the three chapters in Division I of this yearbook. These three studies provide the reader with information that raises important questions regarding the context in which we prepare our nation's teachers. The authors present insights that prompt us to consider the attributes of those in the teacher workforce and pose alternatives to how we might better understand what we do in our programs. We are also prompted to recognize that we might learn valuable lessons from educators in other nations as we strive to prepare teachers for the 21st century. Specifically, we read each piece in an attempt to "flesh out" what the authors tell us about abilities, attributes, and dispositions of the strong professional as we consider the following challenges:

1. Teachers will have to have an in-depth understanding of their communities to understand linkages with state, national, and global societies.
2. To articulate their professional judgments with greater authority, teachers will have to assume the role of researchers using various modes of inquiry and will have to effectively communicate the results of these efforts to a diverse constituency.
3. Collaboration will play an ever-increasing role in the teaching profession. To appropriately meet the needs of each student, teams of professionals working with a variety of agencies along with the parents/guardians will make decisions regarding the educational process.
4. Individuals must be personally and professionally committed to diversity and have a solid understanding of social and cultural issues. Banks (1993) advocates knowledge that

> consists of concepts, paradigms, themes, and explanations that challenge mainstream academic knowledge and that expand the historical literacy canon that knowledge is not neutral but influenced by human interests, that all knowledge reflects the power and social relationships within society, and that an important purpose of knowledge is to help people improve society. (p. 9)

5. Teachers will have a strong commitment to the process of continuously improving classroom instruction. Teachers will be school-based managers with a commitment to continuously improving instruction. Working as a team, they will employ multiple sources of data to make instructional decisions (Bonstingl, 1992) and manage the learning environment.

6. Critical thinking and decision making will become even more critical components of teaching as the complexities of the profession increase, as will the ability to reflect on one's own teaching, the disposition toward continued professional development, and a willingness to mentor and coach other professionals in a constructive manner.

7. Imagination and innovation will have to become an increasingly important part of teaching and learning process. Teacher education programs and the public schools will have to modify their cultures to encourage and to reward teachers who develop new and exciting ways to provide meaningful learning experiences for students.

There seems to be little disagreement that there will be significant changes in the way in which we educate students in the public schools. Teacher educators, perhaps as a matter of survival, will have to continue to develop and implement programs that enable their students to successfully serve as leaders in shaping such changes. Kenneth Sirotnik (1995) defined leadership as the "exercise of significant and responsible influence" (p. 236). As leaders, teachers will have to continuously assess the context and content of their programs, using relevant information from the many stakeholders who offer multiple solutions to the increasingly difficult task of preparing teachers for the 21st century.

The Three Chapters

What follows are three chapters that address the topic of the context in which we prepare our nation's teachers. In Chapter 1, McNergney, Regelbrugge, and Harper present a sound rationale for education that prepares individuals to participate in a global society by linking local communities with the world at large. They stress the importance of education that celebrates diversity through global perspectives on multicultural education. This chapter presents the results of the study of multicultural education in the countries of Singapore, India, South Africa, England, and Denmark. The authors highlight approaches to multicultural education in each country and programs that have been developed to enhance student understanding and appreciation of diversity.

In Chapter 2, Striedieck takes us into an elementary methods classroom via a case study that provides insights about how diverse learners participate differently in this particular setting. Reflecting the assumptions inherent in postmodern and feminist ideologies, this study uses participant observation, document analyses, and in-depth interviewing to further our understanding of multiple cultures and perspectives.

Rollefson and Smith provide important data regarding the talent loss in the teacher workforce in Chapter 3. This piece presents interesting information related to the literary scores and salaries of teachers as compared with those of other white-collar professions. This study, using a national database, questions many of the previously held assumptions about the teaching workforce.

References

Banks, J. A. (1993). *Approaches to multicultural curriculum reform in multicultural education: Issues and perspectives.* Boston: Allyn & Bacon.

Barone, T., Berliner, D. C., Blanchard, J., Casanova, U., & McGowan, T. (1996). A future for teacher education: Developing a strong sense of professionalism. In J. Sikula, T. Buttery, & E. Guyton (Eds.), *Handbook of research on teacher education* (2nd ed., pp. 1108-1149). New York: Macmillan.

Bonstingl, J. J. (1992). Quality revolution in education. *Educational Leadership, 50*(3), 4-9.

Schwartz, H. S. (1996). The changing nature of teacher education. In J. Sikula, T. Buttery, & E. Guyton (Eds.), *Handbook of research on teacher education* (2nd ed., pp. 3-13). New York: Macmillan.

Sirotnik, K. (1995). Curriculum overview and framework. In M. J. O'Hair & S. J. Odell (Eds.), *Education teachers for leadership and change: Teacher education yearbook III* (pp. 235-242). Thousand Oaks, CA: Corwin Press.

1 Multicultural Education in a Global Context

Robert F. McNergney

Laurie A. Regelbrugge

Jeffrey P. Harper

Robert F. McNergney is Professor of Educational Studies at the University of Virginia. McNergney has coauthored two books and has edited four. His writing has appeared in the *Handbook of Research on Teacher Education, Educational Researcher, Journal of Teacher Education, The Washington Post,* and *The New York Times.* His research interests include work on case-method teaching and learning and the relationship of educational research and the press.

Laurie A. Regelbrugge is Vice President at The Hitachi Foundation, a U.S. philanthropic organization established in 1985 by Hitachi, Ltd., of Tokyo. She has had professional assignments in Japan, Indonesia, Jordan, and France and has taught social studies at the secondary level in public schools.

Jeffrey P. Harper, Ph.D., is a counselor and an independent consultant on international and global education issues and programs. He has extensive international experience in Denmark, England, Germany, India, Singapore, Thailand, and Zaire. Harper's current research interest is the internationalization of higher education. He is author of *The Directory of International Education in Virginia Higher Education.*

ABSTRACT

We argue for educating for participation in a global society by celebrating cultural diversity, both locally and internationally. We do so by reporting the results of a study of multicultural education in five countries—Singapore, India, South Africa, England, and Denmark—and by exploring issues across cultures within a country and across countries. We contend that multicultural challenges in any given locale or country are a subset of the multicultural challenges worldwide. To advance this understanding, we urge educators to explore life as it unfolds in communities around the world. These cases can be used to encourage both children and adults learn to live, play, and work together successfully.

We use this chapter, first, to argue for educating for participation in a global society in ways that celebrate cultural diversity, both locally and internationally. Second, we report results of a preliminary investigation of multicultural education in five countries—Singapore, India, South Africa, England, and Denmark, and we raise additional questions for study.

The Global Context

As we approach the 21st century, there can be no question we live in a multicultural, global community, one in which the actions and aspirations of individuals affect the lives of others in profound ways. Although we exist as members of a global community, we are still educated primarily to be loyal, law-abiding, productive citizens of a given nation-state or cultural group.

People live in different regions of the world, speak different languages, and adhere to different religious or philosophical principles, but all are affected by global forces—social movements, global production and commerce, and technological and environmental change. The popular cliché, "Think globally, act locally," challenges people to recognize that their local actions have global implications and that global forces affect local conditions. The phrase accurately reflects that most action is local. Most people attend first to primary needs in their communities: feeding, clothing, and educating the children; caring for the sick and elderly; adhering to, and in many cases participating in, local government policies and administration.

Although people around the world recognize increasingly the global context within which their action occurs, far fewer understand how to make sense out of global issues relating to local decisions, actions, and education (Regelbrugge & Moultrie, 1995). Delwin Roy (1991) acknowledged that "in practice, the two poles of the community-to-global continuum are complementary. There are no issues so exclusively global or grassroots in dimension or context as to justify the segregation of causes or solutions" (p. 3). If we are to live as global citizens we need to think of ourselves and others as members of a "community" that must attend to both global and local issues. We also need to acquire the practical skills that allow us to integrate problems and solutions in local and global terms.

Transportation and communication technologies have brought previously isolated groups into far greater, more intimate, and more frequent contact, thereby exposing them to subtle and stark differences of perspective and worldview (Roy, Banzhaf, & Regelbrugge, 1993). These technologies have helped disseminate cultural icons, bring attention to conditions of human suffering and devastation, rally support for reform efforts, and assist human migration. Trademarked products, such as Levi's blue jeans and Coca Cola, cars made by Volkswagen or Toyota, and services such as VISA credit cards or DHL courier, are now available virtually anywhere in the world.

Trends toward globalized culture have been countered by movements to preserve cultural identity. Indigenous populations globally have fought strenuously to protect their native knowledge and cultures against policies designed to overwhelm or assimilate.

The coinciding hegemony of the Cold War and post-World War II reconstruction efforts in West Germany and Japan provided the impetus for a massive building of industrial infrastructure and military capacity in the northern hemisphere. Although many argue that the Cold War prevented numerous conflicts, there have been frequent wars and violent conflicts since the end of World War II, and a disturbing increase of these conflicts since the end of the Cold War. The world's political geography was recast with independence movements over five decades that have essentially removed colonial rule, if not always real control.

The results include vastly expanded productive capacity and subsequent intense competition for markets, rampant technological development with broad civilian application, the growth of a global marketplace and integrated information and knowledge-driven markets, accumulation of vast resources within a global private sector, and a growing chasm between the fortunes of the rich and the poor—countries, whole regions, and individuals. The corporate sector now stands alongside the public sector in the scope of its command and control over resources, and its influence is growing, whereas the capacity of nation-states is declining. For many people, the standard of living and conditions of life are vastly improved from this industrial development. In most parts of the world, however, environmental degradation, human overpopulation, disease, poverty, and despair have escalated. The gap between rich and poor has widened as measured by increasing numbers of both wealthy and impoverished people.

Throughout the world, there is evidence of social strain resulting from the rapidity and pervasiveness of change incurred over the last 50 years. Some 5% of the world's population is living in a place other than their "home" country. The ravaging of communities by violence, poverty, and lack of hope has created turmoil. There is growing confusion about what a community even is. Many cling to community as family, neighborhood, or some geographic area. Others choose to identify their communities in terms based on heritage, experience, profession, beliefs, or even class. No doubt we are all members of many communities, but these differing identities can lead to conflict and misunderstanding. In many places around the world, there is turmoil from historical conflicts and ancient enmity never resolved.

Nowhere are the challenges of living and learning in a multicultural society felt more acutely than in schools around the world; for by virtue of their work, schools must look to the future as they operate in the present. Countries as diverse as Brazil, Canada, Denmark, New Zealand, Singapore, South Africa, and the United States, to mention but a few, have sought in varying degrees to shape educational policies and to deliver services that reflect the diversity of their peoples. Each nation exhibits strengths and limitations in these efforts, and each might well learn from the others. Indeed, we might expect educators to be among the first and most important people to learn about others, and about themselves in relation to others, if young people are to grow with a vision of what constitutes a flourishing global multicultural society.

Multicultural Education in Five Nations:
Contexts, Constructs, and Questions

Multicultural education, broadly defined as what schools do where more than one self-identifying group occupies a common geography, can be found around the world in a wide variety of national and local contexts and operating within an equally wide variety of constructs. The member-defined characteristics of particular group identity can include the dimensions such as socioeconomic class, caste, religion, race, tribe, political philosophy, economic theology, culture, national origin, history, and language. The combinations of these characteristics are seemingly endless. Generally speaking, multicultural education encourages or celebrates diversity.

During the 1993-1994 academic year, a study group from the University of Virginia traveled to Singapore, India (Delhi), South Africa (Cape Town), England (the London boroughs of Holloway and Ealing), and Denmark (Aalborg and Odense). These countries were selected because (a) they exhibited various combinations of difference within their "mixes" of difference, (b) educators in them were developing strategies for enhancing mutual understanding across dimensions of difference, and (c) the likelihood of finding English used as either the language of instruction or commonly used in professional discourse was high. (This latter point was important because of our plan to work on videocases for instructional use in the United States and elsewhere. See Herbert & McNergney, 1996a, 1996b.)

The contexts, constructs, lessons, and questions that follow do not make up an exhaustive list of contextual factors that affect multicultural education in each nation; they may not even be the most important elements. We simply want to acknowledge some factors that might influence comparative multicultural education for teachers and others interested in educational problems. Practitioners in the field of comparative education warn against overly generalized accounts of educational systems. We believe these practitioners make good sense.

Singapore

Singapore is a small island nation at the southern tip of the Malay Peninsula of roughly three million citizens with few natural resources and no agricultural base of its own. Its advantages are its geographical location at the "crossroads" of the world, an excellent deep water port, a stable national government, a liberalized free market economy, and well-educated and productive human resources. Singapore is a consumerist society of immigrants, a newly independent democratic country, and a multi-ethnic society with Chinese as the majority (76.9%), followed by Malays (14.6%), Indians (6.4%), and "others" (2.1%) (Lee, 1991).

Education is an important issue in Singapore. Education is perceived as providing two primary functions: (a) to foster national consciousness and national identity in a multicultural society and (b) to develop Singapore's natural resource—its people—by providing the necessary experience, knowledge, and skill for modernizing the country and equipping the country as an independent commercial and industrial city state (Cowan & McLean, 1984). Singapore's education system reflects these functions in its structure. There is an emphasis on technological and scientific education as well as an organized effort to acknowledge and maintain the cultural identities of its subgroups within an overarching national identity. The national language of trade, government, and education is English. The school system "streams" students according to "ability," with the "brilliant" students streamed into an advanced bilingual course of study, the "above average" students streamed into the normal bilingual course of studies, and the "average" students streamed into the ordinary, monolingual (English) course of study. All students are required to have some study in the language of their own cultural group in addition to English. With the exception of one school solely devoted to Chinese students engaged in Chinese language of instruction, all schools are racially and ethnically integrated. There is currently a trend toward site-based management of schools in Singapore with the intent of fostering a creative and innovative curriculum.

A Construct of Multicultural Education in Singapore

In Singapore, along with other Chinese-influenced societies in Asia, "a great deal of pressure is brought to bear on the young to shine academically [because in a highly credentialed society] most graduates expect their degrees automatically to open doors to well paid jobs, whether in government service or the private sector" (Tasker, 1985, p. 36). The task facing multicultural education in Singapore is to ensure a minimum of inequality across socioeconomic groups and across cultural groups in a society where "success" depends on educational attainment. In addition, to minimize unrest among the different ethnic groups, multicultural education in Singapore is constructed to provide a high degree of equality of opportunity (Lee, 1991).

Multicultural education occurs both formally and informally throughout the nation's schools. Texts and courses acknowledge historical roles played by various groups in the formation of modern Singaporean culture. The arts that are offered in schools also reflect the richness of their heritage. Because the nation is so small geographically, and virtually devoid of natural resources, schools must develop Singapore's most important resource—its human capital. Education that is multicultural promotes conformity to a standard view of citizenship, yet educators attempt to acknowledge that nation building requires recognition of people's most deeply held ancestral beliefs and cultural values.

At Anderson Secondary School, for example, students—Chinese, Malay, Indian, and others—are grouped into classes that reflect the cultural composition of the community. Anderson is ranked academically in the top 10 of the 150 high schools in Singapore. The school runs a split schedule, which means there are two groups of teachers and two groups of students (but only one principal) that occupy the premises. The tremendous pressure on the system requires that educators capitalize on every opportunity to encourage students to interact with one another as Singaporeans. Thus, extracurricular activities of clubs and sporting events are viewed as important opportunities to build a common sense of community.

Lessons and Questions

In Singapore, an explicit, coordinated, and proactive governmental program is in operation for national economic development. Three distinct cultural groups constitute Singapore's population. What purposes might "multicultural education" serve in Singapore? How and why might the concept of multicultural education in Singapore be different from concepts in other democratic states? With great cultural differences regarding attitudes toward education present, how might educational planners and administrators address the philosophical differences between "equality of outcome" and "equality of opportunity" in Singapore?

India (Delhi)

India is a large country that occupies the majority of the landmass of South Asia. It has the second largest population in the world, with more than 900 million people. After a long period of colonial occupation by Great Britain, India became independent in 1947 and began the huge task of nation building and the establishment of institutions. Today, India is basically a traditional rural society with aspects of modernization reshaping it in urban centers and rightly boasts of having the largest democracy in the world (Singha, 1991). Nevertheless, it is a nation of incredible diversity and disparity; topographical, climatic, religious, linguistic, racial, cultural, ethnic, caste, class, regional, economic, and educational difference abounds.

Educational flux has been a historical necessity in India since independence because India wanted education to be a vehicle of progress and social resurgence. An analysis of the existing educational system would easily highlight two of its most important features: It is gigantic, and it does not begin to meet the needs of its citizens (Singha, 1991). More than 700,000 schools in India employ more than 3,600,000 teachers for 120,000,000 students! Eighty-four percent of India's school-age population is within one kilometer of a primary school. In 1986, where schools existed, 40% had no chalkboards, 60% had no drinking water, 27% had no toilet facilities, and 27% had a single teacher for three or four grade levels. The literacy rate has risen from 16% in 1951 to 36% in 1981, although the absolute numbers of illiterate have risen from 300,000,000 in 1951 to 430,000,000 in 1981. These figures should be seen in the perspective of the disparity between many excellent educational opportunities in large urban areas, some of which rival any in the world, and the lack of educational resources in rural habitations (Singha, 1991).

A country as large and populous as India presents many seemingly intractable educational problems. These include the financing of education, developing a relevant curriculum for postsecondary-bound and occupation-bound students, teacher education, and examination equity. In India, where between 60 and 70 children could be given primary education for the cost of training one university student, approximately half of the nation's children fail to finish primary school, whereas the country as a whole produces more university graduates than it can productively employ. Since independence, more than 100 committees and commissions at the national level have diagnosed the malaise affecting the Indian education system and given valuable suggestions for revamping it, but the desired results have been elusive (Aggarawal, 1992).

A Construct of Multicultural
Education in India

India, as a "new" nation, is keenly aware of the necessity to build a nation that is cohesive and stable if it is to succeed. Aggarawal (1992) contends that the traditional and deep-rooted social practices of class and caste discrimination are at odds with India's modern, democratic constitution. By national policy, although with uneven application, India is dedicated to the "removal of disparities and to equalize educational opportunity by attending to the specific needs of those who have been denied equality so far" (p. 3). Furthermore, multicultural education is undertaken with the aim of promoting an integration based on appreciation of common national goals and ideas while protecting the languages and cultures of minority groups who have been educationally deprived or backward. The challenge to multicultural education has been to create national and emotional integration, that is, to help individuals "attain a particular kind of consciousness in every citizen of the Republic of India which will enable him or her to feel that he or she, transcending the primordial divides of India's ancient society, thinks and acts as a citizen of India first" (Lakshmi, 1989, p. 95), as a counterforce to those in society who attempt to exploit the negative influences at work in India.

The content and delivery of multicultural education may be as diverse as India itself. For example, at the KATHA school in Delhi some 600 students—Hindus, Muslims, Christians, Jains, Parsis, atheists—learn to work together on common literacy and life skills necessary for survival. The school began as a "crèche" or nursery for babies. The teachers care for babies and thus free the older girls to get an education in something they call the "Girl/Child Program"—a program designed to address gender oppression in the slums of Delhi. The mothers come for classes and learn how to cook and bake and to sell their wares to support their families. Teachers provide the women not only with life skills but also with the confidence necessary to earn a living for themselves and their children.

In marked contrast to the slum school, multicultural education in Sardar Patel Vidyalaya, a privately funded school in New Delhi, is a sumptuous example of multicultural education. The school is occupied by students with an even greater array of beliefs and philosophies than KATHA. Every morning begins in the British tradition with a convocation. The principal and various students lead the school in song and moral teaching. The content of these presentations is sometimes nonsecular but most often religiously inspired. Across the year, the convocations are meant to shape a pluralistic vision of human beliefs. The school is alive with art and music. Academic studies seem not to be ends in themselves but vehicles for the transmission of knowledge about India's many cultures.

Lessons and Questions

India is a country with a huge and diverse population with distinctive regional differences. Great disparity exists between the haves and the have-nots. Some contemporary political parties in India have aligned themselves with the interests of one group over and against the interests of other groups for political gain in a practice known as "vote banking," to the possible detriment of national unity. Are there parallels to the practice of vote banking in other democracies? If so, what are the consequences for multicultural education? In India, the slogan "unity in diversity" is promoted as a theme to define the ideal goal for India's society. Are there any similar slogans or themes in other democratic states that guide national projects of multicultural education? If so, what are they, and what are their intents? If not, what factors or forces militate against such practices?

South Africa (Cape Town)

South Africa is a nation in transition. With the ending of the institutionalized racial segregation, apartheid, and the founding of a democratic majority rule government, South Africa is faced with the vestiges of an educational system marked by profound disparity and resource inequity. After years of the apartheid regime, characterized by a high degree of conflict and little room for dialogue on educational alternatives, South Africa has become a nation where less than 1% of the White population is counted as illiterate whereas 67% of the Black population, 12% of the so-called colored population, and 6% of the Indian population are counted as such—and the rates for women are less (Unterhalter, 1991, p. 162).

Pundy (1991) argued that the change to democratic rule does not guarantee immediate educational equality. Given current economic projections, it is unlikely that the postapartheid economy will be capable of generating sufficiently high growth rates, in the short term, to enable the state to fund education for all at the premajority rule level of expenditure on White education. Some argue that these economic constraints will entail lowering the educational expectations of both the privileged minority and the historically deprived majority. To be sure, severe economic conditions, wherever they exist, will limit opportunities for learning.

A Construct of Multicultural
Education in South Africa

The arrival of majority rule in South Africa will bring "nonracial" schools. The related issue of providing schools to the majority of Blacks who had previously been deprived of adequate educational opportunities and who speak different languages, compounds the problems facing multicultural education. What multicultural education in South Africa will look like in the future is not yet known. There are, however, some examples of nonracial schools that existed before majority rule.

In 1990, legislation was enacted that made it possible for hitherto segregated White schools to admit children of other races (Penny, Appel, Gultig, Harley, & Muir, 1993). Before this allowance, schooling was undertaken by "own culture" schools, where "own culture" corresponded to race, ethnicity, and language. The decision to integrate individual White schools was put in the hands of the White parents—many chose the course of integration. Whether these schools can be regarded as effective sites for the development of a "new" nonracial South African educational culture, as distinct from the kind of school culture that exists in exclusively African schools at present, remains highly problematic. The use of the terms *race free, nonracial,* or *raceless* to describe integrated schools instead of *multicultural* creates a complex set of issues. In the case of non-White students attending primarily White schools, unless students of other races can present a raceless persona—a formidable feat attained at considerable cost—they are unlikely to be successful in their new schools. Although motivated by the best of intentions, racelessness is, in effect, little more than a euphemism for the cultural attributes of the dominant middle class.

Under these conditions, multicultural education has a tremendous task of defining its goals and objectives. If education will be uniform for all South African children, and not a multitiered system with different curricula for different groups, the relationship between culture and knowledge will need to be understood more as a changing dynamic than as a set of accepted, transcendental "givens." Whether or not multicultural education in South Africa will be able to overcome internalized assumptions about the primacy of difference and promote unity in diversity, as in India, is yet to be decided. Among many segments of society, there appears to be the will to construct a new society in South Africa, and the schools will have a major part to play.

"Model C" schools were the first previously all-White schools to commit themselves to educating Black and so-called colored students. For example, Camps Bay High School and Westerford High in Cape Town are working to involve these students in virtually every aspect of school life (McNergney, 1994). Sometimes the efforts are designed to integrate Black and so-called colored students into the existing system—teach them the same content in the same classrooms in the same way. At other times, educators try to preserve Black or tribal culture by capitalizing on community customs, mores, and languages (for examples, see "Project Cape Town: Education and Integration in South Africa," a multimedia case on the World Wide Web at http://curry.edschool.virginia.edu/~tedcases/).

Lessons and Questions

In South Africa, a minority group dominated a majority group. Now that official apartheid policies have ended, what might be the goals of multicultural education? Might the goals for multicultural education in South Africa be different from the goals of multicultural education in other democratic societies? If so, how and why? If not, why not?

Great Britain (Urban)

During the 1950s and 1960s Britain experienced major labor migrations to urban centers from their former African, Asian, Afro-Caribbean, and other colonies (Tomlinson, 1990). Following the flight of young White families to the suburbs in the 1980s, many inner cities had wards largely inhabited by racial minorities. Britain is now firmly a multiracial, multicultural society; the presence of cultural, religious, and linguistic diversity is an integral part of the continuously evolving British culture (Pumfrey & Gajendra, 1990).

The collection of information on race and ethnic origin is rare in England (McAdams, 1993). The most reliable projections are that by the year 2000 the non-White population of Britain will be 5% to 6% and the concentration of minority population in urban areas will increase (Tomlinson, 1990). In 1988, only 2% of the teachers in England and Wales came from ethnic minorities and only 2.5% of the teachers in training were ethnic minorities (Shaw, 1990).

A Construct of Multicultural
Education in Great Britain

British education is characterized by a national curriculum, externally administered terminal examinations, a public/private divide, and a multiethnic, multifaith, and multilingual student population. Since the mid-1970s, Labour and Conservative governments have rightly seen the need to reform the education system to help meet changing national needs and to create a different kind of society (Hargraves, 1993). Great Britain is in a time of great educational change and uncertainty—a time when the role, funding, and centrality of multicultural education are open to intense debate. As King (1993) observed, by statute, multicultural education is a professional responsibility of all teachers. All schools are to engage directly with issues of racism, racial discrimination, and disadvantage and to eradicate racism and prejudice within their own structures and policies. There are essentially four strands that are interwoven under the umbrella of multicultural education in Britain: (a) intercultural understanding and harmony, (b) global awareness and knowledge, (c) equality of opportunity and access for all, and (d) freedom from racism and discrimination.

How do these strands play themselves out in British schools? Certainly in many ways, but one unusually creative attempt to educate a changing culture in the United Kingdom can be found in the work of the Association of Science Educators Multicultural Education Working Party, chaired by Kabir Shaikh (Thorp, 1991). This group identified a range of teaching methods designed to incorporate issues of race and equality in science teaching. They did so to emphasize the "potential of science to enhance the curriculum by drawing on the richness and diversity of cultures and on the practice of science, now and throughout history . . . (and) the powerful role of science teaching for combating racism and prejudice in society" (p. vii). In short, the group has developed a science curriculum that provides teachers with materials and ideas for integrating cultural studies with scientific investigation.

The Ealing Education Centre, located in the borough of Ealing west of London and a remnant of the teacher movement, conducts courses and seminars on multicultural education for teachers in the system. Ealing schools are populated heavily by immigrant children from Asia (many of whom are Sikh) and from Africa (Zaire). Some 100 languages are spoken in the borough. Multicultural education here is meant to capitalize on children's knowledge, not to socialize them to a particular national view.

Curriculum and instruction are intended to promote natural and easy exchange of ideas within and across cultures.

Lessons and Questions

England has seen, and continues to see, tremendous waves of immigration from its former colonies. Culturally, ethnically, linguistically, and racially different immigrants and their succeeding second and third generations account for large percentages of the populations of many major cities in England. "Whether the schools [in England] will be harnessed to the cause of racial harmony or whether they will be used as instruments by which one social group will seek to sustain its advantages may well be critical in determining the future harmony of English society" (Thorp, 1991, p. 10). To what extent have schools in other nations been "harnessed to the cause of racial harmony" or "used as instruments by which one social group will seek to sustain its advantages"? Do these polarized concerns enter in any way into the conceptualizing and planning of multicultural education in other countries? If so, in what form? If not, what factors or conditions inhibit such inclusion?

Denmark (Odense and Aalborg)

Denmark is a small country of 5 million inhabitants composed of a nearly homogeneous ethnic group. In 1992, immigrants formed only 3% of the population (mainly from North and West European countries) (Husen & Postlethwaite, 1994). Denmark's membership in the European Community (EC) has brought with it greater obligations to accept refugees from the developing world, however. Danish citizens enjoy one of the highest standards of living in the world. McAdams (1993) noted that a steeply progressive income tax system effectively eliminates great disparities in wealth and provides financing for an extensive welfare state. Denmark provides an example of an educational system that is not challenged by disparities of wealth, large and varied ethnic subcultures, and fragmented governance. In addition, because it has been ethnically homogeneous, liberal, moral, and progressive, Denmark does not possess historically institutionalized forms of prejudice. Because it has been one of the most homogeneous countries in the world, however, Denmark has no experience base from which to develop multicultural policy and practice. The presence of new groups of immigrants and refugees offers a challenge to Danish society and institutions to create from scratch, as it were, a fresh response to "difference" within its borders.

A Construct of Multicultural Education in Denmark

The Danes do not maintain a "melting pot" philosophy. As is often the case in small countries, the maintenance of national cultural identity in the face of cultural hegemony from neighboring large countries becomes a national obsession. Immigrants and refugees in Denmark are not expected to become Danish. Their ethnocultural identities appear to be respected and great efforts are made to help "foreigners" in Denmark maintain their own cultural practices and languages. Newcomers are given instruction on "the Danish way" of doing things and Danish language as an aide to economic success and societal harmony, not as a program for cultural integration (Faborg, 1993). Danish schools make structural accommodations to address the needs of foreign children. Multicultural education is implicit in the curriculum as a part of instruction in egalitarian ethics, morality, and cultural sensitivity.

As Sanne Nielson, a teacher in Odense, explained, multicultural education is meant to be active:

> I have some knowledge. I want them to learn something. Many have found out that you can't just take your knowledge and put it in them. . . . They are drawing it, they are painting it, they are working with it with their fingers, we have music about it. (Faborg, 1993)

When asked if Danish teachers try to help immigrants keep their culture or become Danes, another teacher said,

> I think it is very important that they have some good experiences here at school. We have to make sure we don't mock. Of course we talk about their culture. We had a philosophical discussion about God and believing in God the other day. This Arab boy said I have another religion, and then he made a prayer for us in this language—a Muslim prayer. And then this Danish girl made a Danish one—a Christian one. And we had a Buddhist one too. . . . We don't notice any more the color of the hair and the skin—

we don't talk about it. But of course, we have some problems with our gymnastics—some girls must bath alone, no one else can see them. But these are small problems. (Faborg, 1993)

Lessons and Questions

Until recently, the Danes have been a homogeneous ethnic group with no significant minority population. The increasing numbers of refugees from the world's "hot spots" as well as "economic refugees" from the less prosperous parts of Europe create new challenges for schools and for a society that must provide jobs for people. With its traditions of liberal, progressive, and egalitarian social and economic policies, Denmark would seem an ideal laboratory for multicultural education. Although Denmark does not have historically institutionalized forms of racial and ethnic prejudice to overcome, it also does not have an extensive historical experience base in addressing issues of "difference" within its own borders. Taking Denmark as a "clean slate," we might ask what forms multicultural education could reasonably take. Are there positive lessons from other countries that might benefit Danish multicultural education? If there are, what are they? If there are none, why?

Conclusion

In many parts of the world, educators confront needs to restructure and redefine their school communities to adjust to the demands of a more diverse, integrated society. Yet schools around the world, and at most grade levels, remain framed primarily by one cultural context and one academic orientation. How can we transform education so learners more easily navigate multiple perspectives, recognizing both diversity and commonality of human experience? How can we make best use of technologies to help people solve problems and pursue productive, sustainable futures? How can we ensure that all children have access to excellent educational opportunities and that all children experience success? How can we support teachers and parents to transform schools into places that encourage the acquisition of a more inclusive worldview? These and related questions grow increasingly prominent in a global community.

Education is critical in preparing people to participate effectively in both global and local societies. Teachers, as key service providers, play a central role in that preparation. They create the climate in which multicultural understanding and critical thinking can be fostered or undermined. Teachers have the responsibility for preparing students from all ethnic, cultural, economic, and ability backgrounds to address problems not yet identified using tools yet to be created. The challenge is to construct education in a global context, within which can be placed the more familiar ethnic, local, or disciplinary strands of thinking. Educators, more than any other group, will be expected to prepare people with a broad sense of communal purpose and the responsibility needed to sustain a diverse global community.

References

Aggarawal, J. C. (1992). Preface. *Education policy in India: 1992. Retrospect prospect.* Delhi, India: Shipra.

Cowen, R., & McLean, M. (Eds.). (1984). *International handbook of education systems.* Chester, UK: Wiley.

Faborg, A. (1993, December). Unpublished interview. Denmark: Aalborg.

Hargraves, D. H. (1993). Preface. In A. S. King & M. J. Reiss (Eds.), *The multicultural dimension of the national curriculum* (p. vii). London: Falmer.

Herbert, J. M., & McNergney, R. F. (Eds.). (1996a). *The case of Columbus, New Mexico: Educational life on the border.* Multicultural Videocase Series. Washington, DC: AACTE.

Herbert, J. M., & McNergney, R. F. (Eds.). (1996b). *The case of Deming, New Mexico: International public education.* Multicultural Videocase Series. Washington, DC: AACTE.

Husen, T., & Postlethwaite, T. N. (Eds.). (1994). Denmark: System of education. In *The international encyclopedia of education* (2nd ed., Vol. 3, pp. 1453-1461). Oxford: Pergamon.

King, A. S. (1993). Introduction. In A. S. King & M. J. Reiss (Eds.), *The multicultural dimension of the national curriculum* (pp. 2-10). London: Falmer.

Lakshmi, S. (1989). *Challenges in Indian education*. New Delhi, India: Sterling.

Lee, W. O. (1991). *Social change and educational problems in Japan, Singapore, and Hong Kong* (pp. 11-52). New York: St. Martin's.

McAdams, R. P. (1993). *Lessons from abroad*. Lancaster, PA: Techtonic.

McNergney, R. F. (1994, December). Videocases: A way to foster a global perspective on multicultural education. *Phi Delta Kappan, 17*(4), 296-299.

Nielson, S. (1993, December). Unpublished interview. Denmark: Aalborg.

Penny, A., Appel, S., Gultig, J., Harley, K., & Muir, R. (1993). Just short of fumbling in the dark: A case study of the advent of racial integration in South African schools. *Comparative Education Review, 37*(4), 412-433.

Pumfrey, P. D., & Gajendra, V. K. (1990). Issues in urban education. In P. D. Pumfrey & V. K. Gajendra (Eds.), *Race relations and urban education: Contexts and promising practices* (pp. 1-12). London: Falmer.

Pundy, P. (1991). Financing educational transformation in South Africa. In E. Unterhalter (Ed.), *Education in a future South Africa: Policy issues for transformation* (pp. 98-123). Oxford: Heinemann International.

Regelbrugge, L., & Moultrie, L. (1995). The role of diversity in sustainable community development. *Issues and Views*. Washington, DC: Hitachi Foundation, 2-4.

Roy, D. A. (1991). A foundation for the future. *Hitachi Foundation 1991 Annual Report*, p. 3.

Roy, D. A., Banzhaf, J. A., & Regelbrugge, L. (1993, August). Global citizenship: What is it and who needs it? *Issues and Views*. Washington, DC: Hitachi Foundation, 1.

Shaw, J. W. (1990). A strategy for improving race relations in urban schools. In P. D. Pumfrey & G. K. Verma (Eds.), *Race relations and urban education: Contexts and promising practices* (pp. 109-120). London: Falmer.

Singha, H. S. (1991). *School education in India: Contemporary issues and trends*. New Delhi, India: Sterling.

Tasker, R. (1985, July). Education: A system geared for the best and brightest. *Far Eastern Economic Review, 129*, 36-37.

Thorp, S. (Ed.). (1991). *Race, equality, and science teaching*. London: Lavenham.

Tomlinson, S. (1990). Race relations and the urban context. In P. D. Pumfrey & G. K. Verma (Eds.), *Race relations and urban education: Contexts and promising practices* (pp. 13-17). London: Falmer.

Unterhalter, E. (1991). Can education overcome women's subordinate position in the occupation structure? In. E. Unterhalter (Ed.), *Education in a future South Africa: Policy issues for transformation* (pp. 147-176). Oxford: Heinemann International.

2 The Representation of Multiple Cultures and Perspectives in One Preservice Elementary Teacher Education Class

A Case Study From a Postmodern Feminist Perspective

Iris M. Striedieck

Iris M. Striedieck is Assistant Professor in the Department of Curriculum and Instruction, the Pennsylvania State University, University Park, Pennsylvania. Her research interests include issues of equity, mathematics education, and supervision.

ABSTRACT

This case study research was designed to describe and interpret how one teacher educator defines and makes meaning of the concept of multiple cultures and perspectives in the context of her elementary education methods course.

In-depth interviews and participant observations were conducted with the teacher educator, and narrative portraits were crafted from them. From the portraits of the teacher educator and class events emerged themes of conflict, voice, position, and power—themes that suggested connections between events of the class and broader social issues.

Collectively, these results suggest that the experiences of prospective teachers and the composition of the class serve as a basis for more holistically making meaning of multiple cultures and perspectives in elementary teacher education. As evidenced in this study, such an approach enabled prospective teachers to conceive of culture as extensive patterns of similarity and difference and encouraged a perspective-taking of culture as inclusive of all individuals.

Calls for the inclusion and evidence of multiculturalism in teacher education are varied. Gay (1986) states that in a time period "of demands for educational excellence, increased teacher competence in pluralistic school settings, and equality of opportunities for ethnically diverse students, more concerted and systematic attention must be given to multicultural teacher education" (p. 157). More specifically, Gay (1983) suggests the following:

> Preservice professional preparation should include *knowledge* about ethnic and cultural diversity, the *creation* and *selection* of instruction materials that reflect ethnic and cultural pluralism, and the *translation* of their knowledge about ethnicity into multiculturalized plans and strategies for instruction. (p. 82)

Taking a perspective that underscores the significance of considering social and political influences, Gollnick (1992) asserts that "the task for teacher education is to help teacher candidates begin the process of critical examination of the practices of educators and schools [and] . . . understand the influence of culture on their teaching styles and on the learning styles of students" (p. 69). Clarken and Hirst (1992) observe that "we know much about diverse cultures, but our schools of education teach little to help teachers understand these cultures" (p. 8).

These findings suggest a need for research in teacher education that critically and holistically examines practices in classrooms, transcending piecemeal efforts of reform to be more inclusive of multiple cultures and perspectives. In response to such calls, this case study was designed to describe and interpret how one teacher educator defines and makes meaning of the concept of multiple cultures and perspectives in the context of her elementary education methods course, and to describe and interpret how selected prospective elementary teachers understand and make meaning of this concept as manifested in this course.

Attempting to understand participants' experiences with and conceptions of multiple cultures and perspectives entails an effort to elicit their point of view. Questions that were investigated include the following:

- What is the context of participants' past experience that shapes their meaning of education that imbues multiple cultures and perspectives?
- How do the factors of participants' lives interact to help them understand education that imbues multiple cultures and perspectives?

Integrated Conceptual Framework

The study design and data analysis reflected assumptions inherent in postmodern and feminist ideologies. In essence, it is my belief that postmodern feminism is fundamentally a movement for emancipation from hierarchical structures of knowledge and power and a commitment to morality, social justice, and equality for all individuals. Hence, voice, defined as "the discourse that is created when people define their own issues in their own ways, from their own perspectives, their own terms—in a word, speak for themselves" (Secada, 1995, p. 156), and position in society become critical parameters through which meaning and knowledge are created. By crafting narrative portraits of the participants in this study and projecting their own words, the parameters of voice and position, among others, were keenly taken up.

When considered in the context of education and research, this conceptual framework stresses the need for a greater degree of participatory interaction between learners and providers of education and between researchers and participants. Attention is also given to how diverse groups and individuals participate differently in educational programs.

Methods and Data Source

This research design used in-depth interviewing, participant observation, and document analysis as tools of inquiry. Data were collected throughout one semester.

The Pennsylvania State University was chosen for this research study. This study focused on an instructor of a required core course in the elementary teacher education program who exemplified notions of multiple cultures and perspectives in her curriculum and pedagogy. The instructor, Christine, and the course she taught served as an *intensity sample* (Patton, 1990) that provided insights into the phenomenon of interest. In this chapter, participant observation is highlighted and serves as the focus for an excerpted portrait of the class.

Participant Observation

Participant observation makes it possible to "understand a program or [phenomenon] to an extent not entirely possible using only the insights of others obtained through interviews" (Patton, 1990, p. 25). My role as a participant observer included audiotaping each class and taking field notes that would assist me in reconstructing the events of each class. As Patton (1990) aptly states, "The challenge is to combine participation and observation so as to become capable of understanding the program as an insider while describing the program for outsiders" (p. 27).

Seven class observations were originally made throughout the semester; three are presented here. Through consultation with Christine, classes were selected for observation as those that would be most insightful to the study.

Together, transcriptions of the audiotapes and my field notes created a portrait of each class observation. Where verbatim excerpts were used, words are set off as quotes within the narrative.

Moments Captured in the Class

This semester-long course was designed to assist prospective elementary teachers in developing a personal sense of art and, subsequently, creating learning activities for elementary-aged students to do the same. The participants, primarily sophomore and junior elementary education majors, met twice a week for two hours each meeting.

Portrait 1—The First Day of Class
(1/9/95)

How many of you have taken an art course at the university? How many of you have taken an art course during high school?

. . . How many of you are afraid of art? . . . I wanted to give everyone an idea where everyone else was . . . that we're all somewhat on an equal ground.

Wearing a long-sleeved, multiflowered print dress with laced leather boots and standing in the front of the room, Christine begins the introduction to her course by asking students to share what their experiences with art have been. Her series of questions attempts to demystify art as a technical skill and to present it rather as a concept open for interpretation, something that everyone can do. Her introductory remarks segue into a discussion of rituals, aesthetics, and culture. Christine's own response to her question, What is art? is "There's no right answer, there's no wrong answer." She elaborates by stating, "Art in our culture reflects who we are and our relationship to our surroundings."

After presenting students with a brief history of art education so that they "have some background of where we're going this semester," Christine explains the approach of Discipline-Based Art Education (DBAE) as the format that she will use in this class. Art education presented in the format of DBAE holistically includes discussion or attention to the four elements of questioning, history of the culture or style of art being presented, critical analysis, and production of the art piece.

Christine reserves a review of the syllabus for the latter part of class. She indicates to students that they will be expected to be involved in determining the grading criteria for each different portfolio project that is required and describes this as "an ongoing working process." Each portfolio project represents a collection of the student's artwork, his or her reflection on a given issue, and the connections the student makes to children's learning. As a final point of discussion, Christine spends considerable time talking about how students will be working in small groups to complete assignments for the class. She focuses on the process for selecting members for group work. Although she emphasizes the element of freedom of choice, she presents practical suggestions for forming effective and functional groups. Conflict, Christine states, is something "you're going to have to learn how to work out."

The context of group work is set up to reflect the six different grade levels in elementary schools. As such, each group is formed by interest in teaching a particular grade level, and all portfolio work and lesson plans developed by the group will be age appropriate.

As a wrap-up activity, Christine asks each person in the room to provide a brief introduction to the rest of the class, stating, "I think it's important that we get to know who we are." Christine begins by introducing herself:

> I'm Christine Morris. I've been teaching in the public school system for 15 years and at the university level for 4 years. I have taught behavior disorder students and autistic children. I was also a cultural arts teacher. That's when you're interrelated, so I taught dance, music, visual arts, theater, and literature in one course. I have taught in an art museum. I have had a dance studio. I still do artists in residency, which means I go into public school systems and I am the artist of the week or the month. I like that. I get to do the fun stuff and really get the kids rowdy and then leave. I'm married, I have two boys, one is fifteen. He's a freshman at the high school and the other one is in seventh grade. I have taught from preschool through adult students. I think the oldest one may have been around 88. So I've had a wide range of students. I love teaching. I'm very open. I'd love to have an informal classroom.

Portrait 3—Discomfort as a Learning Opportunity (1/16/95)

As an organizer for their quilt project, Christine assists students with the process of developing a conceptual map. Perched on a tabletop with feet resting on a chair and adorned in a brilliantly colored outfit consisting of a cotton top, multipatched skirt, lime-green sash, red stockings and shoes, and a ceramic beaded necklace, she demonstrates how to create a unit web by identifying and writing issues connected to quilts in the circles and squares drawn on the board.

"Now, do I have any volunteers who might want to read their sentences about quilts?" This invitation elicits responses from four students, and Christine launches into a cultural story of one quilt she brought in that had been made by her grandfather. In the course of discussing the history and culture of several other quilts, she points out how they can "function as a cover or can provide a great source of comfort as something that warms the soul." Whether talking about the Amish, South American Indian, African American, or Appalachian heritage, or raising political and social issues such as war, health, rituals, friendship, birth, and death, Christine consistently connects the notion of quilts to children's experiences. She does this by pointing out how young children have favorite security blankets, by demonstrating how to sensitively discuss sexuality or issues of gender with sixth-grade students, and by identifying messages embedded in the stories told through quilts.

As an approach to learning, Christine uses the display of quilts, together with a slide show of how other artists have developed and conveyed the function of quilts, as a medium by which to examine issues. She entices students to engage in a critical reading of quilts by writing on the chalkboard and orally posing the following questions: "(1) Is quilting art? (2) If the quilt is used, does that mean it's not art? (3) Is making art with fabric and thread female? (4) Is women's art less valuable than men's art?"

In the course of the resulting discussion, these open-ended questions are explored in the context of various elementary grade levels for their appropriateness in "raising children's consciousness about certain issues." Christine explicitly points out that "the differences that we . . . show through our responses to these questions is our culture—your experiences and your age [for example] will influence your aesthetic responses."

Returning to her invitation to students to share what they know about quilts, Christine notes that student responses to this question provided a baseline from which to decide what additional information she needed to provide students, so that "we all have some [common] understanding of what we're going to be talking about." She attempts to establish a common understanding of quilts through repeated questioning of each student's perceptions and meaning making. In the course of modeling this process and helping her students to make connections to children's learning, she comments, "It's interesting to watch some of you with the questions I asked. The body language—there's a lot of shifting—what does that mean? . . . Right, you're uncomfortable. You don't want to talk about it. I want you to. I want you to think about it."

To conclude this lesson, Christine attempts to help students visualize the process of creating a "paper" quilt square and developing an accompanying story to reflect their culture and life experience. "It could be family or personal or fiction . . . as you want. I'm giving you a lot of choices. I want you to spend time with your group talking about how and what you would teach in your grades, as far as quilts. First, I want you to brainstorm. We've talked about these four questions . . . I want you to think about all of this in relationship to the age that you are teaching."

Portrait 5—Notions of Multicultural
Education (1/30/95)

Today I asked you to come prepared to talk about your experience with multicultural education. Instead of putting someone in the hot seat to raise their hand to begin the conversation, I
thought we would do like we did last class and go around from
table to table and have one or two of you discuss what . . . experiences you have had.

Christine asks students to rearrange tables into a circle. In light of the
open-ended invitation to speak, almost all students offer a response to
Christine's request. The stories that unfold provide both shared and
unique life experiences, for shared and unique reasons. A palette of
student responses follows:

Student 1: I haven't had very much experience with it, but I've
talked about it in some of my classes. We just briefly touched upon
it, but I haven't had any . . . from what I remember in high school.

Student 2: I've not been exposed to it in the classroom other
than up here in a professional setting. . . . [With] literature, I
remember one activity we did was to discuss whether a [particu-
lar] book [which was] written the way a southern Black would
speak was grammatically correct and whether it should have been
published. [The consensus] was yes, that it was wonderful. But
there was one person in the class who thought that because it
wasn't written in real British, that it was wrong and that it should
not be used in school because children would think that that was
correct.

Student 3: I had a cultural anthropology class which went into
it but more like primitive. It wasn't [about] a lot of cultures that
are prevalent today. I mean I would have liked to have taken a
class just on different U.S. cultures or something, but I don't really
believe there is one though. I remember in one educational theory
and policy course, that they didn't go over different cultures as
much, just kind of told us to be aware that there are different

cultures. And to make sure your lessons aren't going to offend other people. Some things you may think is no big deal but to them it's a big deal . . . I just remembered something. The one thing that always stuck out in my mind [inaudible] is that most of the history is written through the white man's eyes, so when we read we should always question. Just because it's written doesn't mean it's right and that can go both ways . . .

Student 4: As far as the U.S. culture and differences, I've been to Europe so I've seen a lot of the European culture and how that differs from the United States. [I've read] *Savage Inequalities*, that pieces the United States up into different districts where they discuss how education is used for their purposes. I've done volunteer work at a juvenile farm, it's like a diversity for kids that have been in trouble. That was primarily African American, maybe two or three Whites out of like five hundred. And that was a very interesting experience to be surrounded by the Black culture, being that I was one of the only White teachers.

Student 5: Within our classes we've talked a lot about multiculturalism and I think I have a personal philosophy of what I believe it is, what I feel it is. I know a lot about it because we talked a lot about it in small groups in classes. But the problem now with some of the people that I've been taking classes with through the years is we are all wondering, How are we going to integrate it? Nobody really knows how to put it into practice. So that's where I'm at.

Student 6: In elementary school there were people there from a lot of different cultures. We never talked about multiculturalism in our classroom. But when you have a school with like 30 people from 30 different countries you just learn about things that way. And so it was never taught to me. I just learned about people from experience. [These cultures and experiences were brought into the classroom.] We did a lot, we focused a lot on creative writing and . . . then we read our stories and so just through that you'd hear different things, how they thought of things. . . . We did a lot of group work and discussion.

Several other students echo tales of limited interaction with culturally diverse people because of school settings that did not outwardly reflect diversity. Students also describe as learning experiences traditional cultural holiday celebrations such as Martin Luther King Day.

As the conversation wanes, Christine responds,

> It's interesting listening to when everybody was talking. . . . I don't mean to be picking words out, so forgive me if that's how it sounds. But it was interesting . . . when you were talking about world cultures [it was about] maps, geography, and facts, and as you stated, not about people. Why was culture attached to the word *world*, why wouldn't it be world facts? Someone talked about nations that we learn about and then forget. Someone else used a descriptive word, *primitive*. And someone else talked about history and that we needed to be very critical about the perspective [presented]. Then the big question, How do you do it?
>
> The reason why multicultural education is so important for me to talk about in art class is because art, more often than any subject, is abused when it come to multiculturalists. Many times teachers feel they are teaching multicultural education because they taught students how to make a Japanese fan or they strung macaroni on a string and say it's a Native American necklace. [Often] . . . the context of the culture is never given. We then have to question, What do children learn? [So my question back to you is] How do we do it?

One student replies,

> I think out of all the multicultural experiences that were talked about, [the one that spoke of] having a project that didn't last for a couple of weeks [was most meaningful]. It was a yearlong thing, and each person individually learned about what their own heritage was as well as that of everybody else. So that's really the idea, in my opinion, but they just don't teach that here in college.

Christine comments,

> I think you bring up a good point in that it was related to their own culture and at the same time, they shared it. How do you do that as a classroom teacher on a yearly basis? If we're going to try to . . . figure that out, what do you think we need to do?

> Let's think about how some culture is put into our public schools, that you know about. One of the ways that culture is integrated in our school systems today is through holidays. What are some holidays?

For the next half hour, Christine lists the holidays that students think of and eventually identifies them as predominantly religious, with a variety of examples of cultural celebrations on ethnic, geographic, and national levels. The conversation results in the observation, as summarized by Christine:

> What you have left are symbols and you don't know . . . what they stand for. . . . The meaning behind the symbols has been removed. So when someone came down and said, "OK, we need to be more open and inclusive," the symbols and activities that had been thought of as oppressive remained, but the meaning behind them was removed. This is often the way cultures are taught. . . . We don't know how to relate the culture. And for me, the best way is to show what we do in schools for holidays about culture. They come from a majority perspective just like you were talking about with the history books.
>
> I can remember when I was teaching, I, too, used my own experiences. I didn't seem to question the fact that I was doing Christmas ornaments in my art class even though I wasn't Christian. I did it because it was expected. Again, authority.
>
> So we have to examine how we can be inclusive and yet try to maintain everyone's rights and have, at the same time . . . [opportunities] to present cultures in an integrated and related way. In your classrooms, you're going to have all these kids . . .
>
> What do you learn when you only have a day or a week set aside? What does that say?

One student responds,

> That the individual that's set aside is only important for that moment.

Christine says,

> I think you're right. In that type of approach you still see that group as different. I'm proposing a different way of teaching

multicultural education, especially when it comes to the arts, because it's something you can do in every subject.

If you remember our discussion about quilts, I talked about Mennonite, Appalachian, African American, and farm communities. Do you remember that? We didn't talk about culture. What did I talk about? So many of you said it so nicely in all of your portfolios.

One student replies,

Personal experiences and the meanings that were cultural?

Christine affirms,

Very good, right. And the similarities that they had when they talked about their experiences of doing the quilt. As people, what do we have that is similar? What states that we have culture?

Most of the class replies with suggestions of tradition, language, food, clothing, belief systems, values, family, and arts. Christine continues,

OK, if cultures all have this and we can agree on this . . . we have to find similarities that we can relate to. How do you relate a culture that may or may not be like you? . . . [Good], compare. Can you think of anything else? . . . OK, learning new ways that you could possibly look at your own self and culture, . . . comparing and contrasting as a learning tool.

As the conversation diminishes, Christine shifts again from paraphrasing students' responses to sharing her own viewpoint:

For me, the things that I find important [are the following]. First, you need to focus on the knowledge of the makers. What I mean is that when you're studying a particular culture, it is nice to go to that particular culture for your information, instead of an outside resource. [Second,] is to [be able to] relate to your own experience and culture. A lot of children in the United States don't believe they come from a culture, . . . that culture is something exotic. So they're growing up thinking they don't have culture. [Third,] be aware of cultural and social biases. You as teachers have the responsibility to check your own biases. And even though you may have a classroom full of children who look just like you, as we've heard today in here from your experiences, it's been a disservice. It's been a disservice not to know. You will not understand or be open-minded if you don't have an experience of others. How do you become aware of your cultural and social biases? . . .

Everyone that talked experienced some incident in beginning to recognize your biases. . . . You have to start questioning yourself on what you're going to be doing. How will I present [my lessons?] You notice I didn't say if you had [certain types of] kids. [You need to be] inclusive and diverse.

After summarizing the discussion thus far, Christine asks, "How do you do it? Let's take an example." She presents the situation of teaching square dancing and discusses ways that reflect both culturally meaningful and disconnected approaches.

Eventually, the discussion returns to symbolism, at which point Christine asks, "Can you teach those particular holidays in a way that allows the meaning of symbols to still be present but in a way that doesn't offend anybody?" Several students voice the concern that it is not possible to avoid "stepping on someone's toes." Another student points out that if such an attempt were made, "you do not have enough time to deal with everyone of them and that's unfair, so you avoid it because you can't do justice to everyone." One more student responds by noting that parents make decisions regarding sending their students to public schools and suggests that parents "have to accept the fact that their students are going to be exposed to not only people of different cultures but also to talk of a different culture." Christine replies,

I understand what you're saying, but I think that's one of the reasons why it's avoided. People have a fear of talking about those things. You bring up a very good point, in that questioning might be the foundation of fear. If you teach children to question, then they're not only going to question things they don't know about but they're going to question things that they do know.

What I want you to think about for next class is along those lines. What choices are you going to make so that you are able to be inclusive and diverse and yet at the same time realistic? Initially, I talked about how . . . if you're going to present cultures, you might want to clue into belief systems, clothing, the arts, food, language, traditions, heritage and history, and values. The other approach, which you've already gone through in doing the quilt portfolio, is to have a common theme and show how different cultures explore that common theme.

Wisdom for Practice in Teacher Education

On the basis of insights gleaned from this study, several important observations can be made regarding teacher education that pervasively includes notions of multiple cultures and perspectives. Perhaps the most salient suggestion is to reconceptualize the compensatory notion of multicultural education as it now predominantly exists to a notion of multiple cultures and perspectives as integral to all aspects of teacher education. In this manner, teacher education that imbues multiple cultures and perspectives is conceived of as ongoing, scholarly, and critical for all teachers to engage in, regardless of their ethnic, racial, and cultural background. The benefit, of course, is for all students, regardless of their ethnic, racial, and cultural background, to engage in equitable learning.

As was evident in Christine's class, notions of multiplicity were central to her teaching and embedded not only in her myriad choice of teaching resources but in her efforts to draw on the everyday experiences and the perspectives of her prospective teachers. For many prospective teachers in this class, Christine's course was their first opportunity to critically engage in and make meaning of cultural diversity.

A second way in which teacher education can benefit from insights gleaned from this case study is to recognize the need to help all prospective teachers realize and identify their cultural selves as a foundation for recognizing their inclusion in the discussion of culture. Evident in the comments made by classmates in general were initial conceptions that culture belonged to Other, and did not include them, by virtue of culture viewed as race.

Through the creation of learning experiences that examined and used notions of conflict, voice, position, and power, Christine attempted to help prospective teachers conceive of culture as broader patterns of similarity and difference, both in their personal lives and in the classroom. Integral to this process was a regard for how prospective teachers' ethnic, racial, and cultural identities shaped their experiences and how they interpreted them. Indeed, it is largely through these human characteristics that meaning making and knowledge construction occur. Corroborating what

Maher and Tetreault (1993) espouse, Christine recognized the importance of the composition of the class as a dynamic factor in shaping classroom discourse, as well as in influencing their meaning-making processes about notions of culture and perspective.

Finally, implications for the way in which teacher educators position themselves as instructors can be drawn from Christine's class. Implicit in the portraits was the influence of Christine's position as the instructor in the class on how students would learn. The role she sought to create for herself was one of colearner with her students. Through her use of myriad open-ended questions, Christine engaged prospective teachers in multiple problem posing and solving, thus allowing students to make meaning through connections to their worldviews. "When instructors move from positions of expertise into collaboration, they may be more inclined to replace traditional classroom hierarchies with more 'open-ended' pedagogies" (Wilkerson, cited in Fitzgerald & Lauter, 1995, p. 743).

As Christine's class portrait keenly demonstrated, by creating such learning environments,

> Students seek mastery on their own terms and in concert with others. . . . Thus, individual mastery is embedded and folded into the social construction of knowledge. It becomes individual and collaborative rather than hierarchical. Rather than achieving one right answer, students make increasingly more sophisticated connections with the topics. (Maher & Tetreault, 1993, p. 24)

Calls for the inclusion of multiple cultures and perspectives in teacher education will not be answered by imposing the use of assembly line models that merely require teacher educators to fit puzzle pieces together, without regard for the characteristics of their schools of education and the experiences prospective teachers bring to the classroom. Rather, by viewing human understanding as a hologram, "pieces" are viewed as images of the whole (Egan, 1986). Metaphorical insights such as this also recognize that

> there are endless ways of being and becoming educated. We may try to specify certain necessary conditions, which may form a "core curriculum," but the sheer diversity of individual students and of social and cultural contexts makes even this a most problematic task. (p. 33)

Providing teacher educators with windows of opportunity into their own and other classrooms is one valuable way in which meaning making both reflects the idiosyncrasies of classrooms and schools and allows broader connections to be made. Such opportunities answer in part the problematic task of creating a core curriculum that adequately considers student diversity by allowing the "core curriculum [to] be rooted in each college's own academic focus, its special approach to the world, and the kind of students it enrolls" (Campbell & Flynn 1990, p. 10). Although each institution of teacher education imposes its own internal limitations on the extent to which social and curricular transformation can occur, there are, nonetheless, myriad ways in which notions of multiple cultures and perspectives may be taken up as means to empower prospective teachers.

References

Campbell, J., & Flynn, T. (1990). Can colleges go back to a core curriculum? *Planning for Higher Education, 19,* 9-15.

Clarken, R. H., & Hirst, L. A. (1992, February). *Enhancing multicultural education in teacher preparation programs.* Paper presented at the Annual Meeting of the American Association of Colleges for Teacher Education, San Antonio, TX.

Egan, K. (1986). *Teaching as storytelling: An alternative approach to teaching and curriculum in the elementary school.* London, Ontario: Althouse.

Fitzgerald, A. K., & Lauter, P. (1995). Multiculturalism and core curricula. In J. A. Banks & C. A. Banks (Eds.), *Handbook of research on multicultural education* (pp. 729-746). New York: Macmillan.

Gay, G. (1983). Why multicultural education in teacher preparation programs? *Contemporary Education, 54*(2), 79-85.

Gay, G. (1986). Multicultural teacher education. In J. A. Banks & J. Lynch (Eds.). *Multicultural education in western societies* (pp. 154-177). New York: Praeger.

Gollnick, D. M. (1992). Understanding the dynamics of race, class, and gender. In Mary E. Dilworth (Ed.), *Diversity in teacher education: New expectations* (pp. 63-78). San Francisco: Jossey-Bass.

Ladson-Billings, G. (1995). Multicultural teacher education: Research, practice, and policy. In J. A. Banks & C. A. Banks (Eds.), *Handbook of research on multicultural education* (pp. 747-761). New York: Macmillan.

Maher, F. A., & Tetreault, M. K. (1993). Doing feminist ethnography: Lessons from feminist classrooms. *Qualitative Studies in Education*, 6(1), 19-32.

Patton, M. Q. (1990). *Qualitative evaluation and research methods*. London: Sage.

Secada, W. G. (1995). Social and critical dimensions for equity in mathematics education. In W. G. Secada, E. Fennema, & L. B. Adajian (Eds.), *New directions for equity in mathematics education* (pp. 146-164). New York: Cambridge University Press.

3 Do Low Salaries Really Draw the Least Able Into the Teaching Profession?

Mary R. Rollefson

Thomas M. Smith

Mary R. Rollefson is a senior survey analyst with the National Center for Education Statistics (NCES), U.S. Department of Education. She has published several reports on teacher supply and demand and serves as the NCES liaison to the National Education Goals Panel.

Thomas M. Smith is the editor of the NCES annual report to Congress, *The Condition of Education.* His research interests include transition from school to work, comparisons of national education systems, and school organization.

ABSTRACT

The hypothesis of talent loss from the teacher workforce was popular in teacher research in the 1980s. Most research supported a progressive loss of talent from the teacher workforce at successive points in the teacher pipeline, from undergraduate preparation through entry to and exit from the teaching profession. This research was limited, however, to samples of undergraduate students in teacher education programs compared with other majors, or to samples of current and former

AUTHORS' NOTE: We want to thank Yupin Bae of Pinkerton Computer Consultants, Inc., for supporting the data analysis presented in this article. An earlier version of this article was presented at the Annual Meeting of the American Educational Research Association, San Francisco, April 1995.

teachers. Data from the National Adult Literacy Survey of 1992 provide an opportunity to test this hypothesis on a nationally representative sample of adults employed in teaching and in other professions requiring a college degree. Prose literacy scores, as a measure of verbal ability, were predicted with key confounding variables held constant. Although expected differences in salary were found, the literacy scores of teachers were not different from those of individuals in other white-collar professions.

Objectives

This chapter uses data from the 1992 National Adult Literacy Survey (NALS) to study the literacy levels of teachers compared with individuals in other professions that may compete with teaching for talented individuals in the labor market. NALS prose literacy scores are the best data on verbal ability that are available on a nationally representative sample of college-educated adults in the labor market. Verbal ability has been identified by research as an indication of teacher quality. The data are used to test the hypothesis, based on earlier research, that those with higher verbal ability select themselves out of teaching, leaving the teaching profession with the individuals of lesser verbal ability.

Theoretical Framework

Teacher quality is the underlying issue in discussions of teacher supply and demand, as imbalances in supply and demand are often resolved through adjustments in teacher qualifications. Economic theory predicts that when the supply of prospective teachers is abundant, school systems can either set higher standards for hiring or pay lower salaries with no effect on quality. On the other hand, when supply is limited, quality may be sacrificed if salaries remain low relative to those in other professions. Traditionally, teacher salaries have been lower than those in many other white-collar professions. The coincidence of comparatively low teacher salaries with the purported teacher shortages of the 1980s has raised teacher quality as an important issue in the education reform debate.

It is assumed in educational practice that teacher quality or effectiveness can be measured, at least in part, through standardized paper-and-pencil tests of academic ability or achievement. Indeed, some policies aimed at improving teacher quality have relied on standardized tests (e.g., the National Teachers Examination) for their implementation. The research basis for this assumption, however, is limited both by the nature of standardized tests as well as the limitations of causal analysis linking teacher characteristics with improved student achievement. What positive research results there are point to teachers' verbal ability as a factor positively related to student outcomes (Darling-Hammond & Hudson, 1986).

A body of research from the 1980s suggests that the teacher pipeline progressively selects individuals of lesser academic ability. At each stage, from the selection of teacher education as a college major, through the acceptance of a teaching position, and the subsequent decisions to continue in teaching, those with lower tested ability and achievement remain in teaching, whereas those with higher test scores select other majors and careers (Murnane, Singer, Kemple, Olsen, & Willet, 1991; Roberson, Keith, & Page, 1983; Schlechty & Vance, 1981). A general phenomenon likely affecting this selection process is the widening career opportunities of women and minorities. Over the past two decades, teaching has had to compete with other professions for the individuals it has traditionally relied on to meet growing demand. Salaries, one obvious factor in the competition for talent, have also remained lower in teaching than in many other professions requiring a college degree (Rollefson, 1993a).

Research Review

Academic Ability and the Teacher Pipeline: The Talent Loss Hypothesis

The hypothesis that the teaching profession progressively loses the more talented individuals to nonteaching alternatives found support from several studies of various points in the teacher pipeline, specifically the following:

- *At selection of college majors:* Those choosing teacher preparation majors had lower SAT scores than noneducation majors (Schlechty & Vance, 1981; Vance & Schlechty, 1982).

- *At college graduation:* Teacher education graduates had lower SAT scores than did those in noneducation fields (Murnane et al., 1991; Vance & Schlechty, 1982).

- *At entry to teaching positions:* Those entering teaching were more likely to be lower scorers on the National Teachers Examination (NTE) and SAT than nonteaching college graduates (Council of Chief State School Officers, 1984; Murnane et al., 1991; Vance & Schlechty, 1982).

- *At exit from teaching:* Those leaving teaching were more likely to have higher NTE and SAT scores than those remaining (Murnane et al., 1991; Vance & Schlechty, 1982).

- *At reentry to teaching:* Those reentering teaching after a break in service were more likely to be lower scorers on the SAT than those who did not return to teaching (Murnane et al., 1991).

- *Overall declines over time:* A comparison of SAT scores of education majors with all college students between 1972 and 1980 showed not only that scores of education majors were lower than the average of all students but also that the differences were increasing over time (Council of Chief State School Officers, 1984). Between 1972 and 1980, the average of all college students dropped by 20 points, whereas those of education majors dropped by 31 points on the math and 29 points on the verbal SAT.

A limitation of those studies comparing education and noneducation majors is the identification of education majors as representative of teachers, whereas at that time about 30% of entering teachers were non-education majors.

Two other studies, failed to support the talent loss hypothesis:

- Heyns (1988), in a comparison of former and current teachers, found that although former teachers had slightly higher ability scores than those who remained in teaching, the differences were small, and of those who left teaching, the higher scorers were more likely to reenter teaching later. In addition, she found that later entrants to teaching (those who pursued other careers and activities after college and before taking first teaching jobs) had higher scores than those who entered immediately after college.

Both of these effects could raise the average talent level of the teacher workforce.

• Alsalam and Hafner (1989), using a hazard model to examine teacher career decisions, found that neither SAT scores nor college GPA were significant in predicting entry, exit, reentry, or duration in teaching when salary and other human capital characteristics were taken into account.

Is Academic Ability a Measure of Teacher Effectiveness?

The assumption of policymakers and practitioners is that the more academically talented the teacher, the more his or her students will learn. The research evidence, however, is mixed. Some studies of the relationship between teachers' IQ scores and student achievement found no relationship (Schalock, 1979; Soar, Medley, & Coker, 1983). Other studies found a positive relationship between teachers' verbal ability and student achievement, and particularly in gains in reading (Bowles & Levin, 1968; Hanushek, 1970; Summers & Wolf, 1975).

Despite the lack of strong research support, it can be argued that test scores can still be an important indicator. Verbal ability scores may matter to the extent that they suggest the ability to convey ideas, a skill important in teaching (Darling-Hammond & Hudson, 1986). More generally, test scores can indicate persons' competitiveness in the labor market and the opportunities to enter other professional fields (Murnane et al., 1991). Literacy, as measured by the NALS, is positively related to employment status and earnings, both indicators of competitiveness (Sum, 1996).

Academic Ability and Education Policy

The position of the education policy community has been that academic ability *does* matter in teaching. The U.S. Commission on Excellence in Education in its report, *A Nation at Risk* (1983), cited the talent loss research in describing the threat to the quality of American education and recommended policies aimed at raising the academic level of teachers, primarily to increase the academic requirements for entry to teaching and to increase salaries to levels competitive with other professions.

Many other policymakers and professional groups concurred, and since the early 1980s, policies to raise standards for the teaching profession have taken many forms. Requirements for academic majors and master's degrees have been promoted for teacher preparation, and the NTE has enjoined some controversy in setting standards for entry to teaching. The practices of granting waivers to those who failed the NTE or emergency certificates to those lacking standard certification suggest, however, that increasing standards for entry does not always produce the intended results, that doing so effectively limits the pool of applicants to the extent that those same standards must be relaxed through waivers to meet demand for new teachers. The more recent work of the National Board for Professional Teaching Standards and the National Council for Accreditation of Teacher Education represents a more systemic approach to raising standards for the profession.

Results of Policy Recommendations
on Teacher Salaries

Teacher salaries, in constant dollars, have risen and fallen dramatically since the 1960s (see Figure 3.1). At the time of the Commission report in 1983, teacher salaries were just beginning to increase from their lowest point since the mid-1960s. Although salaries climbed throughout the rest of 1980s, by 1988 they had just caught up with the high they had attained 16 years earlier in 1972. Since 1988, teacher salaries have risen only modestly above inflation.

Even though the salaries of other professional groups also fell during the 1970s and early 1980s, some researchers report that the salaries of teachers fell even more. Math majors in teaching, for instance, earned 77% of what math majors in business and industry earned in 1973, and by 1981 they earned only 61% (Murnane et al., 1991).

Despite the increases in the late 1980s, by 1991 first-year teaching salaries were still lower than salaries earned by new college graduates in nonteaching jobs in several occupations (see Table 3.1). One year after graduation, teachers earned 65% of what computer scientists and 76% of what mathematicians and physical scientists earned in nonteaching jobs (Rollefson, 1993a). Even when teacher salaries are adjusted to account for length of the school year, most of these differences remain. Data from the same survey conducted in 1987 indicate that the relative standing of first-year teacher salaries compared with first-year salaries in other professions had not changed over those 4 years.

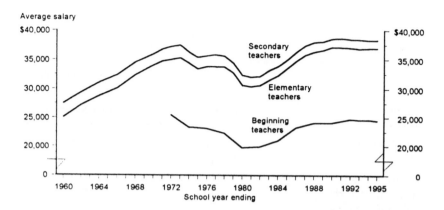

Figure 3.1. Average Annual and Beginning Salaries (in 1995 constant dollars) for Public School Teachers: Selected School Years Ending: 1960 to 1995[a]
SOURCE: U.S. Department of Education, National Center for Education Statistics, *The Condition of Education, 1996.*
a. Plotted points for average annual salary for teachers are even years 1960 through 1968 and all years 1970 through 1975. Plotted points for average beginning salary for teachers are even years 1972 through 1988 and all years 1990 through 1995.

Do Salaries Make a Difference in the Recruitment and Retention of Teachers?

The research evidence is again mixed. Research in North Carolina and Michigan (Murnane et al., 1991) suggests that teachers stay longer in districts with higher than lower salary streams, that lower paid teachers are more likely to leave teaching, especially in their first years, and that higher paid teachers are more likely to return to teaching after a break.

Data from the NCES Teacher Follow-Up Survey on the influence of salaries on decisions to stay in teaching provide mixed results. Of those teachers who left the teaching profession because they were dissatisfied with teaching as a career, only 8% cited poor salary as their main reason for dissatisfaction. On the other hand, when asked what schools could do to encourage teachers to stay in teaching, 46% of all teachers who had left teaching (in 1988) and 38% of leavers (in 1991) said, "[Provide] higher salaries or better fringe benefits" (Bobbitt, Leich, Whitener, & Lunch, 1994). Using more sophisticated modeling techniques with the same data set,

TABLE 3.1 Average Annual Salaries of New Bachelor's Degree
Recipients in Teaching and Other Selected Occupations:
1991

Occupation	Salary	Teacher Salary as a Percentage of Other Salaries
All occupations	$23,632	84%
Teaching	19,913[a]	—
Computer science	30,419	65
Mathematics and physical sciences	26,040	76
Business/management	25,961	77
Writers/artists	22,353	89
Biologists	21,325	93
Communications	19,585	102
Public affairs/social	19,227	104

SOURCE: Data are from the Survey of Recent College Graduates, 1991, and the School and Staffing Survey, 1991, U.S. Department of Education, National Center for Education.
a. Scheduled salary for a first-year teacher based on an average contract length of 9.7 months.

however, neither salary nor satisfaction with salary explained actual attrition behavior of teachers (Arnold & Choy, 1993).

Some researchers, in interpreting the results of research on the talent loss hypothesis, argue that the effect of increased standards has been the opposite of what was intended, that is, that increasing standards at a time when salary increases were not commensurate effectively raised the cost to individuals of entering teaching, thereby creating disincentives. Those with the skills and test scores to compete for better paying jobs were drawn away from teaching.

A Human Capital Model of the Teacher Labor Market

The changes in the teacher labor market since World War II illustrate the effect of increased competition from other professions on the supply of potential teachers. At the end of World War II, teaching was the principal professional opportunity for women and minorities. At that time, 79% of black women entering the labor market after college went into education, but by the 1980s, this had decreased to 24%. Among white women, the change was from 69% to 24% (Murnane et al., 1991).

Human capital theory posits that as alternatives to teaching increase, the teaching profession will increasingly have to compete with other professions for talented individuals. To the extent that teacher salaries remain low in relation to alternative professions (those requiring the same level and type of skills) and to the extent that demand for teachers continues to rise, the teaching profession will lose the more talented individuals to the competition.

Many researchers have studied the balance of supply and demand as it affects teacher quality (National Research Council, 1990). Usually these studies are limited to the context of the education system. Few have studied teacher quality in the context of the larger labor market. The 1992 NALS allows the examination of teacher characteristics in this larger context by providing measures of the literacy proficiencies of teachers compared with those of individuals in other professions, their labor market status, and their earnings. With these data, we can examine the extent to which the teacher labor market has selected individuals of lesser verbal ability than other higher paying professions.

Data Source

The NALS of 1992 is a project of the National Center for Education Statistics of the U.S. Department of Education. Its purpose is to profile the English literacy skills of adults in the United States, variations across major subgroups of the population, and the relation of literacy to key social and economic factors. Literacy was assessed with an array of tasks that reflect the materials and demands adults encounter in their daily lives in prose, document, and quantitative areas. Prose literacy, the dependent variable used in this analysis, is defined as the knowledge and skills needed to understand and use information from texts that include editorials, news stories, poems, and fiction; for example, finding a piece of information in a newspaper article, interpreting instructions from a warranty, inferring a theme from a poem, or contrasting views expressed in an editorial (Kirsch, Jungeblut, Jenkins, & Kolstad, 1993). Of the literacy scales, it is the one that most closely reflects the verbal ability that researchers have tied to teacher quality.

In addition to the literacy tasks, respondents provided information on their demographic characteristics, educational backgrounds, reading practices, and other areas related to literacy. Using IRT scaling methods, respondents received scores ranging from 0 to 500 on prose, document, and quantitative literacy. A nationally representative sample of more than 25,000 adults aged 16 years and older was surveyed.

Methods

The hypothesis tested is that full-time teachers have lower levels of literacy than those employed full-time in other white-collar professions, holding constant a set of confounding variables, including gender, highest level of educational attainment, and age.

In addition to teaching, white-collar occupations, including scientists, lawyers, executives and managers, engineers, physicians, writers and artists, social workers, sales representatives, educational administrators, registered nurses, and sales supervisors and proprietors were entered as dummy variables in the model. Occupations were included when they were deemed reasonable alternatives to teaching for people with similar levels of education and there were enough sample observations to have reasonable statistical properties. Because prose literacy is likely to be related to postbaccalaureate work, the highest level of educational attainment was included in the model as a control variable, along with age and gender.

For this analysis, the NALS sample was restricted to those adults with at least a bachelor's degree who were employed full-time. This left a sample of about 12,500 adult workers, about 900 of whom were teachers. Data were weighted to national estimates. The equations were estimated using a form of Generalized Least Squares regression that considers the complex nature of the survey design (multistaged, clustered, stratified sample).

If teachers have lower prose literacy scores than individuals in competing occupations (holding constant highest level of educational attainment, age, and gender), then this provides confirmatory evidence that the teaching market does select (or retain or both) less able individuals as so defined. If, however, the literacy levels of teachers are no lower than their counterparts in other occupations, then the talent loss hypothesis would not be supported.

Results and Implications

In 1992, teacher literacy scores were similar to other college graduates employed full-time in the occupations of private-sector executives and managers, engineers, physicians, writers and artists, social workers, sales representatives, education administrators, and registered nurses (see Table 3.2). Scientists had measurably higher prose literacy scores, and supervisors and proprietors had measurably lower scores than teachers. As predicted, teachers had among the lowest annual and weekly earnings of all occupational groups.

Other apparent differences in literacy scores of teachers and other occupational groups were not statistically significant, but even if they had been, the differences were still small. After controlling for a set of confounding variables—sex, age, and graduate education (graduate school with and without a graduate degree)—the results changed very little (see Table 3.3). Scientists, lawyers, accountants, and private-sector managers had higher predicted literacy scores than the average bachelor's degree recipient in an occupation other than those presented in Table 3.2. Teachers had predicted literacy scores similar to other occupations.

These results do not support the talent loss hypothesis that low salaries in the teaching profession draw the least academically able college graduates into the teaching workforce. In general, teachers have average literacy skills equal to that of the average full-time employed person with at least a bachelor's degree.

The failure to find the differences in prose proficiency between teachers and other professionals even when the predicted differences in salary were found may be the result of a number of factors, as follows:

1. *Measurement instruments*: The measure of verbal ability, NALS prose proficiency scores, may differ enough from the SAT or the NTE to account for the differences in results. As a measure of the literacy level of the whole adult population, we might suspect that the NALS is easier or less discriminating than the SAT, which is designed for a more selected college-bound population. There is no indication, however, of a ceiling effect or lack of discrimination because none of the occupational groups included in this analysis scored above level 4 when level 5 is the highest literacy level on the scale. Certainly, however, there remain differences in these tests in purposes, content domains, and scoring methods. Further analysis of these differences might enhance

TABLE 3.2 Prose Literacy Scores, Labor Market Outcomes, and Other Characteristics of Full-Time Employed Bachelor's Degree Recipients, by Occupation: 1992

Occupation	Average Prose Literacy Scores	Average Annual Earnings in 1991	Average Weekly Wage Last Week	Average Weeks Worked in 1991	Average Age	Percentage With Graduate Degrees	Percentage Female
Bachelor's degree recipients	334	$38,530*	$805*	49*	40*	35*	38*
Scientists	354*	39,320*	805	49*	36*	43	21*
Lawyers and judges	352	71,223*	871*	49*	41	94*	17*
Accountants and auditors	344	38,463*	832*	50*	37*	28*	38*
Private-sector executives and managers	341	56,044*	1,052*	51*	41	33*	26*
Postsecondary teachers	340	47,867	924	48	45	90*	29*
Engineers	339	48,408*	952	50*	41	32*	8*
Physicians	335	121,120	2,454*	49	44	100*	16*
Teachers[a]	333	25,983	568	45	42	48	71
Writers and artists	332	29,507	589	46	39	33	47
Social workers	332	26,739	551	50*	40	38	60
Sales representatives	328	39,872*	900	49*	42	10*	23*
Education administrators	326	44,130*	888*	50*	49*	79*	57
Registered nurses	326	33,981*	741*	49	38	16*	88*
Sales supervisors and proprietors	316	32,720	669	51*	41	21*	20*

SOURCE: Data are from the National Adult Literacy Survey 1992, U.S. Department of Education, National Center for Education Statistics.

a. Prekindergarten and kindergarten teachers, elementary school and secondary school teachers, teachers in special education, and teachers not elsewhere categorized.

*Statistically significant difference from teachers.

TABLE 3.3 Actual and Predicted Prose Literacy Scores for Full-Time
Employed Bachelor's Degree Recipients: 1992

Occupation	Actual	Predicted[a]
Scientists	354	351
Lawyers and judges	352	344
Accountants and auditors	344	343
Private-sector executives and managers	341	341
Postsecondary teachers	340	336
Engineers	339	339
Physicians	335	329
Elementary teachers	335	**330**
Secondary teachers	335	**328**
Writers and artists	332	331
Social workers	332	330
Sales reps	328	331
Education administrators	326	323
Registered nurses	326	327
Supervisors and proprietors: Sales	316	319

SOURCE: Data are from the National Adult Literacy Survey 1992, U.S. Department
of Education, National Center for Education Statistics.
a. Predicted scores statistically adjust for sex, postgraduate coursework and
degrees, and age.

understanding of the abilities being measured and the effect of the
instruments on the constructs measured.

2. *The supply of teachers*: An important assumption of the research on
   teacher supply and teacher quality has been that the supply of prospective teachers is limited, and that therefore, in periods of lower salaries
   and poorer working conditions, quality of teachers would suffer. This
   was based on reports of declining enrollments in teacher education
   programs and fewer teacher education majors entering teaching immediately after graduation. Earlier research on the talent loss
   hypothesis limited its definition of prospective teachers to individuals
   with an education major, although even at the time it was known that
   not all teachers came from that source. Evidence continues to accumu-
   late that teachers come from other supply sources besides new teacher
   education graduates (National Center for Education Statistics, 1993;

Rollefson, 1993b; Rollefson & Broughman, 1995), and that these other sources may bring individuals of higher ability levels into the teacher workforce (Heyns, 1988). Policies promoting academic majors, as well as dynamics of the marketplace, can influence some of these shifts in supply. In further research, it is important that all supply sources be considered and that differences in ability by source be examined.

3. *Salary as an incentive for recruiting and retaining quality teachers*: An economic assumption underlying much of the talent loss research is that salary is a key factor in sorting individuals along quality dimensions as they enter the labor market. These findings confirm the lower salaries of teachers compared with other professions but provide no support for a deleterious effect on teacher quality. Contrary to expectations, these results raise the question of whether teachers might, in fact, be less responsive to salary incentives than assumed. Perhaps other workplace conditions, such as the shorter work year and opportunities to work with children, compensate for the lower salaries.

4. *Ability as a factor in hiring teachers*: Another underlying assumption of the research is that school systems select teachers on the basis of ability or some quality represented in SAT or NALS scores. It may be, however, that the teacher labor market compared with those for other professions is relatively indifferent to this type of ability, or that such considerations are outweighed by other requirements such as certification or teacher education.

Overall, this finding of no difference between the verbal ability of teachers and other professionals, especially when the hypothesized differences in salary were confirmed, contradicts many long-held assumptions about the teacher labor market. Further research and development activities in this area should (a) develop or examine other measures of teacher ability or quality and how they compare with standard SAT and NTE and NALS literacy measures; (b) use more comprehensive and accurate definitions of the sources from which teachers are hired and compare ability or quality of the various sources; (c) develop and use other hard data measures, beyond salary, of factors that influence decisions of individuals to enter, leave, or return to teaching; (d) conduct more research on the teacher labor market to determine the factors that schools use in decisions to hire individuals; and (e) whenever possible, compare teaching with alternative professions to provide a wider context for understanding the teacher labor market.

References

Alsalam, N., & Hafner, A. L. (1989, March). *An event analysis of entry, exit, and reentry into the teaching profession: Evidence from the high school class of 1972.* Paper presented at the meeting of the American Educational Research Association, San Francisco.

Arnold, C. L., & Choy, S. P. (1993). *Modeling teacher supply and demand, with commentary* (NCES No. 93-461). Washington, DC: U.S. Department of Education, National Center for Education Statistics.

Bobbitt, S. A., Leich, M. C., Whitener, S. D., & Lunch, H. F. (1994). *Characteristics of stayers, movers, and leavers: Results from the teacher follow-up survey: 1991-1992* (NCES No. 95-0313-M). Washington, DC: U.S. Department of Education, National Center for Education Statistics. (ERIC Document Reproduction Service No. ED 374 134)

Bowles, S., & Levin, H. M. (1968). The determinants of scholastic achievement—an appraisal of some recent evidence. *Journal of Human Resources, 3*, 3-34.

Council of Chief State School Officers. (1984). *Staffing the nation's schools: A national emergency.* Washington, DC.

Darling-Hammond, L., & Hudson, L. (1986). *Indicators of teacher and teaching quality.* Washington, DC: RAND.

Hanushek, D. (1970). *The production of education, teacher quality and efficiency.* Washington, DC: Government Printing Office.

Heyns, B. (1988). Educational defectors: A first look at teacher attrition in NLS-72. *Educational Researcher, 17*(3), 24-32.

Kirsch, I. S. Jungeblut, A., Jenkins, L., & Kolstad, A. (1993). *Adult literacy in America: A first look at the National Adult Literacy Survey.* Washington, DC: U.S. Department of Education, National Center for Education Statistics.

Murnane, R. J., Singer, J. D., Kemple, J. J., Olsen, R. J., & Willet, J. B. (1991). *Who will teach?* Cambridge, MA: Harvard University Press.

National Center for Education Statistics. (1993a). *The condition of education: 1993* (NCES No. 93-290). Washington, DC: NCES.

National Center for Education Statistics. (1993b). *Occupational and educational outcomes of the 1989-1990 bachelor's degree recipients 1 year after graduation: 1991* (NCES No. 93-1261-M). Washington, DC: NCES.

National Research Council. (1990). *Precollege science and mathematics teachers: Monitoring supply, demand, and quality.* D. M. Gilford & E. Tenenbaum (Eds.). Washington, DC: National Academy Press.

Roberson, S. D., Keith, T. Z., & Page, E. B. (1983). Now who aspires to teach? *Educational Researcher, 12*, 13-21.

Rollefson, M. (1993a). *Teacher salaries—are they competitive?* (NCES No. 93-450). Washington, DC: U.S. Department of Education, National Center for Education Statistics.

Rollefson, M. (1993b). *Teacher supply in the United States: Sources of newly hired teachers in public and private schools* (NCES No. 93-424). Washington, DC: U.S. Department of Education, National Center for Education Statistics.

Rollefson, M., & Broughman, S. (1995). *Teacher supply in the United States: Sources of newly hired teachers in public and private schools: 1988-1991* (NCES No. 95-348). Washington, DC: U.S. Department of Education, National Center for Education Statistics.

Schalock, D. (1979). Research on teacher selection. In D. C. Berliner (Ed.), Review of research in education (Vol. 7, pp. 364-417). Washington, DC: American Educational Research Association.

Schlechty, P. C., & Vance, V. (1981). Do academically able teachers leave education? The North Carolina case. *Phi Delta Kappan, 63*(2), 106-112.

Soar, R. S., Medley, D. M., & Coker, H. (1983). Teacher evaluation: A critique of currently used methods. *Phi Delta Kappan, 65*(4), 239-246.

Sum, A. (1996). *Literacy in the labor force: Results from the National Literacy Survey.* Washington, DC: U.S. Department of Education, National Center for Education Statistics.

Summers, A. A., & Wolfe, B. L. (1975). *Equality of educational opportunity quantified: A production function approach.* Philadelphia: Department of Research, Federal Reserve Bank of Philadelphia.

U.S. Commission on Excellence in Education. (1983). *A nation at risk: The imperative for educational reform.* Washington, DC: Government Printing Office.

Vance, V. S., & Schlechty, P. C. (1982). The distribution of academic ability in the teaching force: Policy implications. *Phi Delta Kappan, 64*(1), 22-27.

CONTEXT:
REFLECTIONS AND IMPLICATIONS

Thomas Weible

John E. White

In the preceding chapters, we have been exposed to three aspects of context. Chapters 1 and 2 present complementary ideas about multicultural education and its role in teacher education. They are similar in that they both see perspective taking as crucial to multicultural competence. They are different in that one promotes such competence through case studies of whole systems, thus, developing global awareness; the other does so through modeling multicultural teaching and extending an understanding of self as a cultural being to understanding of others as cultural beings. In Chapter 3, the authors address the economic context, namely salaries, and their potential effect on teacher quality.

The Global Context

In Chapter 1, McNergney, Regelbrugge, and Harper remind us of how small the world has become and how similar our concerns are. Although there undoubtedly are still major health and welfare concerns to be confronted, the reality is that worldwide human health is improving, economies are growing, and cultures are bumping squarely up against one another. In short, the world is undergoing rapid change. Concomitant with such dynamic changes are the opportunities and tensions that evolve. These authors propose that comparisons and case studies of multicultural issues in other countries are not only helpful but also a necessary part of preparing teachers for the modern age. They offer us a brief systematic look at the countries of Singapore, India, South Africa, Denmark, and England.

All these countries are attempting to respond to the emergence of previously subordinated or oppressed cultures into the mainstream of more democratic practices. Their approaches are similar and are characteristic of the intercultural, or intergroup, education. James Banks (1994), noted scholar of subjects multiethnic, described intergroup, or intercultural, education in the following:

Activities designed to reduce prejudice and to increase interracial understanding included the teaching of isolated instructional units on various ethnic groups, exhortations against prejudice, organizing assemblies and cultural get-togethers, disseminating information on racial, ethnic, and religious backgrounds, and banning considered stereotypic and demeaning to ethnic groups. (p. 24)

A common feature in these countries is a desire to bring people into the mainstream with as little effect on mainstream operations as possible. They want to maintain the status quo way of conducting a society. Some talk of changing educational structures and approaches but talk little of changing philosophies or purposes as a result of becoming a more inclusive society. In Singapore, we see a promotion of "conformity to a standard view of citizenship" (p. 3) while there exists a "recognition of people's most deeply held ancestral beliefs and cultural values" (p. 3). In India, we find a desire among educators to develop a cross-cultural consciousness that still requires people to think of themselves as citizens of India first. Thus, we see a given: The current economic and governance structures need only minor tuning. Countries need only to ensure equality of opportunity that is respectful of cultural differences. In essence, the dominant culture is telling all others, "Be like us in the economic sphere, and we'll let you be anything you want in others." This doesn't sound very different from what many people say about multiculturalism in the United States.

If the intent of the first part of this chapter is to convince us that we can learn much from comparative studies, it succeeds. There is much to be learned from observing the means by which others organize to operate their systems and resolve their conflicts. These authors make a strong case for being knowledgeable of the whole of a culture whether it be ours or someone else's. In fact, it is through knowing and judging the efficacy of other cultural approaches that we ultimately face questions about the efficacy of our own approaches. Tomorrow's teachers will continue to face a highly diverse population. They need to be supported by a system that understands, appreciates, and accommodates such diversity. Learning about other cultures more deeply should lead us to see diversity as natural and desirable.

The Personal Context

Just as McNergney and his colleagues encourage perspective taking, Striedieck makes the same assertion in Chapter 2, this volume. She suggests that we "reconceptualize the compensatory notion of multicultural education . . . to a notion of multiple cultures and perspectives" (p. 39). In some ways, her chapter complements to the prior one. She finds that the way to multicultural competence is through a teaching approach that requires introspection about self as a cultural being. From such introspection comes an openness to and respect for oneself as a connected person. It's a short step to realizing that other people are also connected persons to other cultures. It is easy to imagine a student who had the benefit of participating in a course like Christine's being able to extend this learning to the case study approach suggested in Chapter 1, and vice versa.

Finally, what Striedieck shows us is a classroom culture that is itself multicultural. She says, "Christine recognized the importance of the composition of the class as a dynamic factor in shaping classroom discourse, as well as in influencing their meaning-making processes about notions of culture and perspective" (p. 40). We see the value of giving students the "opportunity to critically engage in and make meaning of cultural diversity" (p. 39). By so doing, we prepare them to be persons who understand, appreciate, and accommodate diversity.

The Economic Context

As Rollefson and Smith readily admit, paper-and-pencil tests are hardly the most desirable way to determine teacher quality. Because the public perception is that teachers are poorer performers on such tests, however, it is necessary from time to time to examine the data, simply to provide a voice of reason and objectivity when this issue arises. Once again they conclusively show us that teachers as a group are comparable to virtually any other group of professionals. What should be amazing to readers is that they are comparable *even though their annual income is significantly lower than that of their counterparts.*

So what do we do with this information? Perhaps we add it to the wealth of information that David Berliner and Bruce Biddle (1997) have provided for us in *The Manufactured Crisis:*

- Between 1981 and 1991, the average SAT verbal score of those planning to teach rose 13 points and SAT math rose 24. (p. 104)
- 10% of those entering teacher education programs come from the highest fifth of the SAT distribution. (p. 104)
- 50% of all current teachers hold master's degrees or higher. (p. 106)

Also, they noted that prospective teachers go through rigorous academic and character assessments. They question whether those determining such policies (legislators and politicians) would be able to meet the very standards they impose on teachers. They also address the general competency issue. According to them, "roughly 80,000 people die every year—and at least 150,000 more are injured annually—from medical negligence in hospitals." Medical malpractice is the third leading cause of preventable death. More people die that way than from automobiles and firearms combined (Dye, cited in Berliner & Biddle, p. 108). Yet physicians' average incomes, as noted in the Rollefson and Smith study, are greater than $121,000. Perhaps we should ask the quality/salary question about them!

Conclusion

A striking and rather frightening conclusion that we draw from these three chapters is that the profession of teaching is and will be even more demanding and complex than it has ever been. The multiple roles that teachers must perform well are increasing in number and complexity (McIntyre & O'Hair, 1996). The information age is with us, multicultural diversity is the norm rather than the exception, and material incentives to become teachers remain minimal. We have the knowledge base, the expertise, and the incoming talent needed to make great strides in teacher preparation. When the resources match the rhetoric, we then can look forward to taking American education to powerful new levels.

References

Banks, J. A. (1994). *Multiethnic education: Theory and practice* (3rd ed.). Boston: Allyn & Bacon.

Berliner, D. C., & Biddle, B. J. (1997). *The manufactured crisis: Myths, fraud, and the attack on America's public schools.* New York: Longman.

McIntyre, D. J., & O'Hair, M. J. (1996). *The reflective roles of the classroom teacher.* Belmont, CA: Wadsworth.

Processes for Implementing Change in Teacher Education

PROCESSES:
OVERVIEW AND FRAMEWORK

Robert Alley

Carol B. Furtwengler

Dennis Potthoff

Robert Alley, Professor of Curriculum and Instruction at Wichita State University, has published widely in the field of teacher education. His research interests include the future of education, teacher efficacy, and instructional strategies involving motivation and classroom discipline. He is also a member of the ATE Task Force on Teacher Education Certification.

Carol B. Furtwengler is Associate Professor of Educational Administration at Wichita State University. Her specialties include personnel management and evaluation and field-based inquiry. She has published articles about state-level programs for beginning teachers, teacher evaluation, and observation of cooperative learning classes. She also has a book chapter on the assessment of cooperative learning to her credit.

Dennis Potthoff, Assistant Professor of Professional Teacher Education at the University of Nebraska at Kearney, recently completed a stint as coordinator of a professional development school site. He also teaches courses that focus on teacher reflection. Potthoff publishes in the following areas: preservice teacher field experiences, mentoring programs for beginning teachers, portfolios, and school and university collaborations.

Promoting and managing change is at the very heart of productive education. According to Fullan (1993), change is the province of every person within educational institutions, a moral imperative for all who work within such institutions if we are to have a productive educational system. Effecting change within educational institutions is, however, both difficult and problematic. Recently—particularly into the 1970s—the education profession has suffered especially from a lack of confidence in its ability to effect systemic change (Fullan, 1993). But by the late 1970s and early 1980s, a renewal of efforts to institutionalize change, by means of a number of different approaches, was evident. The first of four quite different approaches to renewal to emerge in the late 1970s was the effective schools movement, which demonstrated that schools can make a difference in the lives of their students—even under trying conditions.

In the second approach to renewal, Joyce and Showers (1980), among others, demonstrated the efficacy of inservice and staff development in the process of change. By 1980, Fullan (1993) reported, "We could say that we knew a fair amount about the major factors associated with introducing single innovations" (p. 2).

Then, in the 1980s came the now infamous report A Nation at Risk, which signaled a third approach to change. In this approach, large-scale governmental action came to be viewed as the most likely means of effecting change. Structural change was promulgated through top-down solutions, such as mandated curricula, increased graduation requirements, and minimal competency tests both for students and teachers. The tenor of the times implied that "change agents" from the outside could effect changes independent of the stakeholders most affected by those very changes—students, teachers, administrators, parents, and teacher educators.

By the mid-1980s, the fourth renewal movement, restructuring, began to overlap the top-down efforts so common to that decade of reform (Fullan, 1993). The restructuring movement emphasized reorganization of institutions to encourage change and improvement at the lowest level of the institution (i.e., the individual school or the teacher education department). The resulting combination, greater top-down regulation and accountability along with more "bottom-up" decentralized control and restructuring strategies, occurred at the same time the educational system was under savage attack from numerous fronts. These interactions produced great confusion in the educational community.

Fortunately, the efforts of the past several decades to better understand change also produced greater knowledge about effecting change in education. Successful processes and strategies for institutionalizing change emerged. Recent literature about two such processes—teacher reflection and situated cognition—are discussed below as background to the specific research studies reported in the next three chapters of this yearbook. Both are fundamental to the change process in contemporary educational settings.

Teacher Reflection

The development of teachers' reflective skills is a fundamental element of change currently stressed in most preservice teacher education programs. Peterson and Phelps (1989-1990), for example, suggested that the major question facing teacher educators today is not *whether* reflection experiences should be incorporated into preservice programs but, rather, *how* to do so effectively.

Although great emphasis is being placed on teacher reflection in the 1990s, the idea that reflection is important is not new. John Dewey's interest in preparing reflective teachers with the capability and orientation to make informed and intelligent decisions provides evidence of the longevity of interest in teacher reflection. Renewed interest in teacher reflection began, however, in the 1970s as the research on teaching shifted from teachers' behaviors to teachers' thinking and decision-making processes (Thompson, 1992).

There is a growing awareness among teacher education professionals that the knowledge base of the teaching profession resides, in part, in the actions of exemplary practitioners (Schon, 1987). Consequently, Schon recommended shifting the focus of teacher education research efforts to teacher inquiry and examination of their own practices. Such inquiry is critical for four reasons. The first reason is that reflection is critical because the scientific, technical rationality view, which argues that teacher problems are solved through the application of theories derived through academic research, is inadequate for dealing with the kinds of "messy" and indeterminate situations that teachers most often face in their work. Teachers today are frequently confronted by situations in which the tasks they are required to perform are no longer similar to the tasks for which they were educated. The second reason for emphasizing reflection is to help preservice teachers better understand and account for biases brought about by previous experiences. Pajares (1993) believed it was important for preservice teachers to ruthlessly pursue and judge the accuracy of their belief systems. The third reason for stressing reflection is to prevent errors made when teachers oversimplify complex situations. Ross (1989) contended that preservice teachers tend to oversimplify causal relationships. Teacher educators should, therefore, design assignments that provide opportunities for students to reanalyze conclusions made previously in light of new evidence. The fourth reason for promoting teacher reflection is to use reflection as a tool for bridging the gap between concrete experiences and the formal learning of relevant concepts (Sharan & Sharan, 1987).

Although most educators agree that reflection is an important tool for improved practice, there are a variety of perspectives about how best to promote teacher reflection. Zeichner (1990) recommended the following field-based strategies for promoting reflection:

1. Asking preservice teachers to engage in inquiry, often collaborative inquiry, using an action research format.
2. Restructuring the content and organization of the field experience component.
3. Implementing supervision models, such as peer supervision and clinical supervision, which especially encourage reflection.
4. Developing interactive seminars that facilitate discussion of field-based inquiries in a communal context.

The move toward reflection through the field-based strategies noted blends well with a second process shift, situated cognition, which attempts to embed teacher education instruction into realistic contexts.

Situated Cognition

The history of teaching has been steeped in the didactic method of instruction. The teacher prepares lecture notes, stands in front of the podium or desk, and delivers knowledge to students. Passive students take notes, memorize the notes and the assigned textbook, and demonstrate knowledge of the content on multiple choice or essay exams. Recent demands for changes in instruction and assessment are questioning the value of didactic instruction. Situated cognition, on the other hand, supports problem-based learning. Resnick (1989) identified three underlying assumptions of cognition theory: (a) learning is "a process of knowledge construction, not of knowledge recording and absorption; (b) learning is knowledge-dependent; people use current knowledge to construct new knowledge; and (c) learning is highly tuned to the situation in which it takes place" (p. 1).

Experts in situated cognition, however, go even further and suggest that studying problems in a higher education classroom setting eliminates the contextual situation. Brown, Collins, and Duguid (1988) stated,

> Much school work has become a highly specialized, self-confirming activity in a culture of its own. When, for pedagogic purposes, authentic domain activities are transferred to the classroom, their context is usually transmuted; they become classroom tasks and part of school culture. Classroom procedures are then applied to what have become classroom tasks. As a result, the system of learning and using (and, of course, testing) can remain hermetically sealed with the self confirming culture of the school. As a consequence, contrary to the aim of schooling, success within this culture often has little bearing on performance elsewhere (p. 9).

Vygotsky (1978) promoted cognitive development rooted in social experience with other adults. Situated cognition has built on Vygotskian theory and perceives learning in a social context and as a social phenomenon rather than occurring within the mind of the individual (Orey & Nelson, 1994). Brown, Collins, and Duguid (1988) stated that "knowing (and not just learning) . . . is inextricably situated in the physical and social context of its acquisition and use. It cannot be extracted from these without being irretrievably transformed" (p. 6).

Basically, situated cognition explains the difference between "knowing" and "doing" and explains why many students have "learned" information but cannot access the information when confronted with problems in the real world. This theoretical position believes that all knowledge is situated in contexts or "knowledge resides in a jointly constructed space of mind and the situation in which mind finds itself confronted with a problem" (Silver, 1990).

What situated cognition can bring to teacher preparation programs is the need for students to learn to address and solve problems within the context in which they occur—and this context is not the higher education classroom. Problem-based case studies have contributed a new approach for instruction, but situated cognition extends the ideas further. Situated cognition requires learners to be in the context in a social situation. Educators have intuitively accepted this fact since the time of Dewey, when "learn by doing" was first recognized as an effective instructional technique. Gardner (1991) noted that Dewey's approach to learning supports the cognitive apprenticeship to learning proposed by constructivists and proponents of situated learning. To use multiple intelligences, students must experience the arts, language, and the integration of content. Situated cognition and cognitive apprenticeships provide a constructivist approach for teacher education. Teacher education programs need a curriculum that is anchored (Cognition and Technology Group at Vanderbilt, 1990) in field experiences and professional development schools.

Situated cognition addresses major themes heard in the cry for reform: (a) relationships with the field in clinical settings where curriculum is integrated across content and inquiry areas and (b) instructional methods that emphasis problem-based learning through teamwork. Proponents argue that teaching should incorporate problem-based learning, but the driving force should be on authentic learning experiences for students. Movement must be made from mastery learning of "inert knowledge" that cannot be applied on the job to competence in instruction, classroom management, and reflection that develops inquiry and problem-solving skills. Field experiences, including those in professional development schools, further allow students to fine-tune their problem-identification, problem-definition, and problem-solving strategies within a collaborative, team environment where synergistic activity results in the whole being greater than the parts.

Three Research Reports

How does a teacher preparation program move from didactic instruction to one emphasizing reflection and situated cognition? The chapters that follow report on three quite disparate research efforts to effect changes in specific aspects of three different teacher education programs. In the first (Chapter 4), Bennett reports on her efforts to enhance teacher decision making through the Teacher as Decision Maker Program (TADMP) at Indiana University. Bennett developed a conceptual framework involving seven perspectives that students bring to the teacher education program. She taught the seven perspectives to the students, engaged them in an ongoing dialogue about their beliefs about teaching, and induced them to reflect on that process in new, systematic ways. The reflection forced the students to reconceptualize their roles as teachers.

In Chapter 5, Sanders and Meloth focus upon the underutilization of the cooperative learning model, despite its extensive theoretical base and the more than ample data demonstrating its utility. In particular, the authors explore the need for teachers to "buy into" a different view of the teacher-learning process along with the need to change teacher belief systems related to the nature and purpose of learning. Only then will changes such as those reflected in the adoption of cooperative learning models for teaching be successful.

Foss, in Chapter 6, describes an attempt to implement instrumental change in a preservice mathematics methods course. Specifically, she describes the fundamental changes in the teacher's conceptions of instruction, the teacher's instructional behavior, and the reaction of the preservice teachers enrolled in the course. Her results call attention to the seemingly insurmountable obstacles to change, entrenchment of the teacher candidates' perceptions about appropriate instructional strategies and the overpowering influence these perceptions have on the behavior of the methods instructor herself.

References

Brown, J. S., Collins, A., & Duguid, P. (1988). *Situated cognition and the culture of learning* (Technical Report No. 6886). Cambridge, MA: Bolt, Beranek, and Newman.

Cognition and Technology Group at Vanderbilt. (1990). Anchored instruction and its relationship to situated cognition. *Educational Researcher, 19*(6), 2-10.

Fullan, M. (1993). *Change forces: Probing the depths of educational reform.* London: Falmer.

Gardner, H. (1991). *The unschooled mind.* New York: Basic Books.

Joyce, B. (1987). Reflections on tomorrow's teachers. *Teachers College Record, 88*(3), 390-393.

Joyce, B., & Showers, B. (1980). Improving inservice training: The messages from research. *Educational Leadership 37*(5), 379-385.

Orey, M. A., & Nelson, W. A. (1994). Situated learning and the limits of applying the results of these data to the theories of cognitive apprenticeships. *Proceedings of Selected Research and Development Presentations at the 1994 National Convention of the Association for Educational Communication and Technology, Research and Theory Division.* (ERIC Document Reproduction Service No. ED 373 746).

Pajares, F. (1993). Preservice teachers' beliefs: A focus for teacher education. *Action in Teacher Education, 15*(2), 45-54.

Peterson, S., & Phelps, P. (1989-1990). S.I.R.: A supervisory technique to promote reflection. *The Teacher Educator, 25*(3), 21-24.

Prestine, N. A. (1993). Apprenticeship in problem-solving: Extending the cognitive apprenticeship model. In P. Hallinger, K. Leithwood, & J. Murphy (Eds.), *Cognitive perspectives on educational leadership* (pp. 192-212). New York: Teachers College Press.

Resnick, L. B. (Ed.). (1989). *Knowing, learning, and instruction: Essays in honor of Robert Glaser.* Hillsdale, NJ: Lawrence Erlbaum.

Ross, D. (1989). First steps in developing a reflective approach. *Journal of Teacher Education, 40*(2), 22-30.

Schon, D. (1983). *The reflective practitioner: How professionals think in action.* New York: Basic Books.

Schon, D. (1987). *Educating the reflective practitioner.* San Francisco: Jossey Bass.

Schon, D. (1989). Professional knowledge and reflective practice. In T. Sergiovanni & J. H. Moore (Eds.), *Schooling for tomorrow.* Boston: Allyn & Bacon.

Schulman, L. (1987). Knowledge and teaching: Foundations of the new reform. *Harvard Educational Review, 57*(1), 1-32.

Sharan, Y., & Sharan, S. (1987). Training teachers for cooperative learning. *Educational Researcher, 45*(3), 20-25.

Silver, E. A. (1990). *Treating estimation and mental computation as situated mathematical processes.* Pittsburgh University, PA: Learning Research and Development Center. (ERIC Document Reproduction Service No. ED 342 645)

Thompson, A. (1992). Teachers' beliefs and conceptions: A synthesis of the research. In D. A. Grouws (Ed.), *Handbook of research on mathematics teaching and learning* (pp. 127-146). New York: Macmillan.

U.S. Commission on Excellence in Education. (1983). *A nation at risk: The imperative for educational reform.* Washington, DC: U.S. Government Printing Office.

Van Manen, M. (1977). Linking ways of knowing with ways of being practical. *Curriculum Inquiry, 6,* 205-228.

Vygotsky, L. S. (1978). *Mind in society.* Cambridge, MA: Harvard University Press.

Zeichner, K. (1990). Changing directions in the practicum: Looking ahead to the 1990s. *Journal of Education for Teaching, 16*(2), 105-132.

Zeichner, K., & Liston, D. (1987). Teaching student teachers to reflect. *Harvard Educational Review, 57*(1), 1-22.

4 How Can Teacher Perspectives Affect Teacher Decision Making?

Christine I. Bennett

Christine I. Bennett is Director of the Research Institute on Teacher Education at Indiana University, Bloomington. Her research includes the impact of a multicultural social studies curriculum on African American, Anglo, and Latino youth; classroom climates in desegregated middle schools; the impact of multicultural teacher education on preservice teachers; and teacher perspectives in teacher reflection and decision making.

ABSTRACT

This chapter reports two phases of research associated with the Teacher as Decision Maker Program (TADMP), a graduate-level program for middle and secondary school certification at Indiana University. In the first phase, seven teacher perspectives emerged from the study of 86 individuals from the fields of science, English, foreign language, math, and social studies: Scholar Psychologist, Friendly Scholar, Inculcator, Facilitator of Thinking, Friendly Pedagogue, Empowerer, and Nurturer. Relationships between perspectives and gender, ethnicity, and content areas were also explored. The latest phase examines these seven teacher perspectives as tools for strengthening self-reflection on teaching among preservice teachers in the TADMP.

Two case studies illustrate how the perspectives were developed and how they can be used to initiate and nurture reflective teaching. Reflective teaching is defined as thoughtful decision making that strives to enhance the personal development and academic performance of virtually *all* students. It is a spiral, ongoing process that involves four interactive dimensions: (1) introspection leading to understanding of one's assumptions, values, and beliefs about teaching; (2) consideration of possible alternatives during the planning and interactive phases of teaching; (3) critical analysis of the effectiveness of selected alternatives; and (4) confirmation or revision of beliefs about teaching and/or best classroom practice.

For the past seven years, I have worked closely with a talented group of preservice teachers seeking middle and secondary school certification through Indiana University's Teacher as Decision Maker Program (TADMP). Teaching and conducting longitudinal research with more than 120 TADMP teachers, from 1988 to 1996, has transformed my work as a teacher educator. Over time, I have discovered the power of the initial teacher perspectives my students bring to the program and how these perspectives can become a tool for reflection and professional growth. This report describes the initial phase of research that led to a conceptual framework of seven teacher perspectives: Inculcators, Friendly Pedagogues, Scholar Psychologists, Facilitators of Thinking, Empowerers, Nurturers, and Friendly Scholars. In addition, this chapter explores how these teacher perspectives help preservice teachers gain a better understanding of themselves as well as other teachers and how the perspectives framework strengthens self-reflection and teacher decision making.

Teacher Perspectives

Teacher perspective refers to the personal attitudes, values, and beliefs that help a teacher justify and unify classroom decisions and actions (Goodman, 1985; Rokeach, 1969). Teacher perspective provides the lens through which teaching is viewed, and it affects the way teaching is perceived and interpreted.

A growing number of researchers argue that the impact of teacher education programs can be strengthened by focusing on prospective teachers' initial beliefs about teaching and teaching metaphors and their background knowledge about teaching (e.g., Britzman, 1986; Bullough, 1991; Shuell, 1992). In his review of teachers' beliefs and educational research, Pajares (1992) wrote, "There are good reasons why attempts to understand the beliefs of preservice teachers are essential to teacher education. Researchers have demonstrated that beliefs influence knowledge acquisition and interpretation, task definition and selection, interpretation of course content, and comprehension monitoring" (p. 328). This was certainly found to be true in our initial research with the first two TADMP cohorts, where some students were much more receptive to TADMP assumptions and practices than others (Bennett & Powell, 1990).

Several case studies have shed light on the nature of teachers' perspectives and suggest that reflection and an understanding of perspective can be tools for both teachers and teacher educators to enhance thoughtful practice (e.g., Goodman & Adler, 1985). Johnston (1992) concluded that "teacher educators can no longer be concerned only with imparting knowledge about teaching" but must help student teachers "understand the values, attitudes, and beliefs they bring to preservice teacher education (as well as) plot and monitor their own professional growth" (p. 134). In short, the influence of teacher education programs might be enhanced if teacher educators better understood their students' perspectives.

The research reported here explored the nature of teacher perspectives held by TADMP teachers as they entered the program and the stability of these perspectives during student teaching and the first three years of classroom teaching. Also addressed are questions about teacher perspectives related to gender, ethnicity, and subject area. Finally, this study explored how an understanding of teacher perspectives can be used to enhance reflection and classroom decision making.

The Decision Maker Theme

The decision maker theme provides a conceptual framework that underlies the TADMP program's goals, rationale, university course work, and field experiences. The professional knowledge emphasized is based primarily on the work of Shulman and Sykes (1986), Shulman (1987), and Tamir (1988), as well as my own work in multicultural education (Bennett, 1995a, 1995b). This framework contains seven areas of inquiry (i.e., the nature of the learner, including aspects of ethnicity and cultural styles; the nature of the subject matter; general pedagogy; content-specific pedagogy; school and community contexts; self-reflection on teaching; and multicultural and global perspectives). The program emphasizes teacher expectations and understandings of how ethnicity, gender, socioeconomic background, and special needs and disabilities can effect the teaching learning process.

Within the TADMP, reflective teaching is defined as thoughtful decision making that strives to enhance the personal development and academic performance of virtually *all* students. This reflection is a spiral, ongoing dialogical process that involves four interactive dimensions: (1) introspection leading to knowledge of one's assumptions, values, and beliefs about teaching; (2) consideration of possible alternatives during the planning and interactive phases of teaching; (3) critical analysis of the effectiveness of selected alternatives for personal and program goals and values; and (4) confirmation or revision of beliefs about teaching or best classroom practice.

As a thematic teacher education program, a goal of the TADMP is to strengthen students' pedagogical schemata and to encourage students to clarify their primary teacher perspectives. We use autobiographical interviews, concept mapping, reflective journals, videotaped classroom observations, and stimulated recall interviews to help students develop schemata for teaching that are more complete, well organized, and stable. We continually ask students to rethink their perspectives in light of their personal classroom experiences and school contexts.

Methodology

Participants

The initial phase of research involved 68 preservice teachers who entered the TADMP between 1988 and 1991. These teachers represented a select group in academic preparation and work experience, interpersonal communication skills, and commitment to teaching. They ranged in age from 23 to 51 and came from many careers, including law, banking, business, homemaking, engineering, nursing, theater, social work, and college teaching. Their areas of certification included 20 in social studies, 18 in science, 18 in English, 6 in math, and 6 in foreign language. The group comprised 37 females and 31 males, with 11 African Americans (16%), 2 Asian Americans, and 55 European Americans.

The implementation phase of our research involved an additional 54 TADMP preservice teachers who had entered the program since 1992. As in previous cohorts, these teachers had degrees in mathematics, English, social studies, science, and foreign languages. The group comprised 29 males and 25 females, of which 13 were African Americans (24%) and 41 were European Americans.

Data Collection

On entering the program, all TADMP teachers participated in autobiographical interviews. Our questions focused on family and education histories; sense of ethnic identity; motivations, values, and conceptions of teaching; conceptions of content area knowledge; and the role of schooling in a democratic society. Using free association concept mapping procedures (Beyerbach, 1988), TADMP teachers were asked to construct concept maps around the central organizing concept of "teaching." Maps were created at four strategic points throughout the program: on entry, end of summer course work, end of fall field experience, and end of student teaching. Lessons taught during the TADMP were videotaped and analyzed in follow-up interviews that focused on planning, interactive teaching, and postteaching reflection. All interviews were audiotaped and subsequently transcribed. We also followed six teachers from each of the first three cohorts during their first three years of teaching, using blind classroom observation and follow-up interviews to explore the validity of the perspective model. These observations have helped us strengthen the color wheel analogy and sharpen the descriptions of each perspective as shown in Tables 4.1 and 4.2 (for details of data collection and analysis, see Bennett, 1991, 1994, 1995a; Bennett & Powell, 1990; Bennett & Spalding, 1991).

Overall Findings

Teaching Perspectives as a Color Wheel

As we sought a way to represent the seven perspectives visually, we wanted to avoid linear designs that might suggest a hierarchy or compartmentalization of the perspectives. Thus, we chose the color wheel as both a model and a metaphor for our general stance toward the perspectives (Bennett & Spalding, 1991).

TABLE 4.1 Teacher Perspectives of TADMP Teachers

Teacher Perspective	Description
Scholar Psychologists	Emphasize academic knowledge and understanding nature of the learner; emphasize relevance in the subject area and helping students become intelligent decision makers in the future.
Friendly Scholars	Emphasize academic knowledge and teacher personality characteristics; stress immediate relevance of subject matter; use subject areas to help students solve personal problems and understand current issues and events.
Inculcators	Emphasize academic knowledge; emphasize transmission of fundamental knowledge and values; view teacher as inspirational role model; teach subject matter as cultural literacy.
Facilitators of Thinking	Emphasize thinking.
Empowerers	Emphasize values.
Nurturers	Emphasize teacher-student interaction.
Friendly Pedagogues	Emphasize instructional strategies.

We found that perspectives, like colors, appear most often in "shades." Just as there are few "pure" colors, there are few "pure" perspectives. The color wheel is also intended to suggest a degree of flexibility among the categories. For example, an individual's fundamental perspective may be that of Empowerer, but she can at times act as a Nurturer or an Inculcator.

Primary Colors

Inculcators (*red*) described the transmission of academic content knowledge as central to teaching. Several aspired to transmit "fundamen-

TABLE 4.2 Seven Teacher Perspectives: Description of Classroom Actions of TADMP Teachers

Perspective \ Actions	Classroom Leadership Style	Student Roles/Behaviors	Content Emphasized	Preferred Instructional Strategies	Responses to School Contexts
Scholar Psychologists	Control through connections and questioning	Cooperative participants	Textbook as a resource / springboard	A wide range	Adaptability
Friendly Scholars	Control through charisma and connections	Passive recipients and admiring fan club	Text plus supplementary materials	Lecture	Questioning
Inculcators	Control through authority	Passive recipient or potential disrupter	Textbook as centerpiece	Lecture	Teacher explanation
Facilitators of Thinking	Student self-control through responsibility	Active participants and decision makers	Primary source materials	Higher-level questions	Student projects
Empowerers	Student self-control and teacher charisma	Passive recipients to active participants	Multiple resources	Discussion	Group work
Nurturers	Student self-control through teacher contact	From caring cooperation to testing the boundaries	Textbook plus hands-on materials	Teacher explanation and student seat work	Willingness to adapt
Friendly Pedagogues	Control through performance and continuous activity	From appreciative to captive audience	A rich array of resources to textbook tedium	Discussion	Group work

81

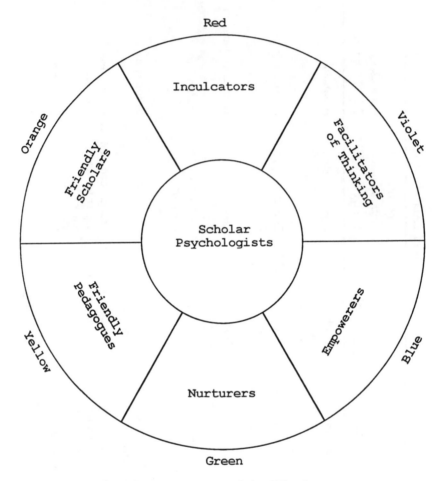

Figure 4.1. Teaching Perspectives as a Color Wheel

tal values" as well. They rarely referred to subject matter relevance, the nature of the learner, or teacher personality characteristics, such as enthusiasm or creativity. They often expressed a desire to "inspire" or be role models. Recurring themes were "control" and "discipline."

Empowerers (*blue*) described teaching as social action or change. They saw academic knowledge as less important than, for example, learners becoming "self-actualized," or "gaining a sense of power and independence and control." Frequently committed to social causes themselves, they hoped to influence students to use political power, understand cultural pluralism, or accept multiple perspectives.

Friendly Pedagogues (*yellow*) defined teaching by lesson preparation and teacher personality characteristics (e.g., "organization" or "enthusiasm"). Most expressed an aversion to "lecture" or to "being boring," and a preference for questioning and discussions. They stressed the importance of preparation and often compared teaching to a "performance."

Secondary Colors

Facilitators of Thinking (*violet*) identified thinking and lifelong learning as the principal goals of teaching. Although often scholarly themselves (and therefore similar to Inculcators), they de-emphasized the importance of content. Their emphasis on "critical thinking," "problem solving," and "learning how to learn" brought them close to the Empowerer perspective, but their recurring focus was cognitive rather than social.

Nurturers (*green*) perceived teaching primarily as interactions with students. They defined good teachers as "open and responsive," "flexible," and "attainable." Because they emphasized the development of the learner and expressed concerns about children as "our future," they resembled Empowerers. Because they de-emphasized academic knowledge, they resembled Friendly Pedagogues.

Friendly Scholars (*orange*) shared with Inculcators an emphasis on the transmission of academic knowledge, but, like Friendly Pedagogues, they stressed teacher personality characteristics such as enthusiasm, humor, and friendliness. Their transmissive view of learning was balanced by a desire to make knowledge relevant and learning fun.

Scholar Psychologists lie at the center of the wheel, representing the murky blend of colors that results from mixing red, violet, blue, green, yellow, and orange. This was the largest and least clearly defined group, who often displayed characteristics of other perspectives. Like Inculcators, they emphasized academic knowledge. Like Friendly Scholars, they wanted to make knowledge relevant. To do this, they often planned elaborate lessons, like Friendly Pedagogues. Like Nurturers, they wanted to be "sensitive" and "available" to students. They were distinguished, however, by several characteristics. They tended to point out relevance for students' future rather than present lives. They used psychological language in describing students, for example, "understanding the nature of adolescent development." They saw themselves as counselors to students, willing to listen to students' problems but not to become personally involved in them.

Teacher Perspectives, Gender, Ethnicity, and Subject Area

Our initial research with 68 preservice teachers revealed some gender and subject area differences in teacher perspectives. An equal number of women and men identified themselves as Scholar Psychologists, the largest category (26.5%). Among Inculcators (16.2%), Facilitators of Thinking (16.2%), and Friendly Pedagogues (10.3%) were nearly equal numbers of men and women. Among Friendly Scholars (14.7%), however, there were more than twice as many men as women, and the Empowerers (10.3%) and Nurturers (5.9%) were all women.

Among the 35 teachers in the TADMP's Fifth and Sixth cohorts were eight Friendly Scholars, seven Scholar Psychologists, six Friendly Pedagogues and Facilitators of Thinking, four Empowerers (one a male), two Empowerer/Nurturers, and two Inculcators. (The self-identification of perspectives within the Seventh Cohort is in process as I write this chapter.) Reflecting a pattern that is evident across the six TADMP cohorts since 1988 ($N + 103$), Empowerers and Nurturers tended to be women, Friendly Scholars tended to be men, and Scholar Psychologists (like the remaining four perspectives) were not associated with gender differences. Six of the eight African American male TADMP teachers identified with the Friendly Scholar perspective, while African American women identified primarily with the Scholar Psychologist or Empowerer/Nurturer perspective.

Scholar Psychologists and Inculcators tended to be science, English, or social studies teachers. Although Friendly Scholars were spread across all the subject areas, one third of them were science teachers. Facilitators of Thinking were primarily in social studies and foreign language. Two of the four Nurturers were in mathematics, and all but one of the seven Empowerers were in social studies or English.

How our understanding of each of the TADMP teacher's primary perspectives developed is illustrated by Cynthia, a mathematics teacher in the Second Cohort. We observed her classroom teaching over 12 months in the TADMP and her first two years of teaching before we analyzed her autobiographical interview. We believe Cynthia is a clear example of the Nurturer, and she agrees with us.

Cynthia

The only child of a factory worker and shipping clerk who eventually bought a liquor store, Cynthia experienced a lonely, somewhat unhappy childhood. She was an excellent student, however, and completed a BA in computer science at a major university in 1973. After graduation, she went to work at an insurance company and attended night school to complete a master's degree in business. She remained with the company for 10 years, moving from programmer to manager of her own systems and development staff, until the premature birth of her twins made it difficult for her to return to work. Five years later, Cynthia and her husband separated, and she returned to the insurance company, earning a good income.

When entering the TADMP in 1989, Cynthia explained her reasons for wanting to teach: "Making a difference. I know I can't change the world, and I don't expect to, but if I can just have one kid feel better about himself, that's important, OK? That's a lot more important than being the vice president of some insurance company." Cynthia described a good teacher as one who "watches you in class. And they pick up on your facial expressions, or they can tell how you react to something. . . . Sensitivity to people's needs is important to me, and drawing (students) out and forcing them to think through it themselves is I think what makes a good teacher."

We visited Cynthia during her prestudent teaching practicum in a seventh-grade math class. A slender woman with long blond hair and large blue eyes that smiled warmly, Cynthia was organized and businesslike. Her sixth-period class was entirely male students, 22 African American and 4 White. The lesson was on polygons. She used visual, auditory, and kinesthetic activities to develop the lesson, which was based on the concept attainment strategy. In the course of 50 minutes, Cynthia interacted with each student several times, and she physically touched each student in an easy manner that they appeared to be comfortable with. Contact with students was facilitated by her arrangement of the desks into a large U shape.

During the follow-up interview, Cynthia explained what stood out in her mind about the lesson:

> I think the kids were on task today. And we did have a good environment today. And I saw kids helping other kids, and that meant a lot to me. Kids working together. And I think a lot of the kids that have trouble with this geometry didn't have trouble

today. They had success today. And they felt good about that. And that made me feel good, too. Some of my kids that would have never gone to the overhead went to the overhead today. And I like that.

After TADMP certification, Cynthia was hired to teach in the high school where she completed her student teaching. We visited her in May (1991) and, after observing several classes, asked her to tell us about them. She responded,

I love all my classes, I do. It's been a real learning experience for me . . . so it took me the first semester to get my own rhythm in. But I love all my classes. They are different. Those computer math kids are wonderful, they are very independent kids. And then I've got the general math kids that don't, aren't interested in school. So I've got a wide range, so I see them both, and I love all of them here. I really care whether they all pass or not.

As in previous visits, we noticed that Cynthia used a lot of positive responses. In less than four minutes of her computer math class we recorded her saying "smart lady," "you guys learn well," "you guys are good, I'm proud of you," "you're great," "you guys are the best math students in the school," "nice work," and so forth. Later Cynthia told us that her math department is excellent. They have won the district's math competition for the past two years, even if

. . . we don't have the best kids, we don't have the brightest kids. They don't come from the best homes, and they don't have the highest IQ, and we still won two years in a row. So it says something about the teachers and the kids working for those teachers.

Each year she decorated her paint-chipped walls with flags: "Say yes to books!" "Have a great day!" "Listen carefully!" "Be happy!" "Smile!" "Think positive!" "We've got class!" One bulletin board had "Math Stars" emblazoned across the top with student papers posted below. Another bulletin board developed the theme "If you can dream it, you can do it!"

Cynthia provides the portrait of a rare and special type of teacher, the Nurturer. She establishes a warm classroom climate where students are genuinely cared for and encouraged to do their best. Nurturers tend to

have more difficulties with classroom discipline, however, than do beginning teachers with different primary perspectives. Understanding of this
potential weakness has helped Nurturers in the TADMP develop a
stronger teacher presence and the ability to be firm without giving up
qualities of fairness and a genuine caring for students.

Implications for Beginning Teachers
and Teacher Educators

Most teachers and teacher educators would agree that knowledge
about one's own beliefs about teaching and learning is essential to becoming an effective teacher. Many teacher educators argue that for beginning
teachers an understanding of one's teacher self is necessary to develop
self-confidence as a teacher, which in turn leads to higher self-expectations
and greater success in the classroom (e.g., Kagan, 1992). Indeed, Kagan
concluded, "Novices without clear self-images as teachers are 'doomed to
flounder.' " Yet even experienced teachers (including teacher educators)
are often unaware of their own beliefs and unaware that there are viable
alternatives to the beliefs they hold. When teachers have not thought about
how their own beliefs, values, and attitudes influence their teaching, they
may react to difficult situations by blaming themselves, their students, the
school, or society when their beliefs do not help them solve problems or
indeed even cause problems (Bennett & Spalding, 1992). How can teacher
perspectives improve teacher decision making?

Beginning with the Fifth Cohort in 1992, I now use the Color Wheel
as a tool for reflection at key points during the TADMP (Bennett, 1994). I
have developed a series of interventions that help preservice teachers
identify the perspectives that are most and least like them, anticipate how
their perspectives might affect their classroom teaching and work with
their mentor teachers, and reflect back on their classroom decision making.
Ronald, a TADMP teacher from the Sixth Cohort, illustrates how an
understanding of teacher perspectives can strengthen reflection on teaching, change, and relationships with mentor teachers. Ronald eventually
identified with the Friendly Scholar perspective but used the entire color
wheel as a tool for reflection on his teaching.

Ronald

The son of a nursing home worker and factory worker, Ronald grew
up in a close-knit family that emphasized education and hard work. After

obtaining a degree in industrial engineering from a Big Ten university, Ronald took a job as a teacher at a Christian school "because they needed somebody who was proficient in math." Although he enjoyed teaching, Ronald left the classroom after one semester to work with a major company for six months. An intelligent, dynamic African American male with exceptional interpersonal skills, Ronald received numerous job offers in his field, and he pursued business and engineering for several years. After learning about the TADMP, he decided to follow his deepest personal convictions and made a career change into teaching. According to Ronald, "A good teacher cares about his or her students. Good teachers have a strong knowledge of what they are teaching, and the ability to get this information across." Ronald was the personification of the Friendly Scholar in the lessons he developed and taught in the education lab, using synectics, humor, and personal charisma to teach math concepts.

When Ronald was introduced to the Color Wheel, he saw himself "most like the Empowerer, with Nurturer second and Friendly Scholar third." He felt that the Inculcator was least like him because "emphasizing knowledge without showing the relevance would be hard for me. Not seeing how something applied to my life was one of my biggest challenges for learning. . . . I feel that academic knowledge is crucial in teaching and want students to feel learning is fun and applicable in the real world."

Ronald's fall practicum took place in two advanced high school math classes where academic achievement was emphasized. At the conclusion of his Ten Day Teach, Ronald identified primarily with the Friendly Scholar perspective. "I really felt at first my teacher also was a Friendly Scholar, and so did she. This was not totally the case. She was very friendly and good, but the core subject matter was too important to be interrupted by many connections to the real world or anything else." He went on to say that his Friendly Scholar perspective "hindered my enjoyment of the teaching experience since I was placed or pushed more into an Inculcator mode, control through authority, etc. Humor and innovation weren't smiled upon. This was a hard pill to swallow."

Thinking about possible areas of weakness, he continued, "I need to be a Facilitator of Thinking as well. And with Friendly Scholars, there is always a potential problem with discipline because students might try to take advantage of their friendly relationship with me."

With classroom teaching experience, Ronald's affirmation of his Friendly Scholar perspective became stronger, but it did not stifle possibilities for change. Placed in a context that was more conducive to an Inculcator perspective, Ronald understood the source of his disease. He accommodated the demands of his high school experience, but his basic perspective did not change. An understanding of his Friendly Scholar perspective helped him identify the source of his frustration without losing respect for his mentor teacher or developing doubts about his own teaching abilities.

Ronald was much happier in his middle school placement during student teaching, where he could teach as a Friendly Scholar, with shades of the Nurturer and Empowerer. After Ronald's first six weeks in the classroom, his mentor teacher wrote this:

> Ronald has a very creative side as well as being very knowledgeable. . . . He seeks to develop activities that engage his students in the learning process. Students who are musically inclined . . . have enjoyed learning two "originals" by Ronald. To help two students learn properties, Ronald taught them songs and motions that would help them learn two mathematical properties. The motions actually gave meaning to otherwise very abstract ideas. Ronald sets the expectations for his classes with style . . . several students have been positively influenced by Ronald's high expectations and have made remarkable improvements.

Ronald illustrates how the Color Wheel can initiate and maintain self-reflection on teaching. It helps preservice teachers make explicit their assumptions about teaching and consider the multiple perspectives from which teaching may be viewed. It encourages them to identify a primary perspective with which they feel most comfortable and to consider how their teaching might be enhanced by incorporating additional perspectives. By portraying the strengths and weaknesses of perspectives derived from the actual classroom instruction of beginning teachers very much like themselves (I use a series of case studies such as Cynthia and Ronald to develop an understanding of the seven perspectives), the Color Wheel suggested ways they might modify their perspectives in various school contexts, should they encounter problems. Having been taught to use the Color Wheel early in the TADMP, many use it as a critical tool for reflection on practice during the Ten Day Teach and student teaching.

The Color Wheel of Seven Teacher Perspectives provides the major framework now used to initiate and nurture students' reflections on their teaching. During observations of their student teaching, for example, I try to view curriculum planning and interactive teaching from their primary perspective, rather than from my own, to help them tune into their strengths and build from these strengths. For example, teachers who are most comfortable with direct instruction, and might therefore favor lecture and be fearful of group work, can be encouraged to develop engaging demonstrations, illuminating visuals, and concrete examples to support their instruction, all of which would be consistent with their primary teacher perspective. With support, however, they might eventually be moved to use discussion dyads that help clarify students' understanding of complex concepts. Likewise, Facilitators of Thinking can be admired for the extensive primary source materials they often integrate into their lessons, yet also be helped to develop lesson closure before time runs out (a frustration they frequently face). Indeed, my own teaching seems to be improving as I develop greater insights into the strengths and potential limitations of my primary teacher perspective.

References

Bennett, C. (1991). The teacher as decision maker program: An alternative for career-change preservice teachers. *Journal of Teacher Education, 42*(2), 119-130.

Bennett, C. (1994, April). *Teacher perspectives as a framework for teacher education.* Paper presented at the annual meeting of the American Educational Research Association, New Orleans.

Bennett, C. (1995a). *Comprehensive multicultural education: Theory and practice.* Boston: Allyn & Bacon.

Bennett, C. (1995b). Preparing teachers for culturally diverse students. *Journal of Teacher Education, 46*(4), 259-265.

Bennett, C., & Powell, R. (1990, April). *The development of professional knowledge schemata and teaching perspectives among career-change preservice teachers: A study of resisters and non-resisters.* Paper presented at the annual meeting of the American Educational Research Association, Boston, MA.

Bennett, C., & Spalding, E. (1991, April). *Teaching perspectives held by preservice and novice teachers in an alternative teacher education program.* Paper presented at the annual meeting of the American Educational Research Association, Chicago. (ERIC Document Reproduction Service No. ED 335336)

Bennett, C., & Spalding, E. (1992). Multiple approaches for multiple perspectives. *Theory and Research in Social Education, 20*(3), 263-292.

Beyerbach, B. A. (1988). Developing a technical vocabulary on teacher planning: Preservice teachers' concept maps. *Teaching and Teacher Education, 4*(4), 337-347.

Britzman, D. (1986). Cultural myths in the making of a teacher: Biography and social structure in teacher education. *Harvard Educational Review, 56*(4), 442-456.

Bullough, R. V., Jr. (1991). Exploring personal teaching metaphors in preservice teacher education. *Journal of Teacher Education, 42*(1), 43-45.

Goodman, J. (1985). Field-based experience: A study of social control and student teachers' response to institutional constraints. *Journal of Education for Teaching, 11*(1), 26-49.

Goodman, J., & Adler, S. (1985). Becoming an elementary social studies teacher: A study of perspectives. *Theory and Research in Social Education, 13*, 1-20.

Johnston, S. (1992). Images: A way of understanding the practical knowledge of student teachers. *Teaching and Teacher Education, 8*(2), 123-136.

Kagan, D. (1992). Professional growth among preservice and beginning teachers. *Review of Educational Research, 62*(2), 129-169.

Pajares, M. F. (1992). Teachers' beliefs and educational research: Cleaning up a messy construct. *Review of Educational Research, 62*(3), 307-332.

Rokeach, M. (1969). *Beliefs, attitudes and values.* San Francisco: Jossey-Bass.

Shuell, T. J. (1992). The two cultures of teaching and teacher preparation. *Teaching and Teacher Education, 8*(1), 83-90.

Shulman, L. S. (1987). Knowledge and teaching: Foundations of the new reform. *Harvard Educational Review, 57*(1), 1-22.

Shulman, L. S., & Sykes, G. (1986). *A national board for teaching? In search of a bold standard. A report for the task force on teaching as a profession.* New York: Carnegie Corporation.

Tamir, P. (1988). Subject matter and related pedagogical knowledge in teacher education. *Teaching and Teacher Education, 4*(2), 99-110.

5 Cooperative Learning, Staff Development, and Change

Adele B. Sanders

Michael S. Meloth

Adele B. Sanders is Assistant Professor at the University of Northern Colorado, College of Education. Her previous research focused on collaborative staff development at a school site. Her current work is developing around ways to determine and meet practicing teachers' professional needs, and middle school partnerships.

Michael S. Meloth is Associate Professor of Education at the University of Colorado at Boulder. His research focuses on how teacher cooperative learning interactions facilitate and support student use of cognitive and metacognitive strategies when learning. An example of his recent work, "Task Talk and Task Awareness Under Different Cooperative Learning Conditions," appears in the *American Educational Research Journal*.

ABSTRACT

One highly regarded instructional strategy that has been proven to meet the needs of a great many and diverse student populations is cooperative learning. According to Meloth and Deering (1994), more elaborate and documented data have been collected on the power and potential of this educational innovation than on any other movement in education. The question, then, is why cooperative learning is being severely underused or ineffectively implemented, as descriptive data suggest.

Two investigations were undertaken to uncover teachers' beliefs about cooperative learning. Independently of each other, the investigators found that (a) instructional innovations involving peer collaboration effectively require that teachers "buy into" a rather different view of the teacher learning process (i.e., that of knowledge construction rather than that of knowledge transmission) and (b) beliefs about the nature and purpose of the teaching learning process, particularly as they relate to peer cooperation, are deeply held, and teachers are not likely to change them without good reason.

Objectives

The two studies described in this chapter explore practicing teachers' and preservice teachers' articulated beliefs about cooperative learning as an instructional strategy. The first study set out to provide a systematic examination of teachers' beliefs about the role that cooperative interactions play in learning to read. Meloth's 45 participants included 15 elementary school teachers who had completed a district-sponsored staff development program on cooperative learning, 15 elementary school teachers who did not complete any cooperative learning staff development program, and 15 precertification students attending teacher education courses at a large southwestern university. All 45 participants were interviewed to uncover their beliefs about instruction.

The second study's goal was to examine three teachers' abilities or inclinations to sustain recent staff development efforts that focused on literacy instruction using cooperative learning teaching strategies. Sanders's reviewed these teachers' articulated beliefs about cooperative learning compared with their practices across three semesters: the first two during the staff development interaction and the third occurring during the first semester of the subsequent school year.

An Examination of the Problem

How teachers teach is affected by many factors, including knowledge of the content, of the students, and of teaching strategies that bring content and pedagogy together effectively. Teachers, regardless of their students' ages or grade levels, need to employ skills that connect with these students' needs while helping them grow academically and socially.

One highly regarded instructional strategy that has been proven to meet the needs of a great many and diverse student populations is cooperative learning. Not surprisingly, then, this strategy continues to find acceptance worldwide. School districts around the country offer staff development programs or encourage their teachers to enroll in independently sponsored workshops emphasizing these methods. In addition, few instructional methods have been as extensively examined as cooperative learning (Meloth & Deering, 1994).

With increasing support for the potential value of cooperative learning as an instructional strategy that benefits students (Johnson & Johnson, 1987; Kagan, 1989; Slavin, 1990), we might expect to witness teachers making fundamental shifts in their practice to include more cooperative interactions to promote student learning. As might also be true for other educational "hot method[s]" (Slavin, 1990), however, cooperative learning's methods were "oversold and [the teachers were] undertrained" (Slavin, 1990, p. 3). Slavin's advice and admonishment: "To do it well takes considerable training and motivation" (p. 3).

Cooperative learning is a method that typically conflicts with teachers' basic beliefs about the appropriate roles of teachers and students in the learning process. It is different in both theory and practice from traditional whole-class instruction. Deering (1992) summed up cooperative learning's break with tradition when he said that cooperative learning approaches "imply, if not require, quite different roles, status, procedures, interaction and evaluation from traditional teacher-directed instruction" (p. 2). Cooperative learning requires teachers to believe in the balance between teacher as informer and teacher as facilitator. To be implemented effectively, cooperative learning requires the alignment of those balanced beliefs with the teaching practice.

This way of thinking, however, runs counter to common classroom practice, where the teacher plays the primary role in identifying and communicating important lesson information (Slavin, 1990). Not surprisingly, then, teachers' articulated beliefs about the benefits of cooperative learning often are not well supported by their practices (Deering, Meloth, & Sanders, 1993; Meloth, 1991; Sanders, 1995; Zeichner & Liston, 1987). Little investigation has been done to characterize those articulated beliefs and practices and the ways in which they are manifested during teaching practice.

Teachers' outright avoidance of the strategy, their use of the language but not the practice, or their frustrations during implementation can be related to their limited knowledge base or understanding of cooperative learning and the underlying rationale for its use, as Slavin (1990) suggested. Not unlike other educational innovations (e.g., whole language, assertive discipline, new math), more time is spent talking about the concept of cooperative learning—explaining and promoting opportunities to investigate and implement the concept in a systematic manner. And though many longtime proponents of cooperative learning acknowledge the power and range of learning that can result from its use, they all agree that it will not happen as a result of a one-shot inservice in the school building or as a result of a teacher education methods course in which it is briefly talked about or played at.

Several scholars (Anderson, 1990; Meloth, 1991; Palincsar, Stevens, & Gavelek, 1989; Peterman & Anders, 1991; Rich, 1990) suggest that discord between a teacher's beliefs and practice can spell failure for the effective implementation of institutional and curricular innovations. Researchers need to enter the "change" picture (Richardson, 1990, 1994) by conducting a knowledge exchange with teachers in a way that elicits teachers' underlying beliefs about teaching and learning, promotes a greater willingness to reflect critically on practice, and helps them identify contextually compatible reforms that are then shaped for the classroom context.

A theoretically sound assumption, then, is that within such a co-constructed or collaborative environment, the reforms derived from those interactions would be sustained. But are they? Although increased effort by teacher educators has been undertaken to identify sources of and the thinking behind the beliefs that guide teachers' practices (e.g., Connelly & Clandinin, 1988; Fullan, 1985; Richardson & Anders, 1994), little investigation has focused specifically on poststaff development ideas about and uses of cooperative learning.

The two investigations described in this chapter took place about two years apart. Meloth investigated his participants' beliefs about cooperative learning use and instructional strategy knowledge and use through structured interviews. He did not observe their classroom practices, yet his findings provide one pane in the window through which to focus on Sanders's subjects, whose belief statements were recorded and whose practices were seen. Through independent analyses of their data, these two authors arrived at similar understandings: (a) instructional innovations involving peer collaboration require that teachers "buy into" a rather different view of the teacher learning process (i.e., that of knowledge construction rather than that of knowledge transmission) and (b) beliefs about the nature and purpose of the teaching/learning process, particularly as it relates to peer cooperation, are deeply held (Palincsar et al., 1989) and teachers are not likely to change them without good reason (Richardson, 1990).

Without "buy in," Meloth (1991) suggests that it is unlikely that teachers will engage in the subtle and not so subtle instructional and curricular decisions and actions that make peer cooperation a successful learning experience. Attempts at changing teachers' beliefs and practices, typically the raison d'être of staff development efforts, need to consider theoretical, empirical, and contextual elements that will reinforce and support teachers' tendencies to make those changes, as evidenced by Sanders's data and those of others (see also Fullan, 1993; Richardson & Anders, 1994). What is of interest, then, are the ways in which teachers, both preservice and "veteran," can be helped to think about and, ultimately, acquire teaching roles and strategies that are congruous with their articulated beliefs about literacy instruction using cooperative learning specifically.

The actual research conducted by each of the authors will be explained next; pertinent and revealing data will be shared in their own right. Following those explanations, data from the two studies will be taken together, revealing patterns of thought and practice that lend support for subsequent conclusions and recommendations.

Meloth's Study Using Interviews

Meloth and his colleagues interviewed 45 subjects from a moderate-sized district in the Southwest. Of these, 30 were practicing teachers and 15 were precertification students. All subjects' participation was voluntary. The practicing teachers were equally divided into "formal knowledge" and "informal knowledge" groups. The formal knowledge group had completed a district-sponsored staff development program on cooperative learning within the past two years. That program involved 30 contact hours over a 10-week period. Teachers completing the course received district credit toward recertification. Teachers in the informal knowledge group were randomly chosen from the remaining pool of volunteering elementary teachers in the district. The precertification students, serving as a control, were currently enrolled in an oral communication course at a local university (a prerequisite for those interested in applying to the University's teacher certification program).

In January 1991, teachers were mailed a letter asking them to participate in a study, if they used cooperative activities during literacy instruction. Those teachers who responded that they used cooperative activities and wanted to be included were then contacted, and a convenient interview time was selected. Phone calls were made to initially unresponsive teachers from the original pool of elementary teachers until 15 teachers for each group (formal and informal) agreed to participate. The first 15 precertification students who volunteered to participate from two sections of the communication course were accepted.

The interview instrument used was adapted from Palincsar et al. (1989) and consisted of 19 questions covering a range of topics focusing on collaborative interactions and learning to read (the wording was altered for the precertification interviews to reflect their nonteaching status). The range of questions spanned their general reasons for using cooperative learning instructional designs, to the selection and actual structuring of the activities, to methods for monitoring and evaluating the students' work. The final question, held to the end so that it would provide no undue influence on their answers to other questions, was,

> Please think of one or two literacy topics or skills that you believe are essential for your students to possess. They may even be ones that are also part of your district's mandated objectives. Would you feel comfortable allowing students to use collaborative methods to learn these topics or skills or would you prefer to teach them directly? Please explain why.

The purpose of this question was to specifically probe teachers' confidence in the effectiveness of learning through collaboration. The participants' responses to this question and those preceding it were read by Meloth and his research colleagues, independently. Categories capturing responses to each question were then constructed. The researchers then met to discuss their categorizations and to make modifications where necessary. Next, each response to a particular question was reviewed jointly by the researchers to determine whether it should be placed in that category. When disagreement occurred, responses were placed in another category or a new category was constructed. Finally, all categories for each transcript were examined and an overall description of each subject's responses was developed.

The pattern that developed across these responses (see Meloth, 1991, for complete information) is the similarity of both teachers' groups to each other and to the precertification students' responses. This suggests the participants' share seemingly "intuitive," gut reactions to the ways in which cooperative learning might be used to benefit students in developing academic knowledge and social skills. Their responses, however, provide much greater conviction for the social benefits of peer-group learning than for cognitive benefits. A clear theme throughout these responses was that "it shouldn't be illegal for students to help each other out when they need to. That sends the wrong message about school." All groups of participants believed teacher modeling to be important because it helped students develop "good group skills."

The major difference distinguishing the "formal" and "informal" groups was in their responses to the kinds of activities that lend themselves to collaboration, with the formal knowledge group describing a much wider range of possible literacy activities (e.g., decoding "games" to discussions of character motives). Finally, all but one teacher (from the formal knowledge group) indicated that they were more comfortable directly teaching essential or district-mandated topics or skills because "if they have to have them, I feel I should make sure they do." The remaining teacher stated that learning essential knowledge could occur through collaboration, but only if activities and interactions were well designed.

The data analyzed to date suggest that even teachers who make the effort to learn more about collaborative methods do not appear to believe that such methods are a primary means to improve students' reading abilities. Instead, cooperation was viewed as a means to improve social skills and to provide the opportunity to solicit assistance from peers when the teacher cannot be present. Surprisingly, precertification students' responses, though less detailed, were similar to the teachers', suggesting that the social skills and knowledge transmission views of teaching are beliefs that remain relatively unchanged, even after learning about and using cooperative methods.

To these participants' articulated beliefs about cooperative learning is added Sanders's beliefs and practices study. As will be seen in the next section, Sanders's participants also spoke about children learning how to work together cooperatively. Despite her participants' enthusiastic statements about cooperative learning, despite their use of that instructional method to teach literacy lessons during the previous academic year (i.e., during an interactive staff development program), the teaching practices Sanders actually observed strongly support Meloth's findings.

Sanders's Study Using Beliefs and Practices

In the fall semester of 1992, Paul Deering led the Cooperative Reading Project (CRP), funded by the McDonnell Foundation, at a metropolitan elementary school in a large southwestern city. He was assisted by Michael Meloth and Adele Sanders. The purpose of the CRP was "to examine and stimulate [teachers'] thinking about cooperative learning literacy instruction" (Deering et al., 1993, p. 3). Seven teachers participated in the year-long project.

During the first half of the CRP, fall semester 1992, teachers were interviewed before and after lesson observations took place (see Deering et al., 1993, for complete description and details). During the second half of the CRP, spring semester 1993, an additional procedure, one-to-one post-lesson feedback sessions between the observed teacher and either Deering or Sanders, promoted opportunities for new constructions of teaching for learning using cooperative learning activities. When the CRP ended in the summer of 1993, data revealed that all participants had increased the cognitive level of their literacy-based cooperative group activities.

Sanders returned to the elementary school for the entire fall 1993 semester to discover whether the teachers continued to have high literacy-oriented cognitive and cooperative group activities. In other words, she wanted to discover whether and to what extent the teachers had sustained the work they had been doing while working with the CRP staff. Three teachers participated in the follow-up study: Brenda, Doris, and Frances. These teachers had been part of the previous year's CRP project, and they were willing to allow Sanders back into their classrooms. They were told that they would be interviewed and observed quite often during the fall semester (about 60 hours each), that they weren't going to receive feedback about their practice, nor were they going to be getting any college credit incentive, as they had during the CRP (they were offered a subscription to a journal of their choice, instead).

Brenda was starting her 6th year of teaching when Sanders's study began, Doris her 23rd, and Frances her 9th. Each teacher had taught elsewhere before teaching at Whitney Elementary School (all participants' and site names are pseudonyms). Each teacher was again teaching in a bilingual classroom environment, having passed the district's Spanish language competency exam. Table 5.1 provides a characterization of these three teachers' teaching assignments during the CRP staff development year (1992-1993) and their subsequent year's assignments during

TABLE 5.1 CRP and Follow-Up Study Participants(*) and Their Teaching Assignments During the CRP Staff Development Project (Fall 1992 to Spring 1993) and During the Follow-Up Study (Fall 1993).

Teacher	During CRP (1992-1993)	During Follow-Up (Fall 1993)
Dana	1-2 mixed, bilingual, double classroom	Maternity leave beginning June 1993
	Teamed with	
Brenda	1-2 mixed, bilingual, double classroom	K-1 mixed, monolingual Spanish, new team partner, double classroom
		Teamed with
Yvonne		K-1 mixed, monolingual Spanish, team partner, double classroom
Nora	1-2 mixed, bilingual, double classroom	Maternity leave beginning March 1993
	Teamed with	
*Doris	1-2 mixed, bilingual, double classroom	2-3 mixed, bilingual, double classroom
		Teamed with
*Frances	3rd grade, bilingual, self-contained	2-3 mixed, bilingual, double classroom

Sanders's semester-long involvement. Worth noting is the "new" teaching assignment each participant faced for the 1993-1994 academic year.

In-depth interviews were conducted three times during the CRP study and three times during the follow-up study. Some of the three teachers' statements about cooperative learning have been excerpted and are presented in Table 5.2. This table shows each teacher's comments across time (CRP, 1992 to 1993, and follow-up, fall semester 1993), and compared with her colleagues' comments. The excerpts reflect a variety of questions asked about cooperative learning. For example, one question asked during the first interview conducted for the CRP was how cooperative learning "fit" with literacy learning. One question asked during the final CRP interview was about the impact cooperative learning had on their classroom during the year. Excerpts from in-depth and post-lesson interviews are represented in the follow-up study row.

As the excerpts show, each of the teachers expresses rather consistent beliefs in the benefits of cooperative learning. Although their comments do not necessarily emphasize literacy instruction, they do express the teachers' beliefs that cooperative learning is a way of helping children understand that they have knowledge and abilities worth sharing with each other. In the first time period, each teacher admits to believing in the potential for cooperative learning "working" in her classroom, though not feeling particularly confident in being able to attain that potential on her own. In the second time period, the trend in comments appears to be one of grand realizations of the potential of successfully used cooperative learning methods in their classrooms. Comments in the third time period (the follow-up study) reflect more diverse responses. From students learning for themselves, to not being the classroom expert, to being aware that fewer cooperative learning lessons were taught during this school year than during the CRP year, the teachers' practices, but not their verbalized beliefs, went on a roller coaster ride.

Brenda's comments emphasize her thoughts about the benefits of students working together and helping each other (cooperating without fighting), and she acknowledges the lack of "formal, jigsaw type" cooperative interactions in her lessons. She also recognizes that she has used fewer cooperative lessons during the fall 1993 semester than she did during CRP, "because there really are a lot of new things going on this year."

Doris's comments revolve around her own learning about the significance of cooperative learning as a way to help children recognize that the adult teacher is not the only classroom teacher. Her comments also indicate her strong feelings about brainstorming as cooperative learning and about direct instruction as a necessary condition for student learning.

Frances's responses indicate her increased appreciation for and knowledge of the ways in which she can design cooperative learning activities so that children can learn. Her follow-up study responses, however, suggest a disappointment in herself for not continuing to use the cooperative learning lessons she had used during the CRP, saying that those lessons "sort of slipped by."

Following are characterizations of the teachers' actual teaching practices during the same time periods, focusing on cooperative learning and literacy instruction (inasmuch as the CRP had such a focus and Sanders's conducted a follow-up study). The actual teaching practices observed

(Text continues on page 105)

TABLE 5.2 Three Teachers' Beliefs About Cooperative Learning and Practice Across Three Time Periods

	Brenda	Doris	Frances
At the start of CRP (Sept.–Oct. 1992)	"They learn from each other, and just sitting there quiet and not talking to each other, well, then it doesn't do any good to have a multi-age classroom"; she wanted to learn more about "having them cooperate with each other . . . it would just be really nice if you could teach them how to take turns within the group, then one to be the person who writes, one to be the person who reads . . . so that they're able to work together and accomplish what they need to accomplish without being an adult there the whole time."	There are "45 teachers in the room and the kids do learn from each other, and that's the way it ought to be . . . I didn't consciously say one day I need to have these kids cooperate; I saw it and it was working"; "I think anything we can do to make the child have confidence and a high self-esteem and feel successful, you know, if it's one more technique, one more method, one more approach. I think we need to [grab] everything we have available to us"; she chose to participate in the CRP because "I would like to get on firmer ground with cooperative learning in literacy groups, and reading and writing processes. I don't feel I know enough about it."	Her cooperative learning practice was "not terribly sophisticated yet; I really do think that it's a very worthwhile way for kids to learn. They learn very well from one another. . . . [I want kids] to look at one another as a resource in the room, rather than the teacher being the only resource"; "I just think the challenge for me as a teacher is to find out the ways in which I can help kids learn cooperatively, by refining the process"; Cooperative learning means that "person A has a role, person B has a role [etc.], and person E stands outside and observes. That's really hard for me to plan, and since I have never planned it, never observed it working, I'm not really sure how it works."

Continued

At the end of CRP (May 1993)	"The children have gotten a lot of practice working in groups, and they are willing to help each other"; "We have other helpers instead of me always being there to help"; their self-confidence increased when they were able to help, "when they were able to say, 'I knew that answer and I helped her with it' . . . but I realized that when I would sit with a group, they would start talking to each other and then I would take over and talk for them . . . instead of trying to get it out of them [I would give] them the answer." She was glad the CRP team had pushed her into implementing cooperative learning, "I don't think that I would have actually implemented a lot of it . . . but when you know you have to do something, you actually do it. . . . I think that next year, I will continue to use them—those that have succeeded and have actually worked."	"I feel like I really have an insight into how valuable [cooperative learning] is; I never really understood it"; "This cooperative thing has really taken hold with me, and I think with the kids, too; that's why I'm going to continue this study next year [Sanders's follow-up]; I see a sense of camaraderie and cooperation in the process; next year we'll start right off with cooperative learning right from the very beginning. . . . I don't think that I will ever regress to the place where I was [when] they weren't cooperating at all."	About the impact of cooperative learning on her classroom and students, she said, "I certainly have included a lot more cooperative learning than I did last year, and I've learned a lot from that. I've really grown in my definition of what a cooperative learning experience is and can be. . . . There have been lots of discoveries that kids have made together that they may not have made by themselves. . . . And I think that was probably the most worthwhile thing that I found about cooperative learning, the ability to discover things together, and picking each other's brain . . . "; She said she would "continue to implement cooperative learning, and continue to explore what other teachers do with it. . . . And next year, I don't know whether I want to say whether I would plan a sequence of lessons to introduce them to cooperative learning, but I'd like to get them into it a little more carefully than I did at the beginning of the year."

TABLE 5.2 Continued

	Brenda	Doris	Frances
During follow-up (Fall 1993)	"When the students learn it for themselves, it's much more meaningful and they get a lot more out of it, or when they're learning from each other, when they have to teach someone else . . . I think it enhances their self-esteem, also"; she said she hadn't implemented any "really structured cooperative learning" lesson, "like the jigsaw," but lessons that had required partners "or three people working together, helping each other read or helping each other complete a project with one person doing the illustration and the other doing the writing and the other reading it to the class"; "A lot of the cooperative learning like the jigsaw . . . we did [last year] that I haven't used much this year, just because there really are a lot of new things going on this year."	"I have pulled back from being the only one that can do the instruction" (10/7/93); "I always want to feel like I'm doing direct teaching, but some-times you have to give them time dur-ing the group to do something, otherwise they don't pick up on it . . . they won't do these things if they don't have an opportunity to practice"; "It's the brainstorming process that really goes into place, where they get ideas from each other"; "We're not islands, we need other people's input, and it's so natural now . . . the kids do it naturally, just easily they slip into it . . . the students really have plugged into cooperative learning"; "They can serve as teachers. I mean I feel that children have taught me a lot and so they can teach each other . . . I have never viewed myself as the expert."	"I don't feel like I went on and accomplished what we started to do last year. There were just too many changes to make at once" (NOTE: Details about this will follow in the next section); "I'm looking at the kinds of things that I started implementing last year and, of course, this is an ideal situation to implement cooperative learning. But, in the sense that we do have a cooperative environment for the reading/writing process, I have not taught the cooperative lessons that I taught last year. So, that sort of slipped by. The children are still working cooperatively in the morning and talking with one another . . . But I haven't actively taught cooperative learning in the grouplike atmosphere that I did last year"; "I was not pleased that I didn't carry over a lot of the more formal cooperative learning lessons that I had prepared last year. . . . If one of the children is at a stage of editing in their book, I will ask the whole group who can help [that child] with checking her spelling words."

during each of the same three time periods are presented in Table 5.3 (compiled from field notes and enriched by audiotape transcripts).

As the descriptions of teaching practices in Table 5.3 show, these teachers all returned to teaching practices most like those seen during the first semester (Fall 1992) of the CRP staff development project. Cooperative learning lessons observed during the follow-up semester (Fall 1993) were not cognitive or collaborative but were mostly affective and teacher directed, as they had been before the teachers' involvement with the CRP team. Having been involved in all phases of the staff development process, Sanders had expected to see no less than what was observed during the spring 1993 semester—the teachers' use of cooperative learning literacy lessons with fairly clear cognitive designs. Why did she have those expectations? Because, as mentioned earlier, the teachers' responses during feedback sessions with one of the CRP team, as well as their comments during whole group sessions and in-depth interview proceedings, were rich in positive language, commitment, and "belief" in the potential for learning by students in cooperative groups.

Those spring semester CRP feedback sessions, opportunities to "stimulate [teachers'] thinking about cooperative learning literacy instruction" (Deering et al., 1993), although not as persistent and probing as those described as practical arguments (Fenstermacher, 1986; Richardson & Anders, 1994), generated new ideas and thinking. The following dialogue is an example of the nature and "content" of the interactions between researcher (staff developer) and teacher during the spring 1993 CRP semester. This interaction, between Paul Deering and Brenda, is an example of the ways in which the CRP team attempted to stimulate teachers' thinking.

Brenda's post-lesson impression was that her descriptive words lesson had failed, only confusing the children because she didn't focus on nouns first. She did say, however, that she had noticed some of her students working with their partners to find their descriptive words collaboratively:

P: Did you do anything in particular to promote the kids helping each other out or learning from each other?

B: No, I didn't, and I realized that after I sat down.

P: Well, at what point might you do that?

B: I think maybe that while I was doing the minilesson (uh-huh) I could maybe, I could, I don't know—role model? have a couple

TABLE 5.3 Teachers' Classroom Practices During Literacy Instruction Across Three Time Periods

	Brenda	Doris	Frances
First half of CRP (Sept. to Dec. 1992)	Two lessons were observed during this time. Both lessons began with teacher instruction, then she started a literacy lesson without connection to teacher-led one. Children sat together, read together, and developed own list of words not known, read about animals and the information learned about them, and in the second lesson, they wrote two sentences about what they do on a cold day (theme of teacher-read book). Getting along and being quiet received teacher attention. (1st + 2nd grade)	Three lessons were observed. Teacher worked with three separate reading groups one at a time around her table, each group involved in group idea generation; teacher does writing and facilitating of story extensions. During second observation, teacher led reading groups and suggested they draw pictures for the books they were writing; one student sat in Author's Chair for writer's workshop and was asked by teacher, in front of group, whether students' questions and comments are helpful to the writing of the story. (1st + 2nd grade)	Five lessons were observed. Children were given variety of "people doing things together" activities to do: read together and rate each other's pace, volume, expression; small group work with teacher on word-attack skills; carefully partnered and planned task for two students on poem and locating onomatopoeia; students work together to use picture clues to "read" story; pairs work together to determine main idea from self-selected book and see how title does or doesn't give hint about book's story. (3rd grade)

TABLE 5.3 Teachers' Classroom Practices During Literacy Instruction Across Three Time Periods

	Brenda	Doris	Frances
First half of CRP (Sept. to Dec. 1992)	Two lessons were observed during this time. Both lessons began with teacher instruction, then she started a literacy lesson without connection to teacher-led one. Children sat together, read together, and developed own list of words not known, read about animals and the information learned about them, and in the second lesson, they wrote two sentences about what they do on a cold day (theme of teacher-read book). Getting along and being quiet received teacher attention. (1st + 2nd grade)	Three lessons were observed. Teacher worked with three separate reading groups one at a time around her table, each group involved in group idea generation; teacher does writing and facilitating of story extensions. During second observation, teacher led reading groups and suggested they draw pictures for the books they were writing; one student sat in Author's Chair for writer's workshop and was asked by teacher, in front of group, whether students' questions and comments are helpful to the writing of the story. (1st + 2nd grade)	Five lessons were observed. Children were given variety of "people doing things together" activities to do: read together and rate each other's pace, volume, expression; small group work with teacher on word-attack skills; carefully partnered and planned task for two students on poem and locating onomatopoeia; students work together to use picture clues to "read" story; pairs work together to determine main idea from self-selected book and see how title does or doesn't give hint about book's story. (3rd grade)

kids role model, helping each other out maybe. (OK) I don't know.

P: That seems like a good idea, because that was kind of like the meat of the task. You know, figure out what are descriptive words. How do you know it's descriptive?

B: Yeah, and how could you help, yeah, how could you help each other out? If you're not sure if it's a descriptive word, what can you do? (post-lesson interview, 2/17/93)

What can be seen in this interaction, and others, is Paul's conversational language, connections between the teacher's comments and his probing comments, and encouragement. Using Brenda's level of knowledge, experiences, and goals, and the researcher's knowledge, goals, and established trust, Paul attempted to push Brenda's thinking about her beliefs and practice and about ways she might think about achieving her goals. Whole group sessions with all teacher participants across the entire CRP period occurred with similar emphasis on teachers' ideas and questions, rather than on researchers' notions of what should be seen, done, or thought.

Now let us review the question of these three teachers' ability to sustain the cooperative learning practices they had been experimenting with. Several data sources contribute to our understanding of each teacher's thinking about her classroom practices and her ability to sustain the work of creating cognitively rich cooperative learning and literacy lessons for her students: pre- and post-lesson interviews, classroom comments during observations, and in-depth interviews (three during Sanders's study). Although the teachers were asked, during the second of two exit interviews, to respond to a question about influences on their former cooperative learning practice, a list of probables had already been emerging out of the data. The teachers' responses are shown in Table 5.4 and were constructed from the actual responses they made in answer to the specific interview question and from other, unsolicited yet related comments they made during other data collection activities (pre- or post-lesson interviews, "asides" during lesson observations).

Brenda's, Doris's, and Frances's influences, as shown in Table 5.4, have at least two commonalities: questions and doubts about their own Spanish language proficiency, and their school-time opportunities for planning. The reality, as they lived it, involved a greater demand on their ability to meet their students' first- and second-language needs, in particular be-

Table 5.4 Influences Mentioned by the Three Teachers That Reduced
Their Abilities to Sustain Cooperative Learning Literacy
Instruction

Brenda	Doris	Frances
Spanish language proficiency; teaming with new partner; preparedness + time; interruptions (meetings); classroom materials	Spanish language proficiency; teaming + collaboration; planning (+ the time to do it); classroom materials (not enough, not in Spanish); parental pressures; interruptions (testing, public address system)	Spanish language proficiency; classroom management; planning (+ the time to do it); self-efficacy issues

cause only one fourth of the students received their instruction in Spanish during the CRP year and three fourths of them required such instruction during the follow-up semester. This new population of students required more and/or new materials as well as lessons that provided for greater learning differences than previously encountered. Another aspect of the reality that the teachers lived is the reduced opportunities for planning—alone or with their teammate. Planning lessons that provide rich cognitive interactions among group members does take time, and when a teaching team is in charge, planning at the teacher level typically precedes planning at the detailed activity level.

It is not enough to say, however, that the teachers discontinued their cooperative learning for literacy instruction use exclusively because of the factors and issues mentioned. After all, Frances, for one, mentioned that she still had the lessons she had put together and tried during the CRP semester but hadn't used them. Could her and her colleagues' discontinued practices mean that their belief in their new group of students' abilities was different from the CRP students they had been teaching? (That belief network is beyond the scope of this chapter but is worth exploring.)

It is not enough to say, as Guskey (1986) does, that teachers change their beliefs after they change their practice. Were that truly so, each teacher might have sustained much more of her cooperative learning literacy instruction than she had, because each had successfully imple-mented several such lessons during the CRP staff development year, albeit, with a different population of students. It is also not enough to say, as Richardson, Anders, Tidwell, and Lloyd (1991) do, that teachers change their beliefs *before* changing their practice, because each teacher spoke frequently and emphatically about the benefits attributed to their students learning from each other, rather than exclusively from the teacher.

Implications

What, then, is left to say? What, then, is the answer, the reason for Sanders's participants not continuing to practice their beliefs by teaching as they talked? And what can be said of the teachers in Meloth's study who went through cooperative learning "training" and retained their commitment to teacher as director and giver of knowledge? Also, ul-timately, what might be done during staff development—defined as addi-tional higher education course work, inservice training, or small group interactive thought-and-practice sessions—to achieve a higher degree of or less temporary sustained change? Some clues can be found somewhere within or between existing cooperative learning and teacher change litera-ture.

Sharan and Sharan (1987), for example, claim the answer to sustaining change lies in reflection—that, they say, "is the bridge between the con-crete experience and the formal learning of relevant concepts" (p. 24). The CRP team and teachers did reflect (see Brenda and Paul's conversation earlier). Cooperative learning challenges teachers' often "intuitive" sense of what teaching means and should look like. The uniqueness of a coopera-tive learning orientation and the demands on teaching and learning that it makes, Rich (1990) believes, "may have [a] profound impact on decisions made consciously or unconsciously regarding the adoption and im-plementation of innovations like cooperative learning" (p. 88).

According to Richardson (1994), a single focus for a staff development effort—either theory or practice—"will not bring about substantial change. Genuine changes will come about when teachers think very differently about what is going on in their classrooms and are provided with the practices to match the different ways of thinking" (p. 102). The CRP team worked with the teachers' knowledge and experiences to con-struct mutually compatible and effective literacy lessons that used cooperative learning methods but did not provide the specific practices for them to use.

Teachers' perceptions of their roles as teachers, of the way children learn, of the environment in which they teach are not easily changed. It takes more than a course, inservice program, or a year of co-constructed understandings to affect the teachers' behaviors in the long term. If time emerges as the answer to helping change last, time to reflect and build bridges or time to argue practically about misaligned beliefs-to-practices, then 1-day workshops, higher education course work as typically taught, or short-term, on-site research (staff development) projects for teaching faculty cannot succeed in fostering sustained thought shifts. If time emerges as the best answer to the question of sustaining teacher change, will work with practicing teachers require lengthy, highly interactive longitudinal sessions to promote permanence?

Cooperative learning requires conceptualizing teaching and the teacher's role in ways different from "the norm." The questions that remain, and continue to mount, show teachers (and soon-to-be teachers) needing more than courses and more than yearlong conversations about what they want (and need) to do in the classroom. If the learning environment of which the teacher is a part is unaccustomed to people working and collaborating together, why should we expect teachers to see their students as capable of meaningful, cognitively rich collaboration?

In his book *Change Forces,* Fullan (1993) cited two reasons for the failure of reform efforts in education: "The problems are complex and intractable," and "the strategies that are used do not focus on things that will really make a difference" (p. 46). Fullan cited "the learning core—changes in instructional practices and in the culture of teaching toward greater collaborative relationships among students, teachers and other potential partners" as "the hardest core to crack" (p. 49). Waiting to crack it once teachers are in classrooms working with children may not be the optimal time because there is so much for them to focus on and do at this time. Perhaps they will be overwhelmed, as Frances was, with so many changes to make at once. Teachers and teachers-to-be need more than courses in which the instructor tells them what they need to think or courses in which there are activities to perform similar to those that their own students might be asked to do. Traditional coursework and even some nontraditional processes, such as co-constructed staff development efforts, continue to be less than adequate strategies for helping teachers make and sustain change in the complex, demanding environment in which teachers work.

References

Anderson, W. T. (1990). *Reality isn't what it used to be.* San Francisco: Harper & Row.

Connelly, F. M., & Clandinin, D. J. (1988). *Teachers as curriculum planners: Narratives of experience.* New York: Teachers College Press.

Deering, P. D. (1992). [Unpublished proposal for the Cooperative Reading Project]. Prepared for Denver Public School, Planning Research and Program Evaluation Department, Denver, CO.

Deering, P. D., Meloth, M., & Sanders, A. (1993, April). *An examination of teacher thinking during a collaborative effort to improve elementary cooperative learning literacy instruction.* Paper presented at the annual meeting of the American Educational Research Association, Atlanta, GA.

Fenstermacher, G. (1986). Philosophy of research on teaching: Three aspects. In M. C. Wittrock (Ed.), *Handbook of research on teaching* (3rd ed., pp. 37-49). New York: Macmillan.

Fullan, M. (1985). Change processes and strategies at the local level. *Elementary School Journal, 85*(3), 391-421.

Fullan, M. (1993). *Change forces.* London: Falmer.

Guskey, T. R. (1986). Staff development and the process of teacher change. *Educational Researcher, 15*(5), 5-12.

Johnson, D. W., & Johnson, R. T. (1987). *Learning together and alone: Cooperative, competitive, and individualistic learning* (2nd ed.). Englewood Cliffs, NJ: Prentice-Hall.

Kagan, S. (1989). The structural approach to cooperative learning. *Educational Leadership, 47*(4), 12-15.

Meloth, M. (1991). Enhancing literacy through cooperative learning. In E. Hiebert (Ed.), *Literacy for a diverse society: Perspectives, practices, and policies* (pp. 172-183). New York: Teachers College Press.

Meloth, M., & Deering, P. (1994). Task talk and task awareness under different cooperative learning conditions. *American Educational Research Journal, 31*(1), 138-165.

Palincsar, A. S., Stevens, D. D., & Gavelek, J. R. (1989). Collaborating with teachers in the interest of student collaboration. *International Journal of Educational Research, 13*(1), 41-53.

Peterman, F. P., & Anders, D. (1991, April). *Changing teachers' and researchers' beliefs through shared construction of meaning.* Paper presented at the annual meeting of the American Educational Research Association, Chicago.

Rich, Y. (1990). Ideological impediments to instructional innovation: The case of cooperative learning. *Teaching and Teacher Education, 6*(1), 81-91.

Richardson, V. (1990). Significant and worthwhile change in teaching practice. *Educational Researcher, 19*(7), 10-18.

Richardson, V. (1994). The consideration of teachers' beliefs. In V. Richardson (Ed.), *Teacher change and the staff development process: A case in reading instruction* (pp. 90-108). New York: Teachers College Press.

Richardson, V., & Anders, P. (1994). The study of teacher change. In V. Richardson (Ed.), *Teacher change and the staff development process: A case in reading instruction* (pp. 159-180). New York: Teachers College Press.

Richardson, V., Anders, P., Tidwell, D., & Lloyd, C. (1991). The relationship between teachers' beliefs and practices in reading comprehension instruction. *American Educational Research Journal, 28*(3), 559-586.

Sanders, A. B. (1995). Sustaining teacher change: What are the influences that make or break it? (Doctoral dissertation, Boulder, CO). *Dissertation Abstracts International, 42*, 1A.

Sharan, Y., & Sharan S. (1987). Training teachers for cooperative learning. *Educational Leadership, 45*(3), 20-25.

Slavin, R. E. (1990). *Cooperative learning: Theory, research, and practice.* Boston: Allyn & Bacon.

Zeichner, K., & Liston, D. (1987). Teaching student teachers to reflect. *Harvard Educational Review, 57*(1), 23-48.

6 A Teacher's Reconceptualization of Mathematics Teaching

A Paradox in Teacher Education

Donna H. Foss

Donna H. Foss is Associate Professor of Mathematics Education at the University of Central Arkansas. Her research interests focus on preservice teachers' beliefs, conceptions of mathematics, and mathematics teaching and learning. She was awarded the ATE Dissertation of the Year in 1995. Her most current publication is "Preservice Elementary Teachers' Views of Pedagogical and Mathematical Content Knowledge," coauthored with Robert C. Kleinsasser.

ABSTRACT

This study investigates a teacher educator's conceptions of mathematics and mathematics teaching and learning during her experience as a mathematics methods instructor in a preservice elementary education program. Thompson (1992) claimed virtually nothing is known about whether students' views of mathematics influence teachers' instructional decisions and actions. Motivated by this research void, this study describes the changes in the methods teacher's conceptions and discusses the relationship between her new conceptions, her

AUTHOR'S NOTE: The preparation of this manuscript was supported in part by the University of Central Arkansas Research Council but does not reflect the university's position, policy, or endorsement.

instructional behavior, and the preservice teachers' reactions. As this experienced teacher educator changes dramatically, the powerful influences of her students' conceptions and actions become factors in her metamorphosis. The results allow teacher educators to see not only the entrenchment of teacher candidates' perceptions but also the profound influence of these conceptions on their methods instructor. In seeking to learn why reform efforts fail, we need future research to elucidate the link between preservice teachers' beliefs and the instructional behavior of their teacher educators.

Objectives and Perspectives

This study is one component of a larger investigation of elementary preservice teachers' conceptions of mathematics teaching and learning during their mathematics methods training (Foss, 1993). In the research process, the methods instructor's beliefs become an important focus. In a synthesis of research on teachers' beliefs and conceptions, Thompson (1992) claimed that virtually nothing is known about if and how students' views of mathematics influence teachers' instructional decisions and actions. Motivated by this research void, the primary objectives of this study include (a) documenting a teacher educator's conceptions while teaching a mathematics methods course, (b) describing the changes in her conceptions, and (c) discussing the implications of the relationship between her new conceptions, her instructional behavior, and the reactions of her methods students.

Grouws (1991) claimed that the general nature of teachers' beliefs about learning, instruction, and mathematical knowledge affects instructional decision making and should be an integral part of future research. What teachers know is how to carry out tasks and connect their conceptions to instructional performance (Fenstermacher, 1994). This may be a form of the practical knowledge Elbaz (1983) describes, involving experiential knowledge, informed by theoretical knowledge of subject matter, integrated by the teacher's personal beliefs, and oriented to the particular situation. In his study of a beginning teacher, Lee (1994) asserted that it is not enough to simply catalog perceptions but, rather, the underlying motivations and beliefs and how crucial the context of the situation is to those beliefs must also be researched. The influence of students' views, however, is missing from current research on practice.

Russell (1987) encouraged educators to recognize that teachers do think about and learn from the experiences of teaching. Richardson (1994) described a new perception of teacher change that concentrates on teachers' practical reasoning and suggested that teachers try activities to see if they "work," and consequently make changes. She added that teachers change all the time, and these changes are sometimes dramatic. Beneath this theory is the question: What factors influence these changes? As the experienced teacher educator in this study changes dramatically, the powerful influences of her students' conceptions and actions become factors in her metamorphosis.

Data Collection and Analysis

The objectives of this study require considerable description, so triangulation is employed to clarify the context of the educational environment (Williamson, Karp, Dalphin, & Gray, 1982). Detailed descriptions from observations of 16 class sessions and 18 practica and 69 interviews are collected in the form of field notes, tape recordings, transcriptions, and videotapes to document the interactions within the course and the teaching practice (practica). The interviews allow participants to respond to open-ended questions at least three times during the one-semester course, including interviews with the instructor and multiple casual conversations. Materials such as lesson plans, grades, written assignments, teaching evaluations, and examinations are also sources of data.

Following Spradley's (1979) model analysis, patterns related to the participants' conceptions are identified by reviewing and coding the data. Using a procedure similar to the Constant Comparison Method by Glaser and Strauss (1967), thematic differences and similarities across all data sources are analyzed to illustrate the participants' conceptions and actions. During the analysis, the change in the methods teachers' conceptions is apparent and is therefore adopted as a line of analysis separate from the main data analysis.

Data Source

The participants in the study are the methods instructor and the 22 preservice teachers enrolled in a mathematics methods course (3 credit hours) of the elementary teacher education program (undergraduate) at an accredited (NCATE) liberal arts college in the south central region of the United States. The methods instructor, Diane Solo, has 10 years of teaching experience, developing a constructivist approach over the 5 years previous to the study. The course is designed to include mathematics content and pedagogy, which are to be studied in tandem. The preservice teachers are elementary education majors, 1 male and 21 females (average age of 26 years). Pseudonyms are consistently employed in the reporting of all data, and at no time did the methods instructor review the data.

Although this study is centered on the instructor, the preservice teachers' conceptions should be described briefly, focusing on three themes involving mathematics that emerged from the data: knowledge, methods, and good teaching. The preservice teachers view mathematical knowledge as basic skills and arithmetic operations in everyday life such as grocery shopping or checkbook balancing. Their conceptions of teaching methods are based on practice, memorization, undeveloped interpretations of instructional tactics, and the belief that, because of innate abilities, children learn mathematics on their own. Their perceptions of good teaching emphasize teacher attributes such as flexibility, patience, and discipline. The preservice teachers' conceptions resemble closely those reported by Anderson, Holt-Reynolds, and Swidler (1994): (a) teachers' attributes are more important than teachers' methods; (b) textbooks are boring; (c) although activities are nice, there is not always enough time nor is it necessary to include them consistently; and (d) if students are motivated and teachers provide explanations, learning will take place. More details about the preservice teachers' unwavering conceptions can be found in Foss and Kleinsasser (1996).

Results

The results are divided into four sections: the methods teacher's conceptions, the preservice teachers' reactions, the lecture, and the resulting paradox.

The Methods Teacher's Conceptions

The mathematics methods instructor, Diane Solo, is confident enough to invite a researcher to observe her teaching. She had on many occasions been vocal about her view of education as a complex but collaborative effort. Her most discernible characteristics are constant reflection on her own teaching and respect for the research process. Employing the curriculum and evaluation standards published by the National Council of Teachers of Mathematics (1989), Diane describes her philosophy as compelling preservice teachers to "experience mathematics, not do exercises in a textbook." She declares, "I'm a constructivist. . . . I can provide experiences where you teach yourself. . . . So, it's got to be interactive, active, concrete, and within context. . . . You have to create the images upon which the abstractions are developed."

Diane confronts the preservice teachers with constructivism weekly. In this setting, the preservice students are guided to make discoveries, that is, constructivism is manifested by the teacher's presenting situations in which mathematics emerges, to be detected and interpreted by the participants (Goldin, 1990). Diane believes that if she provides the experiences and creates the images, the preservice teachers will be induced to think about teaching mathematics in active, interactive classrooms using concrete materials. The following are excerpts from an interview in which Diane describes her position.

> I'm glad, kind of, that you're interviewing me, because sometimes I worry that you, I guess because you're watching me, and my students see some of the things that I do as kind of gimmicky or trivial. . . . But everything I do, I'm trying to create images for them and I can talk about it, but I don't think that they experience it unless I actually bring it in. . . . I'm really getting kind of daring and every time I teach the class, I think I get more daring. . . . So, I'm trying to make it a new experience for them and I'm trying to create images that they will take with them.

> My number one goal is to get the students to become, not to need me, to get the students independent of me, give them experiences that will help them think about mathematics, so then they can think without me. . . . And my second goal is that I want the students to see the beauty of mathematics, to be excited about mathematics so that they can communicate that to the children they teach. . . . I see myself as a coach and what I do is I think about the things that they need to know about human growth and development, collateral learning, about the structure of the discipline . . . and then think about what experiences do I need to provide in order for them to understand these things. . . . And so, mainly, I see myself as providing experiences. (first interview)

Three components layer Diane's methods: delivery systems, mathematics content, and educational theory, each playing a significant role in almost every class session, integrated by her organizational finesse. Although more emphasis on a single aspect emerges in each class session, the interlocking of these elements is the essence of her method. To stimulate collaboration and spontaneity, Diane employs cooperative learning, presentations, mathematics activities and games, role playing, discussions, student reporting, and calls for reflection. Although Diane limits the use of a presentation model, a small portion of each class session involves her providing historical or theoretical information. She often concludes a group activity by describing a real experience with elementary children and then soliciting suggestions from the preservice teachers. Emphasizing continuous reflection, she merges personal experiences, colorful analogies, and sample encounters with children. She explains what she wants the preservice teachers to do when they become teachers: "Giving a lecture is not what I want them to do, so I am not going to lecture." Diane yearns to conduct a thought-provoking course, providing experiences that will impress the students with mental images not merely of activities to be duplicated but images of how to think about mathematics teaching. Her aspirations remain high as she anticipates each class session with enthusiasm.

The Preservice Teachers' Reactions

With this vision of Diane's teaching in mind, let us look at one example of the preservice teachers' reactions. Following her usual effort to engage the students, she wants the preservice teachers to plan mathematics lessons and to describe and reflect on their difficulties; then she can provide an immediate riposte. After discussing preparation of lesson plans, distributing samples, and confirming important features, she divides the class into groups of three and assigns 30 minutes as a planning session. The following excerpts from field notes are typical examples of the eagerness, vacillation, and lack of interest with which some of the preservice teachers reacted.

Group 1: Marie, Sue, and Wendy selected a lesson on place value and then wrote their objectives and goals first, calling them out and then writing. "Have each child show and explain. What about the relationship between ones and tens? We want the children to be able to group the numbers. I don't know what else we can put down." It seemed like this group stayed on the topic the entire 30 minutes, talking loudly and enthusiastically. Sue made a suggestion and Marie discussed it. "Hey, this is like what the girl did on the video," said Marie. "Yes, but we are concentrating on second grade and beginning more basically," Sue replied. Wendy shook her head, yes, and made the notes. They continued a discussion until the teacher called time.

Group 2: Kevin, Wanda, and Hope discussed teaching fractions for about 20 minutes of the allotted time, mentioning goals such as better understanding of fractions and how fractions are used in everyday life. Then it seemed that they began discussing generally the problems of teaching. For example, "You can't change anyone. You have to change within yourself." The conversation digressed to a discussion of yesterday's campus events regarding the honor system. . . . Then Hope said, "OK, do we need anything else?"

Group 3: Marge, Mona, and Betty began their discussion. Marge said softly, "This is so stupid." Betty and Mona did most of the talking and planning, while Marge wrote something on the lesson plan sheet. Marge went into a daydreamlike stare, while Betty and Mona discussed teaching fractions. Marge broke her stare when Betty asked her what she thought. Marge said, "Maybe split the class in half and give half the class half a cookie and explain they have a half." Mona and Betty just looked at each other and then resumed discussion. Marge looked around the room and seemed to ignore them again. (field notes, March 12)

Despite concerns about transferring ideas to written form, the first group tackles the challenge and connects their ideas to exemplary teaching they had seen on a video. In the second group, members superficially approach the task of lesson planning. Even the time on planning produces only general goals without any specifics. They tend to vacillate, never focusing fully on the task at hand. In the third group, the disinterest of a participant is coupled with a lack of understanding and complete disengagement.

When the class reconvenes, several class members briefly comment about how difficult it is "to put into words." When Diane petitions for more input and gives advice for their upcoming practica, most of the preservice teachers prepare for departure and talk to each other, ignoring Diane. Although a course requirement, eight do not submit lesson plans. This is not the first time the observations expose the disengagement of some of the preservice teachers, but it is the first time Diane reveals her awareness of disinterest when she tells the observer she overheard Marge's remark, "This is so stupid."

The Lecture

Previously, Diane had never lectured. Remember her commitment, "I am not going to lecture." At the ninth classroom observation, however, she declares to the observer that she has material she wants to "give" to the preservice teachers, so she will just tell them. As she discusses two educational philosophies, her enthusiasm seems to momentarily fade as she moves back and forth and almost nervously announces, "I'm going to do quite a bit of talking today, and so you may want to take down a few notes," pointing to an overhead projector transparency.

Diane calls the main theme of the lesson, problem solving, "the number one focus of mathematics," which she outlines laboriously, mentioning 11 different strategies. The variety she extols is not braced by the involvement and the concrete materials she typically employs, however, and she controls the preservice teachers' responses by not pausing except when she asks for a show of hands. Summarizing, she advocates the importance of observing to diagnose difficulties:

> What I'm saying is you train yourself to be a diagnostician, but the best, your teachers, the people who will train you, are your students. So you watch your students. You know, are they rubbing their eyes? Are their hands bothering them? Are they wiggling? If they're not getting their work done, that's a symptom of something and you have to start thinking that way. (ninth classroom observation)

Diane again lectures again at a session not well attended before the practica and at the last class session scheduled as a practicum debriefing, at which time the preservice teachers' questions involve completion of course requirements, with no mention of their practice teaching experiences.

The Paradox

After class, a preservice teacher, Marie, mentions to the observer that even though the class was different (lecture instead of activities), "it was probably good for the class to get all that information because some have been saying they are not learning anything in here." In a later interview, Diane suggests this paradox:

> It's gonna be a strong pull to go back to the textbook, because, I know even for me, it was harder to teach this way in some ways. It's less secure. The days that I just did problem-solving lectures, I felt very secure. And yet, I bet they learned less in those two days. . . . Although they may have felt like they learned more because it was more traditional. (second interview)

Because she is seemingly ensconced in her definition of an interactive classroom environment, Diane's secure feeling while lecturing seems contradictory to her characteristic teaching. The reactions of the students and Diane's abrupt change lead us to look more closely at her final interview. At the end of the course, Diane continues to issue forceful statements regarding her decision to teach mathematics methods in a nontraditional manner.

> The way we've been training teachers hasn't worked. I mean, they go out there and they use the damn textbook. . . . Why not do something entirely different, because what we're doing isn't working? It absolutely is not working! The way I feel is, what have we got to lose? . . . There's hardly any risk involved, because I don't think we can be doing any worse than we are. (third interview)

As Diane responds, her concerns and realizations force her to review and adjust the knowledge, methods, and good teaching she expects of the preservice teachers.

Knowledge

For Diane, the preservice teachers' knowledge development includes critically examining current educational research. Diane mentions here for the first time reducing the requirements because of the preservice teachers' writing skills, while merely hoping the preservice teachers will read more on their own.

The journal article critiques. . . . I think three is a good number because one doesn't give you any breadth at all. . . . I have in the past required as many as six, which I think is even better. . . . I'd really like to have them read an article a week and react to it, but as you can see from their writing, it's very hard for them to write. . . . So, I think six is kind of unrealistic, although I would like for them to be reading more than three articles in an entire semester. Hopefully, they read some on their own that they didn't write about.

Another reason why I give those three journal article critiques is because I think that teachers have to be good communicators, and part of communicating is being able to write. And as you also can see, there are some students in the class that are very poor communicators . . . and that comes through in their writing. . . . I hope that they are learning some mathematics, learning some new methodologies by reading those articles. . . . They became familiar with some journals, mainly with the *Arithmetic Teacher*, but good grief, at least they know that now! At least now, they know where to go when they get out in the classroom and need ideas . . . and they didn't know that before! (third interview)

Although espousing written communication as significant to knowledge development, Diane reaches for evidence of the preservice teachers' progress but, once again, reduces her expectations. Subsequently, Diane speaks of her insecurity regarding acquisition of mathematical content knowledge.

The danger in that is that there are gonna be some students who go out there, and you can probably name them as well as I can, who really don't have the content down very well. The only hope I have is that they will teach themselves. . . . What we have to hope is that if they're doing well in their other courses, they're capable of learning it and teaching themselves. . . . But knowing that, I'm giving up. I don't have a real good handle on how well they know the content. And that concerns me, but I don't know what to do about it.

The thing that bothers me most about the class and the evaluation is I really don't have a good idea of what their math skills are, how well they know the content . . . they take the PPST, which is a basic skills test. . . . If they pass that test, they do have a basic knowledge of mathematics. . . . And we require college algebra. If they can make it through college algebra, then my assumption is they are able to look at the textbook and read the teachers' manual and understand the math. (third interview)

Adopting the preservice teachers' conceptions of how children learn, Diane deduces that if they are successful in other courses, then they are capable of teaching themselves mathematics. Making certain assumptions without substantiation, she does not totally renounce the preservice teachers' capabilities but, instead, rationalizes a narrower view of their knowledge development. Surrendering her previous emphasis on logic, reasoning, and problem solving, Diane acquiesces to basic skills as the major component of their knowledge.

Methods

Having relinquished responsibility for developing the preservice teachers' mathematical content knowledge, Diane turns her focus to methods and plans for the next semester.

So, I decided not to focus on that [mathematics content like fractions] but to focus on now: What do you think about when you get ready to teach fractions? Because that, they're not gonna get it anywhere, if they don't get it in my class. (third interview)

Although claiming the hope they will teach themselves, Diane implies that if they don't learn methods in this course, the preservice teachers are not equipped to learn methods once in the school systems. Diane's conceptions of knowledge and methods are clearly compromised by the reality of the preservice teachers. Expecting the third aspect, good teaching, to parallel the preservice teachers' depictions, we found instead, the following denouement.

Good Teaching

Returning to her discussion of the disappointing aspects of the mathematics methods course, Diane expresses disillusionment and frustration.

The only other thing that I do want to add: There are some students in the class that I really am not sure have the intellectual ability, I guess, to be good teachers. . . . And part of it is an alertness, inquisitiveness . . . I'm not sure. . . . John Dewey said there aren't enough people who are capable of being good teachers to fill the classrooms, and I think he's right. . . . So, we're going to graduate a whole lot of students that are gonna be just mediocre, because there just aren't enough people who have whatever it is that it takes. . . . And you just see it, you just see it in their eyes. You see it in their lesson plans. You see it in their work. . . . You can't light the fire. You can't make it, I don't know what, and I don't know how to do it. (third interview)

What Diane dialogically concludes from the preservice teachers' examinations, assignments, and grades (A = 7, B = 14, C = 1), her intuition now contradicts.

[Is there] some way of keeping them out? [pause] I don't think so. You know? I don't think, because they pass the tests. They pass the courses. Sometimes they even get A's. . . . Because it's sort of an intangible thing. It's like the difference between somebody who paints pictures and an artist. I mean, what is it? How do you measure it? And it's like they're painting by number and then there are others who go in and create these beautiful paintings! And I don't know . . . I don't even know how you measure it or how you could even say to somebody, "I think you're gonna be mediocre, so I'm not gonna recommend that you go out and student teach." (third interview)

Facing the decremental possibilities of change, Diane spirals to sadness and hopelessness, as she contemplates the preservice teachers entering elementary classrooms.

The thing that's bothersome to me about that is that if it doesn't happen here, it's not gonna happen, because the school culture is such that . . . if the spark isn't here, it will never happen out there in the schools. . . . The environment [school] isn't right for it to happen. It's got to happen here or I don't think it's gonna happen. It might. I mean, if you get a dynamic principal. . . . If the fires don't get lit here, they're not gonna get lit. And that's kind of sad.

We've gotten much more rigorous, but they go to another university and finish out at that university. We turn them down and the next thing I know, they're student teaching and they're supervising teachers. . . . So, anyway, that bothers me, but I'm beginning to let go of that, too . . . I just have to do the best I can . . . I can't take on the problems of the world . . . And there will be some [preservice teachers] and you know which ones they are. You know as well as I do. But you think, "Well, I hope my child's not in that person's classroom." (third interview)

In this unexpected response, Diane explains how her institution had established higher standards and, as a result, suffered enrollment decline when preservice teachers transferred elsewhere. As she descends from hopefulness to disappointment and despair, she lets go of her vision of good teaching.

Discussion and Implications

Referring to our initial theoretical perspectives of this study, teachers try activities to see if they work and make changes, sometimes dramatic (Richardson, 1994). The methods instructor, Diane Solo, believes she can be a constructivist, but her beliefs are dramatically recast, if not reconceptualized. Although she believes in the importance of teaching for understanding, she moves from an active approach to the traditional lecture. Diane yearns for the preservice teachers to think differently about mathematics education, but although she is advocating appraisal and synthesis, some are nonplussed or disinterested. Her aspirations for the preservice teachers to transform their knowledge beyond the basics, construct their own mathematical knowledge, and develop instructional prowess are shattered. In the end, she no longer expects content knowledge other than basic skills, and she consoles herself with the hope that they will learn on their own, just as many of the preservice teachers believe children do.

When Diane changes to lecture, she confesses to feeling more comfortable. This paradox is dramatic evidence of her metamorphosis. The preservice teachers' operative participation declines and tension develops in some instances because of their belief that they are not learning unless they are being told what to do. Personal factors, time constraints, or her perceived acceptance by the preservice teachers may have interfered with Diane's attempts to teach through constructivism. Regardless, when the students disengage and she realizes her efforts are foiled, Diane gives up. The preservice teachers' reactions undermine the methods teacher's attempts to provide instruction in a different way. As she so aptly declares, "Your teachers, the people who will train you, are your students." Diane had been trained by her students, altering her beliefs to fit the preservice teachers' conceptions of teaching and learning.

Diane's final remarks about the preservice teachers are disconcerting to teacher educators and may leave the mathematics education community with a feeling of powerlessness. A teacher who senses the constructivist basis of modern reform falls victim to the politics of an educational system. Her decision to propel the preservice teachers through the program, despite her doubts regarding their capabilities, may not have been an individualized decision. For instance, if Diane had assigned failing grades, her record of failures might be viewed as representative of her teaching credibility. Instead, grades became unrealistic forms of flattery that the preservice teachers could interpret as readiness. As happened earlier, if Diane had not awarded passing grades, the preservice teachers might have transferred to another institution—then not only would the program be at risk, Diane also would be at risk. The economic, political, and social pressures to move students through a program may have produced standards unrelated to learning.

Regardless of the subject matter, learning environment descriptions are inadequate unless students are studied (Kleinsasser, 1993). Furthermore, educational research has neglected to reveal how students' views influence teachers' instructional decisions (Thompson, 1992). One major reason for this research chasm is that many teacher education studies omit the beliefs and conceptions of the participants and the possible links between students' conceptions and their teacher's instructional behavior. This study enables us to see teacher education in a new way, revealing not only the commonly known entrenchment of teacher candidates' conceptions but also the profound influence exerted on their methods instructor's beliefs and practices. The implications are far-reaching. If preservice teachers reject the beliefs and practices of modern reform, and their conceptions can influence changes in the instructional behavior of their teacher educators, learning to improve mathematics instruction may remain intractable.

In seeking to answer why reform efforts fail, this study provides evidence and suggests future research endeavors. A teacher who begins with a commitment to reform mathematics education returns to traditional practices. The reactions of her students, whose conceptions contrast with her own, eventually reduce her fervor and alter her vision. How often do students' beliefs interfere with the instructional behavior of their teachers? If this is atypical, why do the conceptions of preservice teachers remain so entrenched? If this is commonplace, then beliefs, not just strategies, must be changed. The meaning constructed from the data suggests future research agendas should seek not only to further illuminate the influence of preservice teachers' beliefs and actions on the instructional behavior of their teachers but also to develop ways to reduce the external pressures that impede reform.

References

Anderson, L. M., Holt-Reynolds, D., & Swidler, S. (1994, April). *Prospective teachers' responses to opportunities to rethink beliefs about learning and teaching.* Paper presented at the annual meeting of the American Educational Research Association, New Orleans.

Elbaz, F. L. (1983). *Teacher thinking: A study of practical knowledge.* London: Croom Helm.

Fenstermacher, G. D. (1994). The knower and the known: The nature of knowledge in research on teaching. In L. Darling-Hammond (Ed.), *Review of research in education* (pp. 3-56). Washington, DC: American Educational Research Association.

Foss, D. H. (1993). *Elementary mathematics methods: A cultural scene in the teacher preparation act.* Unpublished doctoral dissertation, University of Memphis.

Foss, D. H., & Kleinsasser, R. C. (1996). Preservice elementary teachers' views of pedagogical and mathematical content knowledge. *Teaching and Teacher Education, 12*(4), 429-442.

Glaser, B., & Strauss, A. (1967). *The discovery of grounded theory: Strategies for qualitative research.* Chicago: Aldine.

Goldin, G. A. (1990). Epistemology, constructivism, and discovery learning in mathematics. In R. B. Davis, C. A. Maher, & N. Noddings (Eds.), *Constructivists views on the teaching and learning of mathematics* (pp. 31-47). Reston, VA: National Council of Teachers of Mathematics.

Grouws, D. A. (1991). Improving research in mathematics classroom instruction. In E. Fennema, T. P. Carpenter, & S. J. Lamon (Eds.), *Integrating research on teaching and learning mathematics* (pp. 199-215). Albany: State University of New York Press.

Kleinsasser, R. C. (1993). A tale of two technical cultures: Foreign language teaching. *Teaching and Teacher Education, 9*(4), 373-383.

Lee, R. W. (1994, April). *Perceptions of a beginning teacher.* Paper presented at the annual conference of the American Educational Research Association, New Orleans.

National Council of Teachers of Mathematics. (1989). *Curriculum and evaluation standards for school mathematics.* Reston, VA: Author.

Richardson, V. (1994). Conducting research on practice. *Educational Researcher, 23*(5), 5-9.

Russell, T. L. (1987). Research, practical knowledge, and the conduct of teacher education. *Educational Theory, 37*(4), 369-375.

Spradley, J. P. (1979). *The ethnographic interview.* New York: Holt, Rinehart & Winston.

Thompson, A. G. (1992). Teachers' beliefs and conceptions: A synthesis of the research. In D. A. Grouws (Ed.), *Handbook of research on mathematics teaching and learning* (pp. 127-146). New York: Macmillan.

Williamson, J. B., Karp, D. A., Dalphin, J. R., & Gray, P. (1982). *The research craft: An introduction to social research methods.* Boston: Little, Brown.

PROCESSES: REFLECTIONS AND IMPLICATIONS

Robert Alley

Carol B. Furtwengler

Dennis Potthoff

Another thing about reflection—it's hard. It's hard because one must analyze what's transpired and, to some degree, make a value judgment about it. And if the reflection is honest, it can mean that a teacher may have to alter his/her style or completely chuck something that he/she worked hard to develop. It seems to be much safer and more secure not to reflect, because one doesn't have to change that which he/she doesn't see as being wrong.

—Richert, 1990, p. 526

Each of the three research studies in this section attempted to effect change through a different process: reflective teaching for thoughtful decision making in one case, teacher's beliefs about cooperative learning in another, and a constructivist, as opposed to a traditionalist, approach to teaching in the third. In the end, two were largely unsuccessful in their attempts at effecting change and one approach, using reflective teaching, showed more promise.

These three studies highlight two fundamental points. First, they reveal how difficult it is to change teachers' practices. For professionals, it is often more comfortable to revert to traditional, known, proven approaches to instruction than to seek new ways of doing things. Second, these studies also reveal that asking teachers to reflect about personal belief systems and confront those beliefs in a systematic manner is one promising strategy for effecting change.

Changing
Teachers' Practices

The ultimate in frustration and discouragement for teacher educators who are trying to change preservice teachers' views of appropriate teaching practice was described by Foss. Her analysis of the actions of the mathematics education instructor (Diane), who concluded that she must adapt to the traditionalist expectations of her students and revert to a didactic model of instruction, underscored the difficulty of the change process. The preservice teachers described by Foss, unable to adapt to an interactive classroom using a constructivist approach to learning, conveyed their displeasure and prompted Diane's return to traditional approaches to instruction. Preservice (and sometimes inservice) teachers often resist faculty attempts to model innovative practices. In Diane's case, the cultural norms of traditional approaches to instruction in higher education effectively raised the question, "Who adjusts to whom?"

Sanders and Meloth met similar reluctance to consider alternatives to traditional approaches to instruction in their studies of both preservice and inservice teachers. They found it difficult to convince inservice teachers to "buy into" a different view of the teacher learning process, even though the value of cooperative learning is supported by a vast body of literature. As they put it, "Teachers are not likely to change them [beliefs] without good reason." The question is what constitutes good and justifiable reasons for change in the minds of teachers? One senses, perhaps, that research-based support may be the wrong kind of evidence. Sanders and Meloth also found that "the social skills and knowledge transmission view of teaching are beliefs that remain relatively unchanged, even after learning about and using cooperative methods." The teachers in the Sanders and Meloth studies saw cooperative learning primarily as a vehicle for improved social skills rather than as a fundamental model of instruction with the capability of improving students' reading abilities.

The Foss and Sanders and Meloth studies, albeit very valuable, are very frustrating to teacher educators who seek ways to change the educational process and are often frustrated by their inability to effect that change.

Confronting Teachers' Belief Systems

Conversely, Bennett, who directly addressed the belief systems of her students, was able to report success in helping them modify their current practices. Her students examined their own beliefs and came to understand that those beliefs shaped their classroom practices. Bennett, for her study, hypothesized that preservice teachers' beliefs about teaching affect their actions in the classroom and then designed a project to help preservice teachers examine their beliefs as a means to effect change in their practice. As she said, "We continually ask students to rethink their perspectives in light of their personal classroom experiences and school contexts." Bennett's study demonstrated the need to encourage—dare we say, force?—preservice teachers to recognize and lay bare their teaching perspectives and biases so they will change their instructional and teaching styles. In Bennett's program, students were continually asked to rethink their perspectives in light of their personal experiences in school contexts.

Of Bennett's seven teacher perspectives, Inculcators best represent the traditional model of teaching whereas Facilitators of Thinking describe those who have moved away from textbook learning to active participation in the learning process. Ronald, a student in her study, saw himself as an Empowerer and pointed out, "Not seeing how something applied to my life was one of my biggest challenges for learning." His reflection was a powerful comment about an inherent problem with traditional teacher education programs, decontexualization of learning (Brown, Collins, & Duguid, 1988) that results in "inert" knowledge rather than competence.

Summary and Conclusions

One difficult issue that emerges from the three studies is this: Do teachers change their beliefs after they change their practice, *or* do they change their practice after they change their beliefs? Furthermore, how do teacher educators help preservice and inservice teachers change the cultural norms about teaching and learning that exist in schools? Bennett's program, which encouraged teachers to reflect on and understand their own teaching perspectives and biases, may be part of the solution. Collectively, however, these studies suggest the need for simultaneous change of belief and practice. Furthermore, they suggest that teachers must also reflect on their belief systems while they are implementing changes in practice.

But reflection comes with a price. With time a premium in teacher education programs, devoting time to reflection may mean reduction in time devoted to instructional strategies or foundational background knowledge. Furthermore, teaching models employing constructivist approaches consume precious time. Content may be sacrificed to enhance process, leaving teachers with a limited knowledge about effective teaching strategies and skill-building techniques. For professionals, balancing competing demands is a central issue.

Modeling desired teacher practices is essential in teacher education programs if the profession is to see significant change in practice. The ultimate irony in all too many programs is exemplified by the notion of a professor lecturing about strategies necessary to implement cooperative learning. Also, teacher educators must reflect on their own practice to assure themselves that they model appropriate practices for their students. Perhaps the most significant point made by Bennett was that her own teaching improved as a result of her development of further insights into the strengths and potential limitations of her own perspective of teaching. She modeled teacher reflection in the adaptation and improvement of her own instruction.

The importance of context in the learning process, as postulated by Silver (1990), is also demonstrated by the three studies in this section of the yearbook. Teacher educators must develop programs that mirror the context(s) in which their students teach. Field-based models, such as professional development schools, are possible steps toward relevant situated learning. The development of such programs, one hopes, will make change more likely.

Teacher educators need to find a way to address the challenge of changing teachers' beliefs while instituting reform in both the methods and location of instruction. Foss supported the importance of preservice teachers' belief systems by referencing Grouws (1991), who argued that the general nature of teachers' beliefs about learning, instruction, and mathematical knowledge affects instructional decision making.

No doubt, teacher educators can anticipate resistance to effective change in their programs. Change is especially difficult when fiscal problems cause administrators to press for increased credit-hour production or other ways to serve more students with the same resources. The current "consumerism" approach to working with students will place further pressures on faculty to surrender to student likes and desires. When such trends abound, teacher educators must step back, reflect, and place the importance of meeting both student needs and the needs of the profession in perspective. Without doubt, improvement of the profession hinges on teacher educators finding the courage and steadfast commitment to change. As Fullan (1993) put it, "Change is too important to leave to the experts" (p. 93).

References

Brown, J. S., Collins, A., & Duguid, P. (1988). *Situated cognition and the culture of learning* (Technical Report No. 6886). Cambridge, MA: Bolt, Beranek, & Newman.

Fullan, M. (1993). *Change forces: Probing the depths of educational reform.* London: Falmer.

Grouws, D. A. (Ed.). (1991). *Handbook of research on mathematics teaching and learning* (pp. 127-146). New York: Macmillan.

Richert, A. (1990). Teaching teachers to reflect: A consideration of programme structure. *Journal of Curriculum Studies, 22*(6), 509-527.

Silver, E. A. (1990). *Treating estimation and mental computation as situated mathematical processes.* Pittsburgh, PA: University of Pittsburgh, Learning Research and Development Center. (ERIC Document Reproduction Service No. ED 342 645)

DIVISION III

CURRICULUM:
OVERVIEW AND FRAMEWORK

Sandra J. Odell

Sandra J. Odell has been Professor and Director of Undergraduate
Studies at Western Michigan University and recently joined the facul-
ty at the University of Nevada, Las Vegas. Dr. Odell has published
Mentor Teacher Programs, chapters in several monographs and books,
as well as many journal articles on the topics of teacher induction and
mentoring. She has served on the ATE National Commissions on
Teacher Induction and the Role and Preparation of Mentor Teachers.
She currently co-chairs the Commission on Novice Teacher Support.
The first three ATE Yearbooks were edited by Dr. Odell with Dr. M. J.
O'Hair. Dr. Odell maintains a career-long research interest in teacher
development, teacher induction, and mentoring in the context of
collaborative university/school district programs.

The three chapters that constitute the curriculum division of this volume
illustrate the complexity of developing curricula for teacher education.
This complexity goes beyond curriculum occurring at all levels of teacher

education discourse, including the preparation of teachers, the induction of teachers into the profession, and the planning of an advanced program of study for graduate students, as the subsequent chapters address. Indeed, the complexities of curricula are evident in all knowledge domains and are equally a matter of concern whether the curriculum deals with classic English language instruction or contemporary issues of multicultural pluralism. Curriculum, defined primarily as the content of teacher education, that is, as the courses and associated school experiences (Howey & Zimpher, 1989), does not stand alone. It is influenced by other commonplaces of education, namely the learner, the teacher, and the social milieu in which the teaching and learning process occurs (Schwab, 1973).

Although the chapters in this division of the ATE Yearbook do not deal explicitly with all of the aforementioned commonplace elements of education and their interactions, the chapters do address a number of important curricular dimensions. Specifically, the chapters focus on developing a conceptual framework for a teacher education curriculum, understanding the influence of subject matter knowledge and pedagogy on teaching, understanding the impact of teachers' beliefs and dispositions on learning to teach, and determining the impact of social contexts on teaching. To provide the reader a framework for better understanding the subsequent chapters, an overview of these particular aspects of curriculum is presented next.

Developing a Conceptual
Orientation for Programs

A first matter of importance in developing a curriculum is to specify an underlying conceptual framework. The National Council for the Accreditation of Teacher Education (NCATE, 1995) emphasizes the import of having a well-articulated, shared conceptual framework for a program in teacher education. The framework for an individual program is expected to define the professional commitments, dispositions, and values that support the program. Moreover, the framework should provide the philosophical and programmatic purposes that undergird the course of study for students and should reflect multicultural and global perspectives. The expectation from NCATE is that the conceptual framework and knowledge base, which support a professional education program, rest on established and contemporary research, the wisdom of practice, and emerging education policies.

Establishing teacher education programs that have a conceptual orientation, which includes a view of teaching and learning as well as beliefs about learning to teach, can give direction to the practical activities of teacher preparation such as program planning, course development, instruction, supervision, and evaluation (Feiman-Nemser, 1990a, 1990b). The knowledge base for a teacher education program is developed when the faculty members who teach in the program collaborate to agree on a consistent and shared vision of teaching that pervades the courses and experiences that constitute "a program" in teacher preparation.

Too often the education of teachers includes simply a collection of courses taken by students who are preparing to be elementary or secondary teachers. Students are exposed to an array of disconnected research and theories where emphasis depends on the individual instructor rather than on a combined and thoughtfully determined hierarchy of courses and experiences that are inextricably linked. Teacher education faculties find the development of a programmatic conceptual framework difficult and time-consuming. It requires an articulation of beliefs, underlying principles, understandings, and expectations not often easily agreed on by academicians. This can result in factions of faculty disagreeing about how to proceed and ultimately resorting to maintaining the status quo. Unfortunately, it is often the case that only when an NCATE visitation is eminent does a rush to develop a consensus around a particular conceptual framework occur.

Despite the time-consuming nature of developing a conceptual framework, the resulting programmatic benefits and clarity make it worth the effort. Howey and Zimpher (1989) emphasized the differences between a curriculum per se and a program in teacher education and focus on the import of developing a conceptual framework to guide teacher education program development. Recognizing that curricula and programs are not mutually exclusive, they define a curriculum as the course work and associated experiences for students and define a teacher education program broadly as more than the sum of the courses and related experiences. Specifically, they stated,

> Programs have one or more frameworks grounded in theory and research as well as practice; frameworks that explicate, justify, and build consensus around such fundamental conceptions as the "role" of the teacher, the "nature of" teaching and learning, and

the "mission" of schools in this democracy. These frameworks guide not only the nature of curriculum as manifested in individual courses but, as well, questions of scope; developmental sequence; integration of discrete disciplines; and the relationships of pedagogical knowledge to learning how to teach in various laboratory, clinical, and school settings. . . . Conceptually coherent programs enable needed and "shared" faculty leadership to engage in more generative and continuing renewal by underscoring collective roles as well as individual course responsibilities. (p. 242)

It seems reasonable, then, to conclude that a definitive conceptual framework is a paramount precondition for creating a coherent teacher education program. The Guyton, Rainer, and Wright piece (Chapter 7) is an interesting description of one faculty's effort to develop a conceptual framework for a graduate teacher education program.

Focusing on Subject Matter
Knowledge and Pedagogy

There is little debate that subject matter is an essential component of teacher knowledge and is a necessary commonplace in education. A plethora of studies over the past decade (e.g., Ball, 1991; Ball & McDiarmid, 1990; Buchmann, 1982; Grossman, 1989; Wilson, 1989; Wineburg & Wilson, 1988) underscores the point that strong subject matter knowledge provides a basis for learning to teach in the more ambitious and adventurous ways that are being advocated by current educational reformers (Mosenthal & Ball, 1992). Going beyond the mere understanding of the facts associated with a subject, coherent subject matter knowledge also involves understanding the relationships and interconnectedness among the concepts of the subject. In addition, subject matter knowledge entails being able to use the logic and structure of the subject to solve problems. Shulman (1986) asserted that teachers should understand the content of a subject at least as well as a subject matter major in a field and must also understand "why it is so, on what grounds its warrant can be asserted, and under what circumstances our belief in its justification can be weakened or even denied" (p. 9).

Shulman (1986) proposed that there also exists a body of pedagogical content knowledge that is unique and central to teaching. Pedagogical content knowledge is distinguished from subject matter knowledge in that it extends beyond the content of a discipline to include its relationship to teaching the particular content. Pedagogical content knowledge entails understanding what makes topics easy or difficult for learners, and how different learners can conceive of content as a result of their background experiences. It sets teachers apart from pure subject matter specialists. Teachers should have the ability to know and represent the ideas of a subject; to offer powerful examples, analogies, and illustrations of the subject's content; and to explain and demonstrate the content so that others can understand.

A third category of knowledge defined by Shulman (1986) is curricular knowledge, which includes an understanding of the range of available teaching materials, texts, visual aids, and films, as well as other alternative curriculum materials for a particular topic in a subject area. Broad curricular knowledge also includes understanding the relationships across subject areas and the relationship of a particular subject to content in the same subject area across grade levels. Curricular knowledge equips teachers to relate the content they are teaching to other subjects and allows teachers to link content to what may have come before or may come after in students' schooling.

The combination of strong subject matter knowledge, pedagogical content knowledge, and curricular knowledge is essential to good teaching. In Chapter 8, Elizabeth Spalding presents an enlightening study of the relationship between subject matter, pedagogical knowledge, and curricular knowledge and raises further the issue of teachers' beliefs and dispositions about teaching.

Understanding the Influence of Beliefs and Dispositions on Teaching

As students enter teacher education programs, they bring with them beliefs and dispositions about teachers and teaching, learners and learning, subject matter, and the contexts in which teaching and learning occur (Lortie, 1975). Researchers across the disciplines of anthropology, social psychology, and philosophy are congruent in defining beliefs as "psychologically held understandings, premises, or propositions about the work that are felt to be true" (Richardson, 1996, p. 103). As opposed to beliefs, knowledge depends on a "truth condition," that is, knowledge requires evidence to back it up and it is held as true, worthwhile, and valid by a community of scholars (Green, 1971, in Richardson, 1996). Beliefs are not necessarily firmly grounded and warranted; they represent propositions accepted by an individual, and they are psychological concepts different from knowledge.

Richardson (1996), in her recent review of the literature on teacher beliefs, explains the genesis of beliefs as personal experience, experience with schooling and instruction, and experience with formal knowledge. She noted that personal-experience factors such as ethnic and socioeconomic background, gender, religious affiliation, and geographic location generally influence a person's beliefs. In addition, one's own experience as a student in preschool, elementary school, middle school, and high school provides a 12- to 15-year long apprenticeship resulting in deep-seated beliefs about teaching and schooling (Lortie, 1975). Furthermore, beliefs about the nature of subject matter develop as a result of years spent inside and outside of school learning about subjects and how they are learned.

Interestingly, and generally speaking, prior beliefs are a consistent predictor of how prospective teachers think about teaching as it relates to subject matter, their underlying philosophical and theoretical orientation to teaching, and their view of children and how they learn. In recent years, studies that explore the influence that beliefs have on learning to teach have gained prominence in the teacher education literature. In particular, researchers have explored the extent to which the entering beliefs of teacher education students can change and develop as they are studying to be teachers (e.g., Hollingsworth, 1989; Holt-Reynolds, 1992, 1995; McDiarmid, 1992; McDiarmid & Price, 1993). It has generally been found that programs designed to change beliefs among participants are considerably more successful and more encouraging with practicing teachers than with preservice students. Richardson (1996) hypothesized that the resistance to change in preservice teacher education may be related to limited practical teaching knowledge. Students seemingly find it difficult, and perhaps impossible, to tie beliefs to teaching practices that have not been tested in the classroom.

Several studies provide reason for optimism that prior practicing teachers' beliefs about teaching can be modified. Evidence that beliefs can be altered has emerged from staff development efforts that use metaphors to reveal teachers beliefs and then examine them, case studies to examine misconceptions about subject matter, and career stories to reconstruct professional self and theory (respectively, Tobin, 1990; Barnett & Sather, 1992; Kelchtermans, 1993, all in Richardson, 1996). Additional research is needed, however, to explore more fully the ultimate question of whether changed beliefs about teaching lead to changed teaching.

Because of the general difficulty of changing teachers' beliefs, Haberman (1993, 1995, 1996) has advocated the differential selection of teacher education candidates who already hold beliefs consonant with best teaching practice rather than attempting to change the less than optimal beliefs and dispositions of some students. To facilitate this differential selection, Haberman (1995) identified 10 "principles of learning" that guide the day-to-day teaching of effective urban teachers and developed an in-depth interview process to determine whether a candidate's beliefs are consistent with these principles. Two chapters in this division, Chapters 8 and 9, by Elizabeth Spalding and Burga Jung, respectively, deal with how beliefs of teachers and teacher candidates influence their teaching. Spalding's study examines how teachers defined and practiced teaching based on their prior perspectives about the subject matter. Jung explores ways in which monocultural preservice teachers' beliefs influence their thinking about teaching multicultural students. This latter work raises the issue of how the extant context influences the teaching/learning process.

Understanding the
Impact of Context on Teaching

As commented on so frequently in the recent literature (e.g., Boyer & Baptiste, 1996; Corrigan & Haberman, 1990; Darling-Hammond & Sclan, 1996; Gage, 1990; Grant & Secada, 1990; Hodgkinson, 1985; Nieto, 1992; Schwartz, 1996), there has been significant change in the sociological environments of schools in the United States during the past 15 years. Literally, one of every four American children is currently living in poverty. With strong movements toward inclusion, more children with special needs are now in mainstream classrooms. Children from families of immigrants are in schools in record numbers, and increasingly large numbers of children with minority language backgrounds are in schools. Demographic trends clearly show that teachers will continue to teach heterogeneous groups of students in American schools with 30% to 40% of students of color making up the school population in the year 2000 (Hodgkinson, 1985).

In contrast, the nation's teaching force has remained homogeneous. White females are expected to remain dominant in the teaching force through the year 2000, despite our efforts to recruit and retain people of color in many colleges of education across the nation. Currently, 87% of female teachers and 9% of male teachers are White and non-Hispanic (Schwartz, 1996).

Among educators, there is the tacit assumption that recruiting a diverse group of people into teacher education will enhance teacher effectiveness. Although much more research is needed to determine the conceptual and empirical limits of this assumption (Grant & Secada, 1990), there seems to be face validity to the assertion that having more diverse models in the teaching profession and selecting individuals into teacher education programs who have strong potential to work in urban contexts are worthwhile (e.g., Haberman, 1996).

In addition to the contextual issue of diversity, other contextual aspects of teaching practice alter the nation's schools by affecting the lives of teachers and students. The within-school variables of school organization, school size and physical plant, school leadership, class size, availability of materials for teaching, level of interaction among teachers, teacher pay, facilities, level of community involvement, leadership, and involvement of specialists in schools are among the myriad of contextual variables that affect teaching and learning. Moreover, overarching external contexts, for example, those of politics and the economy, influence teaching and learning in schools.

Three Research Reports

By way of overview, the matter of curriculum, specifically that of teacher education curriculum, is complex. I have attempted to provide a framework for the reader by discussing the commonplace curricular elements addressed, directly and indirectly, by the chapters that constitute the curriculum division of this yearbook. Although in very different ways, each chapter is provocative in providing insight into the necessary conditions for constructing curricula. Specifically, Chapter 7, "Developing a Constructivist Teacher Education Program," by Edith M. Guyton, Julie Rainer, and Trish Wright, is an instructive example of a faculty at a large urban state university working together to develop a conceptual framework for an early childhood master's degree program based on constructivist theories and principles. Chapter 8, " 'Swallowing an Elephant': The Subject Perspectives of Selected Novice English Teachers," by Elizabeth Spalding is an example of using interpretive inquiry methods to examine how three novice English teachers defined their work, how they acted on their beliefs in the classroom using a "subject perspective" approach, and how context has influenced their teaching. Finally, Chapter 9, "Multicultural Education and Monocultural Students: Curriculum Struggles in Teacher Education," by Burga Jung examines the effect of a course on altering the multicultural beliefs of preservice teacher education students.

References

Ball, D. L. (1991). Teaching mathematics for understanding: What do teachers need to know about the subject matter? In M. Kennedy (Ed.), *Teaching academic subjects to diverse learners* (pp. 63-83). New York: Teachers College Press.

Ball, D. L., & McDiarmid, G. W. (1990). The subject-matter preparation of teachers. In W. R. Houston, M. Haberman, & J. Sikula (Eds.), *Handbook of research on teacher education* (pp. 437-449). New York: Macmillan.

Boyer, J. B., & Baptiste, P. (1996). The crisis in teacher education in America: Issues of recruitment and retention of culturally different (minority) teachers. In J. Sikula, T. J. Buttery, & E. Guyton (Eds.), *Handbook of research on teacher education* (pp. 779-794). New York: Macmillan.

Buchmann, M. (1982). The flight away from content in teacher educa-tion and teaching. *Journal of Curriculum Studies, 14*(1), 61-68.

Corrigan, D. C., & Haberman, M. (1990). The context of teacher educa-tion. In W. R. Houston, M. Haberman, & J. Sikula (Eds.), *Handbook of research on teacher education* (pp. 195-211). New York: Macmillan.

Darling-Hammond, L., & Sclan, E. M. (1996). Who teaches and why: Dilemmas of building a profession for twenty-first century schools. In J. Sikula, T. J. Buttery, & E. Guyton (Eds.), *Handbook of research on teacher education* (pp. 67-101). New York: Macmillan.

Feiman-Nemser, S. (1990a). *Conceptual orientations in teacher education* (Issue Paper 90-2). East Lansing, MI: The National Center for Re-search on Teacher Education.

Feiman-Nemser, S. (1990b). Teacher preparation: Structural and con-ceptual alternatives. In W. R. Houston, M. Haberman, & J. Sikula (Eds.), *Handbook of research on teacher education* (pp. 212-233). New York: Macmillan.

Gage, N. L. (1990). Dealing with the dropout problem. *Phi Delta Kappan, 72*, 280-285.

Grant, G. A., & Secada, W. G. (1990). Preparing teachers for diversity. In W. R. Houston, M. Haberman, & J. Sikula (Eds.), *Handbook of research on teacher education* (pp. 403-422). New York: Macmillan.

Grossman, P. L. (1989). A study in contrast: Sources of pedagogical content knowledge for secondary English. *Journal of Teacher Education, 40*(5), 24-31.

Haberman, M. (1993). Contexts: Implications and reflections. In M. J. O'Hair & S. J. Odell (Eds.), *Diversity and teaching* (pp. 84-89). Ft. Worth, TX: Harcourt Brace Jovanovich.

Haberman, M. (1995). *STAR teachers of children in poverty.* West Lafayette, IN: Kappa Delta Pi.

Haberman, M. (1996). Selecting and preparing culturally competent teachers for urban schools. In J. Sikula, T. J. Buttery, & E. Guyton (Eds.), *Handbook of research on teacher education* (pp. 747-760). New York: Macmillan.

Hodgkinson, H. L. (1985). *All one system: Demographics of education— kindergarten through graduate school.* Washington, DC: Institute for Educational Leadership.

Hollingsworth, S. (1989). Prior beliefs and cognitive change in learning to teach. *American Educational Research Journal, 26*(2), 160-189.

Holt-Reynolds, D. (1992). Personal history-based beliefs as relevant prior knowledge in coursework: Can we practice what we teach? *American Educational Research Journal, 29*, 325-349.

Holt-Reynolds, D. (1995). Preservice teachers and coursework: When is getting it right wrong? In M. J. O'Hair & S. J. Odell (Eds.), *Educating teachers for leadership and change* (pp. 117-137). Thousand Oaks, CA: Corwin.

Howey, K. R., & Zimpher, N. L. (1989). *Profiles of preservice teacher education: Inquiry into the nature of programs.* Albany: State University of New York Press.

Lortie, D. (1975). *Schoolteacher: A sociological study.* Chicago: University of Chicago Press.

McDiarmid, G. W. (1992). What to do about differences? A study of multicultural education for teacher trainees in the Los Angeles Unified School District. *Journal of Teacher Education, 43* (2), 83-93.

McDiarmid, G. W., & Price, J. (1993). Preparing teachers for diversity: A study of student teachers in a multicultural program. In M. J.

O'Hair & S. J. Odell (Eds.), *Diversity and teaching* (pp. 31-57). Ft. Worth, TX: Harcourt Brace Jovanovich.

Mosenthal, J. H., & Ball, D. L. (1992). Constructing new forms of teaching: Subject matter knowledge in inservice teacher education. *Journal of Teacher Education, 43*(5), 347-356.

National Council for the Accreditation of Teacher Education. (1995). *Standards, procedures, & policies for the accreditation of professional education units.* Washington, DC: Author.

Nieto, S. (1992). *Affirming diversity: The sociopolitical context of multicultural education.* New York: Longman.

Richardson, V. (1996). The role of attitudes and beliefs in learning to teach. In J. Sikula, T. J. Buttery, & E. Guyton (Eds.), *Handbook of research on teacher education* (pp. 102-119). New York: Macmillan.

Schwab, T. (1973). The practical translation into curriculum. *School Review, 81,* 501-522.

Schwartz, H. (1996). The changing nature of teacher education. In J. Sikula, T. J. Buttery, & E. Guyton (Eds.), *Handbook of research on teacher education* (pp. 3-13). New York: Macmillan.

Shulman, L. (1986). Those who understand: Knowledge growth in teaching. *Educational Researcher, 15*(2), 4-14.

Wilson, S. M. (1989). *A case concerning content: Using case studies to teach subject matter* (Craft Paper 89-1). East Lansing, MI: The National Center for Research on Teacher Education.

Wineburg, S. S., & Wilson, S. M. (1988). Models of wisdom in the teaching of history. *Phi Delta Kappan, 70*(1), 50-58.

7 Developing a Constructivist Teacher Education Program

Edith M. Guyton

Julie Rainer

Trish Wright

Edith M. Guyton is Associate Professor of Early Childhood Education at Georgia State University, Atlanta. She, along with Julie Rainer were guest editors for a special issue (Summer 1996) of *Action in Teacher Education* on constructivist education. Guyton is an editor of the 1996 *Handbook of Research on Teacher Education* and was editor of the Georgia Association of Teacher Educators journal for six years. She has served on the Executive Board of the Association of Teacher Educators and was president of the Georgia and Southeastern Association of Teacher Educators. Guyton has published numerous articles in *Action in Teacher Education* and the *Journal of Teacher Education.* Her current writing and research focus is on constructivist teacher education, urban teacher education, and cultural diversity.

Julie Rainer is Assistant Professor at Georgia State University. She is an active member of the Association of Teacher Educators, serving on the Professional Journal Committee and the 1995 and 1997 National Planning Committees. She is a member of the NCATE Board of Examiners. Her current research and writing focus is on program development, constructivist teacher education, and urban teacher education.

Trish Wright is a doctoral candidate at Georgia State University in the Department of Counseling and Psychological Services.

ABSTRACT

Program development in teacher education is a complex process. This chapter focuses on three phases of curriculum decision making for an early childhood department at a large urban state university engaged in developing a new master's degree program based on constructivist theories and principles. We were participant observers, and data were collected over a 3-year period from field notes, interviews, and documents. We identified (a) tasks, issues, and decisions for each phase; (b) foundations for change; and (c) faculty struggles in making a paradigm shift. Recommendations for effecting positive change are made.

Constructivist Education

One current focus of change in teacher education involves attempts to develop constructivist teacher education programs designed to prepare teachers who base their teaching on constructivist principles and theories. The philosophy of John Dewey undergirds constructivist education, and Dewey (1938) differentiated this philosophy from traditional education.

> To imposition from above is opposed expression and cultivation of individuality; to external discipline is opposed free activity; to learning from texts and teachers, learning through experience; to acquisition of isolated skills and techniques by drill is opposed acquisition of them as means of attaining ends which make direct vital appeal; to preparation for a more or less remote future is opposed making the most of opportunities of present life; to static aims and materials is opposed acquaintance with a changing world. (pp. 19-20)

Dewey insisted that the competent educator "views teaching and learning as a continuous process of reconstruction of experience" (p. 87). He developed strict criteria for determining what is an educative experience: Experience must lead to positive growth, have continuity, be inherently worthwhile, and provoke change. Dewey also emphasized the "importance of the participation of the learner in the formation of purposes that direct his activities in the learning process" (p. 67).

The literature on constructivist theory and its implications for education are extensive. From a review of the current research, we developed a conceptual framework to organize and report the literature. The literature is organized into three major categories (assumptions about knowledge, assumptions about learning and the learner, and assumptions about teaching and the teacher) and eight subcategories. Tables 7.1 through 7.3 summarize the framework and the relevant literature. The Foxfire Approach (Foxfire, 1990, pp. 4-5) was particularly influential on the processes described in this chapter.

The Foxfire Approach

The Foxfire Fund, Inc. (1990) developed the Foxfire Approach to instruction. This approach evolved over two decades and continues to be enriched by the reflective experiences of thousands of teachers and the pedagogical framework of Dewey's *Experience and Education* (1938). The essence of the approach is expressed in 11 core practices (Foxfire, 1990, pp. 4-5):

1. Work flows from student desire and student concerns.
2. The teacher is a collaborator, team leader, and guide rather than a boss.
3. The academic integrity of the work is absolutely clear.
4. The work is characterized by student actions.
5. Emphasis is on peer teaching, small group work, and teamwork.
6. Connections between the classroom work and surrounding communities and the real world outside the classroom are clear.
7. There is an audience beyond the teacher for student work.
8. New activities spiral gracefully out of the old, incorporating lessons learned from past experiences, building on skills and understandings.
9. Teachers acknowledge the worth of aesthetic experience.
10. Reflection is an essential activity that takes place at key points throughout the work.
11. The work is honest, with ongoing evaluation for skills and content and changes in student attitude.

TABLE 7.1 Theoretical Framework for Constructivism: Assumptions About Knowledge

Nature of Knowledge	Development of Knowledge
A source of power (O'Loughlin, 1991)	Constructed by learners from experience (Cannella, 1992; Cochran et al., 1993; Condon et al., 1993; Dittmer et al., 1993; Greene, 1989; Puckett, 1989)
Uncertain, messy, and negotiated (Mosenthal & Ball, 1992)	
Transformative not reproductive (O'Loughlin, 1991; O'Loughlin, 1992b; Von Glaserfield, 1991)	
	Multiple realities created by user (Cannella, 1992; O'Loughlin, 1991; O'Loughlin, 1992b)
Complex, ambiguous, unpredictable (Cannella, 1992)	
Bidirectional between teacher and student (Belenky et al., 1994; Mosenthal & Ball, 1992)	Constructed by ordering and organizing the world constituted by experience (Condon et al., 1993)
Cognitive and social (Black & Ammon, 1992)	Actively created, not passively received (Cochran et al., 1993; O'Loughlin, 1992a)
Not an objective body of truth with universal value external to the learner (Cochran et al., 1993; O'-Loughlin, 1992a; Puckett, 1989)	Socially constructed not just in mind but in action (O'Loughlin, 1991; Vygotsky, 1978)
Dialectical, not dualistic, not either/or (O'Loughlin, 1992b)	Continually revised (Cannella, 1992; Von Glaserfield, 1991; Vygotsky, 1978)
Connected to the world outside classroom (Belenky et al., 1994; Greene, 1989; Puckett, 1989)	Created by zone of proximal development—knowledge created in collaboration and with guidance from adult (Vygotsky, 1978)
Has multiple frames of reference—class, gender, ethnic, cultural (Grinberg et al., 1994; O'Loughlin, 1992a)	Created using aesthetic experience (Foxfire Fund, 1990)
What one can do with guidance, not just what can do alone (Vygotsky, 1978)	

The Process of Change and Program Development

A review of the literature revealed three contextual categories for program development: (a) higher education, (b) teacher education, and (c) constructivist teacher education. Harrington (1988) suggested that any change must be considered in its context, and this chapter focuses on the specific context of constructivist teacher education.

In the teacher education context, several authors (Daly, 1983; Short, 1987; Tom, 1988) suggested guidelines for redesigning teacher education. Short (1987) suggested that the process of change in teacher education (curriculum decision making) is characterized by the phases of policy making, program development, and program design. Within these phases, he identified tasks and decisions that facilitate curriculum development. Within the context of constructivist teacher education, several current authors (Dittmer, Fischetti, & Kyle, 1990; Etchberger & Shaw, 1992; O'Loughlin, 1992b) described the change process in terms of principles for guiding constructivist planning. O'Loughlin (1992b) described the process as three "principles of emancipatory constructivism": ownership, community, and time. Etchberger and Shaw (1992) concluded that reflection and "cooperative education are ideal vehicles for the construction process to take place" (p. 416).

Other researchers described suggestions for faculty implementing change toward more constructivist programs. Parsons-Chatman (1990) concluded that change appears more on paper than in classrooms and that "self and institutional resistance" must be considered in the process of change. Regan and Hannah (1993) suggested that the "fit between the culture of the school, the individual teacher and her preparation" are important in professional development (p. 311). Finally, Condon, Clyde, Kyle, and Hovda (1993) suggested redefining roles for students and faculty, institutional support, and collaboration as implications for teacher educators involved in the professional development of teachers.

Purpose

This chapter focuses on the curriculum decision-making process for an early childhood education department at a large, public urban university engaged in developing a new master's degree program based on constructivist theories and principles. The process is described from the perspective of the faculty group as it attempts to make a paradigm shift in thought and actions in teacher education. What happens as change occurs (or does not) is the focus rather than organizational change. The larger ethnographic study that generated this chapter has five phases: (a) policy making, the process of making the decision to change; (b) program development; (c) program design; (d) program implementation; and (e)

TABLE 7.2 Theoretical Framework for Constructivism: Assumptions About Learning and the Learner

Nature of Learning	Process of Learning	Nature of the Learner	Outcomes of Learning
Risky (Mosenthal & Ball, 1992)	Based on Piaget—accommodation and assimilation (Black & Ammon, 1992; O'Loughlin, 1991)	Plays an active role in learning (Cobb, 1994; Condon et al., 1993; Grinberg et al., 1994)	Education (understanding), not training (behavioral change) (Von Glaserfield, 1991)
Complex, ambiguous, unpredictable (Mosenthal & Ball, 1992)	Based on Vygotsky—social nature of learning (Cannella, 1992; Cobb, 1994; Vygotsky, 1978)	Has responsibility for learning (Mosenthal & Ball, 1992)	Freedom, responsibility, and growth (Greene, 1989; Grinberg et al., 1994)
Nonlinear (Cannella, 1992)			
Context dependent (Black & Ammon, 1992; Cannella, 1992)	Relative-situation specific (Cochran et al., 1993)	Desires and point of view affect learning (Greene, 1989; O'Loughlin, 1991)	An integration of experiences (Cochran et al., 1993; Condon et al., 1993; Greene, 1989)
Social in nature (Dittmer et al., 1993; Grinberg et al., 1994; O'Loughlin, 1989; O'Loughlin, 1991)	Involves continuous integration (Condon et al., 1993; Greene, 1989)	Learns in active way, through reconstruction of reality (Cochran et al., 1993)	Equality, social justice, and democracy (Grinberg et al., 1994)
Active (Cannella, 1992; Cochran et al., 1993; Dittmer et al., 1993; O'Loughlin, 1991)	Involves construction of concepts, ideas, beliefs (Cannella, 1992)	Curious (Grinberg et al., 1994)	No failure (Gertzman, 1994)
Dynamic, not static (Vygotsky, 1978)	Involves internal processes that operate in authentic interaction with others—teacher and peers (Cannella, 1992; O'Loughlin, 1991; O'Loughlin, 1992b; Vygotsky, 1978)	Wants to learn (Grinberg et al., 1994)	Accretion of life experiences (Cochran et al., 1993; Puckett, 1989)
Uses higher-order thinking (Condon et al., 1993; Von Glaserfield, 1991)			Improvement of human condition (Dittmer et al., 1993; O'Loughlin, 1991; O'Loughlin, 1992b)

Deals with significant concepts of a content or discipline—has depth (Cochran et al., 1993)

Addresses real world problems (Dittmer et al., 1993; Puckett, 1989)

Uses personal knowledge (O'Loughlin, 1989)

Interactive (Belenky et al., 1994; Cannella, 1992)

Spirals new activities from old (Puckett, 1989)

Takes place within context of meaningful whole (Gertzman, 1994)

Evaluated continuously for growth in skills, knowledge, and attitude (Foxfire Fund, 1990)

Starts with a genuine problem (Puckett, 1989)

Flows from student desires and concerns (Greene, 1989; O'Loughlin, 1991)

Characterized by student action (Foxfire Fund, 1990)

Emphasizes peer teaching, small-group work, and teamwork (Foxfire Fund, 1990)

Reflection (Grinberg et al., 1994)

Academic integrity (Foxfire Fund, 1990)

Audience beyond the teacher (Greene, 1989; O'Loughlin, 1991)

Student empowerment (Dittmer et al., 1993; O'Loughlin, 1991; O'Loughlin, 1992a)

TABLE 7.3 Theoretical Framework for Constructivism: Assumptions About Teaching and the Teacher

Role of the Teacher	Process of Teaching
Engages students in constructing knowledge (Black & Ammon, 1992; Dittmer et al., 1993)	Makes subject matter part of child's experience (Greene, 1989)
Facilitates/collaborates/guides (Mosenthal & Ball, 1992)	Incorporates understanding of what is happening with child (Cochran et al., 1993; Greene, 1989)
Understands how students learn, understand, and construct knowledge (Cochran et al., 1993)	Determines how child's growth can be maximized (Greene, 1989)
Inquires into students' understandings (O'Loughlin, 1991)	Relates learning to the student (Greene, 1989)
Continues to learn /inquire (Greene, 1989)	Is contextualized (Cannella, 1992)
As midwife rather than banking model or adversarial doubting mode (Belenky et al., 1994)	Shares experiences with students (Greene, 1989)
As a subject matter expert (Cochran et al., 1993; Puckett, 1989)	Helps expand and articulate latent knowledge (Belenky et al., 1994)
Has high expectations	Supports evolution of students' thinking (Belenky et al., 1994)
Respects and includes all students (Grinberg et al., 1994)	Encourages students to use knowledge in everyday life (Belenky et al., 1994; Greene, 1989)
Welcomes diversity of opinion (Belenky et al., 1994)	Fosters reflection, inquiry, critical consciousness, questioning, challenging (Grinberg et al., 1994)
Accepts students' feelings (Belenky et al., 1994; Greene, 1989)	Converts impulses to educational purposes (Puckett, 1989)
	Bridges school and out-of-school experience (Puckett, 1989)
	Is a political act (Grinberg et al., 1994)

effects on primary grades students. Consistent with Short (1987), the curriculum decision-making process includes the first three phases. Rainer and Guyton (1994) elaborated on the policy-making phase in a previous paper.

Phases one through three focus on the following questions that emerged from a review of literature and preliminary observations: (a) What is the context for curriculum decision making? For example, what are facilitators of and constraints on curriculum decision making? Do critical events or key conditions exist for curriculum decision making? (b) What are the steps and tasks in the process? (c) How do faculty respond to the process? Although this chapter is not focused on describing the program, a brief program description (the product) creates a context for looking at the development process.

Description of the Program

Mission Statement

The mission statement for the program is as follows:

> This program is based on the assumption that learning is a constructive process that builds on the knowledge and experience of the learner. The teacher functions as a collaborator with parents and children to focus on strategies to enhance effective child learning. This master's degree program is designed, therefore, to involve experienced classroom teachers in designing their own program of study for professional growth. The major focus for this collaborative preparation is to assure effective child learning in the classroom.

Admissions

An intensive interview process is one key to the selection process. Foxfire personnel, school-based teachers who have been trained in Foxfire methods, and Georgia State University faculty recruit and select students for the program who must be employed in a school.

Overview of the Program

The program is five academic quarters. Two faculty members (cohort faculty) teach, coordinate the program, and provide consistent guidance for the cohort group. A new concept, faculty on retainer, provides faculty expertise, technical support, resources, and coaching as needed by participants rather than as prescribed by a course schedule. Faculty assigned a course load are retained for approximately 50 contact hours of "access" during the five-quarter program, providing flexible schedules for faculty to meet with large and small groups of participants or individuals and to observe in classrooms. Cohort faculty manage the logistics of this arrangement, as well as other administrative tasks.

An initial experience, a 2-day retreat involving teacher and faculty participants, builds a community of learners. The first retreat was very successful and is reported elsewhere (Guyton, Jones, Rainer, Zimmerman-Parrish, Fortune, & Tate, 1995). Academic experiences include exploring philosophical bases of constructivism; child development; critical thinking; research and assessment; mathematics, science, social studies, and language arts methods and materials; and multiculturalism. Constructivist pedagogy is modeled for teachers by program faculty. Students satisfy program requirements in a variety of settings and experiences, for example, seminars, group or individual projects, curriculum design and implementation, workshops, and action research. Collaborative decisions and continuous assessment are major program components. Indicators created by participants and faculty show levels of competence on a continuum, with benchmarks for periodic assessments. The last benchmark, a capstone experience, is the development and presentation of major projects that synthesize and demonstrate knowledge, skills, and attitudes.

Vygotsky's (1978) notion of students being led by "more capable peers" certainly applies to this program. Program participants, faculty, and consultants are the more capable peers at varying times. Furthermore, "travel by teachers to other teachers involved in similar classroom efforts is one of the most effective means to reinforce effective teaching strategies, build teacher confidence, and maintain the pedagogical integrity of the approach" (Smith, 1991, p. 8). Cohort faculty and faculty on retainer spend time in the classrooms of the teachers, and teachers are encouraged to use each other as resources.

Method

This study was grounded in a constructivist view of teaching, learning, and change that considers constructivism as an orienting framework for discussing pedagogy and instruction (Cobb, 1994). It was further informed by Guba and Lincoln's (1989) "constructivist paradigm" as an alternative to the positivist paradigm of inquiry. In this paradigm, inquiry begins with issues of the participants and emerges through collaborative reconstructions among researchers and participants. Qualitative research methods were compatible with a constructivist perspective and studying change in teachers (Richardson & Anders, 1995) and organizations (Van Maanen, 1979).

The researchers were "active" participant observers (Spradley, 1980) in a 3-year process of curriculum decision making. Observations focused on the events, tasks, and decisions of the faculty groups involved in curriculum decision making. The researchers and a graduate research assistant conducted formal and informal interviews with the group at intervals consistent with the natural events.

Data collection in Phase 1 (June 1992 to December 1992) involved (a) participant observation at an organizational meeting, two workshops, and two retreats involving all departmental faculty; (b) two faculty surveys; and (c) one individual interview and one group interview focused on faculty views about developing a new program, critical events in the process of program development, and faculty reactions to the process. Data collection in Phase 2 (January 1993 to May 1994) involved (a) participant observation during four full-day, off-campus meetings and four half-day, off-campus meetings and (b) four formal and informal interviews with each faculty member focused on changes in faculty ideas about constructivism, personal experiences using constructivism in his or her classroom, reactions to the process of program development and to the program itself, and realities of faculty actually working in the program. The third phase of data collection involved (a) participant observation in weekly planning meetings during the 1994-1995 academic year and in several Summer 1995 planning meetings; (b) written group summaries of tasks, issues, and decisions compiled at each meeting; and (c) a group interview of cohort faculty, faculty on retainer, and administrators (July 1995) regarding the constraints of implementing a constructivist program within the university.

Data analysis used procedures suggested by Lincoln and Guba (1985), Miles and Huberman (1984), and Strauss (1987). First, data (in the form of field notes and transcriptions) were examined, compared, and organized into domains or symbolic categories. Domains were defined, expanded, and examined for patterns across domains. Concurrent data analysis provided direction for subsequent interview questions.

A brief introduction to the group and early childhood department at this university provides a context for this study. The university is a large, urban institution with many nontraditional students. The department has several distinguishing characteristics. Leadership is strong, and decision making is shared with faculty. The 14 faculty members are from diverse academic backgrounds. Faculty and program development are encouraged. There is continual work on improving existing programs and generating new ones.

Findings

This study examines two levels simultaneously: the details and the broader features of the change process. The details include the chronological events, issues, and decisions in the process. The broad features include three phases in the curriculum decision-making process (policy making, program development, and program design); the tasks in each phase; foundations for change; and faculty struggles in making a paradigm shift. The broad features are described with reference to the details.

Curriculum Decision-Making Process

Consistent with Short (1987), this study identified three phases (policy making, program development, and program design). A domain of tasks emerged in the first phase and continued through the next two phases that included understanding constructivism, grappling with issues, and making decisions. A chronological summary of the phases, events, and selected activities in the process is provided in Table 7.4.

Initial Phase

The first phase of the process of developing the constructivist program involved all departmental faculty and consultants from Foxfire. Events consisted of an introductory meeting, two half-day workshops, and two faculty retreats. The first major event was a retreat at the Foxfire Center at Rabun Gap, Georgia, in September 1992. Foxfire consultants conducted a 2-day seminar immersing the group in the history, philosophy, and application of their approach.

In two workshops in October, faculty further explored Foxfire as the basis for a master's program, and consultants modeled the constructivist philosophy. Faculty members studied Dewey's work, discussed issues, reflected, and made decisions to construct policy for the new program and observed elementary teachers using the Foxfire Approach.

At the final event (December 1992) in the first phase, a 3-day retreat, faculty developed a list of desired knowledge, skills, and attitudes for

TABLE 7.4 Phases, Events, and Activities in the Curriculum
Decision-Making Process

Policy-Making Phase
Spring 1992
   One-day meeting with Foxfire directors and teachers
      Explore Foxfire as an alternative master's degree program
Fall 1992
   Three-day retreat at Foxfire Headquarters
   Two half-day workshops
   Three-day retreat with faculty and Foxfire consultants
      Observe, model, analyze, and discuss constructivist principles
      Generate a first draft of program

Program Development Phase
Winter 1993
   Brief organizational meeting
   Two full-day meetings with faculty task group and school-based consultants
      Draft a mission statement
      Generate a list of critical elements
Spring 1993
   Two full-day meetings with faculty task group and school-based consultants
      Discuss programmatic issues such as staffing, marketing, hours, admissions
Summer 1993
   One half-day meeting of faculty task group
      Decided to make this new program our only master's degree
      Presentation of draft of program for submission to university and college
         committees
Fall 1993
   Program approved by university
Winter 1994
   One half-day meeting
      Developed brochure, admission criteria, interview dates, and deadlines
Spring 1994
   Two full-day meetings of faculty task group
      Designated program faculty to develop and coordinate program
      Discussed administrative costs of program
      Developed interview protocol
Summer 1994
   Hired a faculty member trained in Foxfire methods

Program Design Phase
Fall-Spring, 1994-1995
   Weekly meetings of two cohort faculty
   Weekly meetings of cohort faculty, administrators, and participant observers
      Developed specific program implementation strategies
      Worked with other departments teaching courses in the program
      Developed concept for staffing the program
   Event
      Activity

teachers and generated a first draft of a proposal for a new master's degree program. A small group of faculty (seven people) agreed to continue the process of program development without the Foxfire consultants. Tasks in Phase 1 included creating a shared understanding of constructivism, grappling with issues, and making implicit and explicit decisions. It was an intense period during which the group immersed themselves in the history, philosophy, and application of the constructivist approach. They explored the philosophical and programmatic issues and possibilities of changing the departmental approach to the education of teachers. The outcome was a commitment to continue the process and ideas and documents with which to begin.

Second Phase

The second phase of program development consisted of an organizational meeting; four full-day, off-campus meetings with school-based consultants; and four on-campus meetings of a faculty task group. An assistant principal and a kindergarten teacher, both active in constructivist education in elementary classrooms, joined the group. Discussions became more product oriented with less philosophical and process-oriented issues. This stage ended in August 1994.

In a retrospective analysis of the process at the university, Phase 2 included a distinct transitional stage. During this transitional phase, the group produced a few concrete products for the curriculum plan, but "trying out" constructivism and building bridges between the more theoretical phase of policy development and the practice state of implementing a program also were salient activities. After steeping themselves in theory and developing and affirming a guiding philosophy for the program, the group needed a transition period, time to define constructivism in action. Characteristics of the phase were trying out the constructivist approach in a university culture, developing trust in the process through the discovery that constructivism "works," and learning more about what it looks like in action. It also involved confronting challenge and frustration; struggling to hold on to constructivist philosophy within the context and constraints of the "real world"; and resisting the pull of the traditional. This period was a time of defining, confirming, and moving. Movement often meant taking two steps forward and one step back, was not linear, and was often back and forth, but progress was apparent.

Third Phase

The next phase, program design, was held from July 1994 to May 1995. It involved two faculty members who implemented the program (cohort faculty), two administrators (department chair and departmental program coordinator), and the researchers. The two cohort faculty met together all day weekly, and the larger group met for several hours once a week.

The major tasks of this phase included developing course content, staffing the program, developing grading procedures, and developing recruitment and admissions processes. Getting university acceptance of the program, both formal and informal approval, and negotiating inter-departmental participation were ongoing processes. The constraints imposed on innovative program development by the university culture are described in Guyton and Rainer (1996). Persistent issues included what would be fair teaching loads for faculty working in this intensive program; how to make grading consistent with constructivist beliefs; how many students should be in a cohort group; being true to constructivism rather than falling back on more traditional patterns of courses, grades, and so on; and whether the constructivist program should be the only master's program or an alternative. Major decisions involved faculty roles, assessment/grading, and developing admissions processes and are reported in the program overview in this chapter.

Foundations for Change

Data indicated that key conditions for change exist. Structural foundations related to organizational issues include commitment, resources, leadership, and dedicated time (such as retreats). Other foundations applied to characteristics of the group, the ways they interacted and worked together. The characteristics are (a) prior knowledge and experience about developing new programs, (b) the ability to assimilate the theoretical framework of change with what one already believes, (c) group trust and respect, and (d) faculty collaboration and democratic decision making (Rainer & Guyton, 1994).

Collaborations with Foxfire consultants and school-based personnel were particularly instrumental foundations. During the policy-making phase, personnel from the Foxfire Center directed each of the meetings, providing the group with a focus for learning about constructivism. Most important was having a constructivist approach modeled by the Foxfire consultants. Most faculty expressed some impatience with the lack of structure at one time or another but later realized the value of the process.

> I understand the importance of building our background—but something in me says "Let's begin to discuss what all this means for our program." (Survey, 11/92)

> At times I wanted to move on, but it's OK now. (Group interview, 12/92)

Participants believed that having been through the process helped them understand what teachers in the program would experience.

> We've gone through what our students will go through. (Group interview, 12/92)

> This is what will happen with teachers . . . initial doubt. (Group interview, 12/92)

The university faculty credited Foxfire personnel with facilitating program development but believed the faculty had ownership of the program.

> Group leaders kept discussion focused. (Survey 1, 10/92)

> Foxfire identified a good leader for us. (Group interview, 12/92)

> We've gone beyond Foxfire—we can take credit for what's developed. The Foxfire consultant encouraged that. (Group interview, 12/92)

The faculty expressed very positive attitudes about the contributions of the school personnel during program development. They focused on their being able to connect the process to the world of elementary classrooms.

> The school-based people . . . kept us focused on really what we wanted to do when people started falling back on academic ways of accomplishing graduate education . . . they also brought in

points of view not familiar to all of us . . . it was a very positive role. (Interview 3, 11/94)

They bring a lot of real world stuff to us . . . as far as being current with children, being with teachers . . . staff development. (Interview 3, 11/94)

Faculty Struggles in Making a Paradigm Shift

The group of faculty created "shared attitudes and feelings" toward constructivism. This domain emerged from an analysis of interviews with faculty. It was originally defined as including attitudes and feelings about ambiguity; paradigm change; developing conceptions of constructivism; group dynamics; collaboration; and faculty, teacher, and student responses to constructivism. In a further refinement, these concepts shared a common theme in the group's process of making a paradigm shift. That theme was that struggles were inherent in the process: struggles to (a) acknowledge and confront ambiguity, (b) be constructivist, and (c) define constructivism in reality, applied constructivism, for individuals. Field notes and data from faculty interviews define and confirm these struggles.

Acknowledging and Confronting Ambiguity

A continuing struggle for faculty in making a change toward constructivism was the process of first acknowledging and then confronting and dealing with the ambiguity inherent in the constructive process. Ambiguity was described by faculty members as "things left to be solved," "a program that is evolving, shaping itself with things not finalized and that could still go either way," and "not having a clear picture of the program." Being flexible and sharing control was described as necessary to program development, but reactions to ambiguity ranged from "uneasy and uncomfortable feelings" to "frustrated and discouraged feelings."

I think we were not feeling comfortable a lot of the time because we weren't getting the specifics we wanted, but I see that as ambiguity and part of the process. I don't think you can avoid that . . . and there's still ambiguity to be worked out. (Interview, 6/94)

You have to be comfortable with the unknown. (Interview, 6/93)

Trying to Be Constructivist

Another recurrent struggle for faculty was the effort to operationalize a theoretical, philosophical view of constructivism. The group acknowledged a shared, abstract vision of constructivism that needed to be tried out in the university culture. People felt a strong need to "be true to constructivism" in the process of program development and in the specifics of the program developed. Yet there was a strong "tug of the traditional" that kept faculty returning to the old, comfortable ways. The effort took place on two levels: trying to construct a new program and trying to teach college courses using constructivist principles. In the process of developing a new program, faculty (a) dealt with the ambiguity described; (b) learned to be more collaborative, within the department, with other agencies and people, and in the college classroom; and (c) learned to live with shared leadership or what seemed at times to be no leadership. Faculty also struggled with giving up control, maintaining academic integrity, working within the university and school culture, and assessing their students. Signs of these struggles are implied in the following interview data:

We had to put it into the process that the College of Education would like, . . . that would be acceptable. (Interview, 11/93)

But I had to struggle because I'm kind of a control person. And you have to give up control as a teacher to use all of these core practices (constructivist principles). (Interview, 6/93)

It's kind of like a paradigm shift for us in that we're so used to teaching and having our own way that we conceptualize a new program and then all of a sudden it's going to be different. (Interview, 4/94)

Defining Constructivism in Action

Defining constructivism as it looks in reality was a continuing struggle for faculty. It was a process of reconstructing theoretical concepts based on "trying out constructivism," their personal experiences in using constructivist principles. Faculty reexamined concepts such as student-initiated learning, beliefs about children, assessment, collaboration, and their roles in teaching and as change agents.

> Now I don't think I can direct other people's learning. I can . . . support them in doing that and facilitate that and maybe push, stretch, and encourage. (Interview, 6/93)

> Assessment is such an issue that probably the thing I would rather do if I could is to bring them (students) into the process. Whether it's peer evaluations or setting standards together, it's better to have them an integral part of that process. (Interview, 6/93)

Conclusions

An examination of the three phases of curriculum decision making indicates the complexity of the process as suggested by Short (1987). Figure 7.1 depicts a reconstruction of these phases in the curriculum decision-making process: policy making, program development, and program design. An analysis of the phases shows that key conditions enhance the curriculum decision-making process, providing a foundation for the tasks and faculty struggles in making a paradigm shift. These findings expand the tasks identified by Short (1987) and extend the discussion by suggesting a process for accomplishing these tasks.

Findings from this study do not suggest the one right way to conduct curriculum development. They are consistent with notions of self and institutional resistance (Parsons-Chatman, 1990) and with the importance of collaboration and redefining faculty and student roles (Condon et al., 1993). What it does indicate is that the *process of getting ready to change* is an integral component of curriculum development and change in teacher education. Leaders and faculty anticipating programmatic change might consider the following recommendations for change:

1. Develop structural foundations such as time, leadership, and resources.
2. Support interactive group dynamics such as collaboration, trust, and shared decision making.

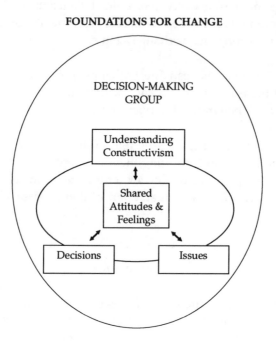

Figure 7.1. A Reconstruction of the Curriculum Decision-Making Process

3. Develop a shared understanding of constructivism by reading, observing, discussing, and reconstructing definitions of an abstract vision.

4. Grapple with philosophical and programmatic issues.

5. Identify implicit and explicit decisions as well as make process and product decisions.

6. Acknowledge shared attitudes and feelings.

7. Acknowledge and confront the struggles inherent in the constructivist process such as ambiguity, control, and academic integrity.

8. Try out the theoretical implications of constructivism in the university classroom.

9. Incorporate constructivist strategies in program development.

10. Allow faculty to personally define constructivism in the context of teacher education.

11. Be prepared to deal with constraints imposed on developing a constructivist program by the university culture.

These recommendations follow from the experiences of faculty at one university. The very nature of constructivism means that any other group experiences will be different, but knowing the processes used and problems encountered by one group may inform another group's work. Similar studies can add to a body of literature revealing commonalities that strengthen these recommendations or suggest others.

References

Belenky, M. F., Clinchy, B. M., Goldberger, N. R., & Tarule, J. M. (1994, Summer). The teacher as midwife. *Hands on Teacher Reader,* pp. 59-62.

Black, A., & Ammon, P. (1992). A developmental-constructivist approach to teacher education. *Journal of Teacher Education, 43*(5), 323-335.

Cannella, G. S. (1992, February). *Constructivist approaches to learning: New directions for learning style theorists.* Paper presented at the Association of Teacher Educators, Orlando, Florida.

Cobb, P. (1994). Where is the mind? Constructivist and sociocultural perspectives on mathematical development. *Educational Researcher, 23*(7), 13-20.

Cochran, K. F., DeRuiter, J. A., & King, R. A. (1993). Pedagogical content knowing: An integrative model for teacher preparation. *Journal of Teacher Education, 44*(4), 263-272.

Condon, M. W. F., Clyde, J. A., Kyle, D. W., & Hovda, R. A. (1993). A constructivist basis for teaching and teacher education: A framework for program development and research on graduates. *Journal of Teacher Education, 44*(4), 273-278.

Daly, N. F. (1983). Redesign of teacher education: Internal change strategies. Paper presented at the World Assembly of the International Council for Teaching, Washington, DC.

Dewey, J. (1938). *Experience and education.* New York: Macmillan.

Dittmer, A., Fischetti, J., & Kyle, D. W. (1990). Constructivist teaching and student empowerment: Educational equity through school reforms. *Equity and Excellence in Education, 26*(1), 40-45.

Etchberger, M. L., & Shaw, K. L. (1992). Teacher change as a progression of transitional images: A chronology of a developing constructivist teacher. *School Science and Mathematics, 92*(8), 411-417.

Foxfire Fund, Inc. (1990). The Foxfire approach: Perspectives and core practices. *Hands on: A Journal for Teachers, 43-44*, 4-5.

Gertzman, A. (1994, Summer). Am I doing it yet: Becoming fluent in Foxfire. *Hands on Teacher Reader*, pp. 65-67.

Greene, M. (1994, Summer). The teacher in John Dewey's works. *Hands on Teacher Reader*, pp. 46-51.

Grinberg, J., Goldfarb, K., & Martusewicz, R. (1994, Summer). Paulo Friere's legacy to democratic education. *Hands on Teacher Reader*, pp. 63-64

Guba, E., & Lincoln, Y. (1989). *Fourth generation evaluation*. Newbury Park: Sage.

Guyton, E., Jones, M., Rainer, J., Zimmerman-Parrish, C., Fortune, C., & Tate, C. (October, 1995). *The power of a retreat experience in developing community in a constructivist master's program*. Paper presented at the annual meeting of the Georgia Association of Teacher Educators and Georgia Association of Colleges for Teacher Education meeting, Savannah.

Guyton, E., & Rainer, J. (1996, February). *Dilemmas involved in developing a constructivist teacher education program in the university context*. Paper presented at the annual meeting of the Association of Teacher Educators, St. Louis.

Harrington, D. (1988, April). *Reform in teacher education: Process to product*. Paper presented at the annual meeting of the American Educational Research Association, New Orleans.

Lincoln, G., & Guba, E. (1985). *Naturalistic inquiry*. Beverly Hills, CA: Sage.

Miles, M. B., & Huberman, M. (1984). *Qualitative data analysis: A source book of new methods*. Beverly Hills, CA: Sage.

Mosenthal, J. H., & Ball, D. L. (1992). Constructing new forms of teaching: Subject matter knowledge in inservice teacher education. *Journal of Teacher Education, 43*(5), 347-356.

O'Loughlin, M. (1989, June). *The influence of teachers' beliefs about knowledge, teaching, and learning of their pedagogy: A constructivist reconceptualization and research agenda for teacher education*. Paper presented at the Annual Symposium of the Jean Piaget Society, Philadelphia. (ERIC Document Reproduction Service No. ED 339 679)

O'Loughlin, M. (1991, April). *Beyond constructivism: Toward a dialectical model of the problematics of teacher socialization.* Paper presented at the annual meeting of the American Educational Research Association, Chicago. (ERIC Document Reproduction Service No. ED 338 559)

O'Loughlin, M. (1992a, April). *The discourse of pedagogy and the possibility of social change.* Paper presented at the annual meeting of the American Educational Research Association, San Francisco.

O'Loughlin, M. (1992b). Engaging teachers in emancipatory knowledge construction. *Journal of Teacher Education, 43*(5), 336-346.

Parsons-Chatman, S. (1990, April). *Making sense of constructivism in preservice: A case study.* Paper presented at the annual meeting of the National Association for Research in Science Teaching, Atlanta, GA. (ERIC Document Reproduction Service No. ED 319600)

Puckett, J. (1989). *Foxfire reconsidered: A twenty-year experiment in progressive education.* Champaign: University of Illinois Press.

Rainer, J. D., & Guyton, E. (1994). Developing a constructivist teacher education program. *Journal of Teacher Education, 45*(2), 140-146.

Regan, H. B., & Hannah, B. H. (1993). Ten teachers teaching: The interplay of individuals, their preparation, and their schools. *Journal of Teacher Education, 44*(4), 305-311.

Richardson, V., & Anders, P. (1995). The study of teacher change. In V. Richardson, (Ed.), *A theory of teacher change and the process of teacher education.* New York: Teachers College Press.

Short, E. C. (1987). Curriculum decision making in teacher education: Policies, program development, and design. *Journal of Teacher Education, 38*(4), 2-12.

Smith, H. (1991). What we think we've learned from six years of outreach. *Hands on: A Journal for Teachers, 42,* 5-13.

Strauss, A. L. (1987). *Qualitative analysis for social scientists.* Cambridge: Cambridge University Press.

Tom, A. (1988). The practical art of redesigning teacher education: Teacher education reform at Washington University, 1970-1975. *Peabody Journal of Education, 65,* 158-179.

Van Maanen, J. (1979). The fact of fiction in organizational ethnography. *Administrative Quarterly, 24*(4), 539-550.

Vygotsky, L. S. (1978). *Mind in society.* Cambridge, MA: Harvard University Press.

8 "Swallowing an Elephant"

The Subject Perspectives of Selected Novice English Teachers

Elizabeth Spalding

Elizabeth Spalding is Assistant Professor in the Department of Curriculum Instruction at the University of Kentucky. Previously, she was Project Manager for Standards at the National Council of Teachers of English in Urbana, Illinois. Her research interests include teacher perspectives, teacher education, and alternative assessment of literacy.

ABSTRACT

This study examined how three novice, middle-school teachers of English defined their work and how they acted on their beliefs in the classroom. The conceptual tool of "subject perspective" was used to achieve the following objectives: (a) describe how the teachers defined and practiced the teaching of English, (b) identify similarities and differences among their perspectives, and (c) identify and describe contextual features that interacted with participants' perspectives. Methods of interpretive inquiry were used. Longitudinal case studies of participants were constructed.

The study found that participants' subject perspectives were coherent and consistent with views they had expressed on entry into teacher education. Some change occurred in the beliefs and practice of Celia, whose perspective clashed with her teaching context. All participants experienced contextual constraints that impeded them from acting on their beliefs about best practice. Implications for preparing preservice teachers and for supporting novice teachers are discussed.

Teaching English is like swallowing an elephant.
        —Jack Glass, second-year English teacher

Jack is one of three middle-school English teachers portrayed in this interpretive study. Creative, enthusiastic, and charismatic in the classroom, he had high expectations of his students and of himself. Nevertheless, he sometimes felt overwhelmed by his responsibilities as an English teacher: teaching about language and literature; developing reading, writing, speaking, listening, and media skills; and encouraging creative, logical, and critical thinking (National Council of Teachers of English, 1982). Small wonder Jack compared teaching English to "swallowing an elephant"!

Only recently have researchers begun asking English teachers what they think their job is or how they go about doing it (e.g., Clift, 1991; Fox, 1995; Grossman, 1990; Grossman & Shulman, 1994; Zancanella, 1991). The aim of this study was to describe the "elephant" of English teaching by rendering an account of the beliefs, actions, and teaching contexts of three teachers who recently entered the profession. By exploring how teachers think about teaching their subject, and by examining how they act on those beliefs in the classroom, we can gain insights into how teacher education programs can better serve preservice and novice teachers.

Theoretical Framework

The conceptual tool of "subject perspective" was used to examine participants' beliefs and classroom actions (Lacey, 1977). Subject perspectives are composed of and expressed in (a) teachers' views of the purposes of education, (b) teachers' views of the role of the subject in achieving these purposes, (c) teachers' views of their own roles, (d) teachers' views of appropriate content, (e) teachers' views of appropriate pedagogy, (f) teachers' relationships with students, (g) classroom ambiance, and (h) the physical appearance of the teacher (Ball & Lacey, 1980; Sikes, Measor, &

Woods, 1985). These eight dimensions formed the framework for data collection, analysis, and reporting.[1] Studying subject perspectives can be an especially appropriate approach to understanding the beliefs and practices of middle and high school teachers, who tend to see themselves as subject specialists and to talk about their work in terms of the subject they teach (Grossman & Shulman, 1994; Grossman & Stodolsky, 1994; Sikes, Measor, & Woods, 1985).

This study was also informed by scholars who have identified various orientations toward the teaching of English (e.g., Applebee, 1974; Ball, 1985; Ball & Lacey, 1980; Barnes, Barnes, & Clarke, 1984; Grossman, 1990). Finally, recent studies of teacher thinking and knowledge, which shared the following assumptions, influenced this research: (a) individuals experience and interpret professional course work and classroom events in quite different ways; (b) these interpretations form part of personally coherent systems of beliefs, values, and attitudes on which teachers base decisions and practice; and (c) understanding what and how teachers know is key to implementing educational reform (e.g., Bullough, Knowles, & Crow, 1991; Elbaz, 1983).

Objectives

The objectives of the study were as follows:

1. Describe participants' subject perspectives.
2. Identify similarities and differences among participants' subject perspectives.
3. Identify and describe contextual features that may interact with the development and expression of subject perspectives.

Program Features and Participants

The TADMP is an alternative teacher education program.[2] It is a selective, graduate-level program for career changers, designed to help teachers become reflective decision makers. Tools for encouraging reflection, including autobiographical interviews and journal keeping, were used by the program director and her assistants for purposes of both research and instruction (Bennett, 1991; Bennett & Spalding, 1992). The three participants were graduates of the TADMP, a common thread that linked them.

Jack, Celia, and Claire had excellent academic records and strong interpersonal skills. They may also have come to teaching by more thoughtful and deliberate choices than many undergraduates with less life experience. Thus, the three participants promised to be outstanding novice teachers. Finally, Jack, Celia, and Claire shared the following characteristics: all (a) taught approximately the same grade span—sixth- through eighth-grade students, (b) expressed clear orientations toward the teaching of English, and (c) taught in contexts that had an observable influence on their teaching. At the time of the study, Jack was in his second year of teaching, Celia was in her third, and Claire was in her fourth.

Methods

Methods of interpretive inquiry include interviews, immersion in a field setting, careful recording of what happened in the setting, analytic reflection on this record, and reporting through description, vignettes, direct quotes, and other descriptive aids (Erickson, 1986). These methods were used in combination throughout data collection and analysis.

Initially, focus group interviews were conducted to allow participants to identify salient issues in their own teaching and to guide the construction of individual interview questions (Morgan, 1988). In the second phase, each teacher participated in two hours of individual, semistructured interviews and was observed during four hours of classroom teaching. Interview questions were constructed to illuminate participants' subject perspectives, including their metaphors for teaching English (Bullough et al., 1991). All interviews were audiotaped and transcribed. Classroom observations were videotaped and field notes were taken. These data were augmented by extensive interview and observation data gathered as participants moved through their teacher education program and into their first years of teaching.

Data were analyzed by adapting Lincoln and Guba's (1985) procedures for unitizing data. The categories used were those aspects of subject perspectives identified earlier; however, other categories did emerge in the course of data analysis. A longitudinal case study of each teacher was constructed (Merriam, 1988). The case reports have been considerably abridged for presentation here. [3]

Case Reports

"Swallowing an Elephant": Jack

Jack's work as a counselor for an adolescent group home convinced him to enter teaching:

> These were people that the system had already lost . . . and I was just giving these people a Band-Aid. . . . I may be too idealistic, but I think I can have a more positive impact on people as a teacher than as a social worker. . . . Plus, I love English. I love talking about it. I like kids—I don't know if I love them yet—but it does dovetail nicely.

He described the purpose of education as "what our country's forefathers put into place as a way of shaping learning, shaping individuals who are raised here, and it's supposed to equip them with the ability to deal with life." English is of "extreme importance" in achieving this purpose:

> Because language is the way in which we communicate. And effective communication can mean the difference between success and failure in our culture. . . . On a less mega-important vein, poetry, literature, creative writing, these things can be joys in a person's life. They can teach so much about oneself, about one's culture and environment and world.

Jack believed that "an excellent teacher is very well versed. They are competent in terms of being able to answer anything . . . even if it's outside the realm of what you're discussing." Confident about his knowledge of English, he expected the TADMP to equip him with "the hows—how do I get this message across? How do I deal with the disciplinary problems? How do I make an effective lesson plan?" Jack hoped that his future students would look to him as a "positive role model" and "an effective teacher," and that they would respect him because "I think you do have to have some respect from them so that they do accept your message to them."

Matched with a wise and experienced mentor teacher, Jack successfully completed his student teaching in an urban high school with a reputation for being a difficult assignment. Afterward, he was hired to teach eighth-grade regular English and an eighth-grade gifted class at Washington Middle School, which serves an urban/suburban population and whose students consistently score well on the annual statewide tests. Jack described Washington as "a great school."

Washington Middle School followed districtwide curriculum guidelines, which included lengthy grammar units in the fall and spring in preparation for the statewide test. Jack questioned the value of these units but accepted them as "something I have to do." Grammar study, however, was not required in the eighth-grade gifted humanities program that was team taught by Jack and a U.S. history teacher. Because the students were studying history chronologically, Jack taught works of literature appropriate to the period. On the whole, Jack was content with the curriculum and felt he had a great deal of freedom to set his own goals for instruction and select important content.

In his first year, Jack had some problems with classroom management, which he later attributed to being "too friendly" with the students. He was also disturbed by the number of students who resisted literature: "I just had to battle with getting students enthused about those things. . . . [I]t was almost like they were struggling, not wanting to get out of their inertia. But once you pushed them out of that inertia, they went along with it." Jack wanted his students to become good readers and writers and believed that they would, if they read and wrote a lot. He taught the required chapters from the grammar textbook but felt he was wasting his time. He eventually abandoned the required spelling textbook, using students' own misspellings as the basis for spelling lessons.

Beginning his second year, Jack was happy: "I have high standards, and it's a struggle to keep that up . . . but it's one of those good kinds of struggles, like going for a long hike in cold weather. . . . I've never questioned, 'Have I done the right thing?' I just feel pretty good about [what I'm doing]." Jack's "high standards" included "exposing" students to great works of literature. By the end of the first nine weeks, his regular eighth graders had read two novels "completely on their own," and had written several short stories and two radio play scripts. Jack stated that writing was his focus: "I really want them to leave eighth grade . . . comfortable in their ability to write an analytical essay. . . . So, the regular kids will write nine or ten for me over the course of the year . . . [and] my tests are always essay exams." Jack spent many evenings and weekends evaluating student papers. This, in addition to his coaching responsibilities, consumed most of his time outside of school.

He strove to make the subject matter "at least palatable, if not exciting" to his students: "That's a real goal. I mean it sounds kind of cheesy to say a love of language and a love of English . . . [but] I want them to have that." Jack found eighth graders more "malleable . . . more willing to participate actively in learning" than high school students. He felt rewarded when he saw students benefiting from his instruction: "So they spend hours reading that novel, just because I said, 'You have to read this,' and they did and they get something out of it . . . it's amazing."

By November, Jack's gifted eighth graders were finishing up a unit on the Colonial Period, having read *The Crucible* aloud and attended a professional performance of the play. His regular English classes were beginning the required 9-week grammar unit. Jack taught the required curriculum three days a week, but he devoted Mondays and Fridays to poetry.

Jack compared teaching English to

> swallowing an elephant . . . it's such a huge thing . . . [there is] reading . . . grammar . . . writing . . . you've got so much stuff. I mean you can't possibly expect to adequately cover it in one year, so you just slowly chip away at it.

This metaphor, pitting the teacher against the subject (an elephant), is consistent with Jack's conception of the teacher as expert and source of knowledge. No role for students is either stated or implied in the image. Jack's metaphor captures the amorphous nature of English as a subject, and reflects the breadth of material he dealt with as a teacher on any given day—ranging from literary classics to the formation of plural possessives. The comparison implies a difficult but doable task, one of the "good kinds of struggles" that Jack enjoyed.

"Conducting an Orchestra of Kazoo Players": Celia

Celia entered the TADMP brimming with energy and creativity and excited about teaching literature. For her, literature had been a source of great personal pleasure, learning, and growth. Believing that the purpose of education was "self-actualization," she hoped to guide her students toward this goal through literature study.

Celia completed her student teaching in an affluent, suburban high school where she taught Honors English. She enjoyed the intellectual stimulation of a mentor teacher whose forte was Shakespeare. She devised creative activities and led successful literary discussions with her students who were bright, motivated, and whose families supported their academic pursuits.

Celia was hired by Blackstone Junior/Senior High School, a 7-12 school. Fewer than 20 miles from a Midwest metropolis, Blackstone served a blue-collar community suffering from the decline of the steel industry. The community and students were far different from any in Celia's experience. She was dismayed by the community's low regard for education and by the sexist, racist, and militaristic views many students espoused. Most teachers at Blackstone were longtime residents of the community; Celia lived in the city and viewed herself as a role model of a less provincial lifestyle.

Blackstone's principal had told Celia she was hired to "create some change." Taking this role seriously, she threw herself into school improvement projects that often set her at odds with other members of the English Department. She disagreed with the school's tracking practices, resented the department's curriculum guidelines, and attributed much of the students' resistance to writing and literature to poor instruction. She found that at Blackstone good teaching was equated with classroom management. She missed the intellectual stimulation she had enjoyed during her student teaching.

Nevertheless, Celia remained enthusiastic as she began her second year. She revamped the junior high reading program, renamed it "Literature," and ordered "huge boxes" of paperbacks to supplement the district-adopted reading textbooks. The students "loved it," and "every one of those kids checked out a book." For her regular high school classes, however, she was handed a curriculum guide and told to use it. Celia disagreed with much of the guide but agreed to "play by the rules," feeling "embarrassed" by her compliance. She assumed additional extracurricular responsibilities, including sponsoring academic teams and the Environmental Club.

By the beginning of her third year, Celia felt she had finally found her "focus": "I think a lot of my enthusiasm before really had to do with content and making the content exciting for them. My focus now has been really on the whole child." Her "primary concern" became "seeing that all the kids are really happy and healthy." Even though Celia preferred an unstructured environment, she responded to her students' lack of social skills by carefully orchestrating classroom activity. She organized her classes into cooperative learning groups. The groups provided the students with structure, encouraged them to accept responsibility for their own learning, and allowed them to practice social skills, goals that had become increasingly important to Celia. She felt most effective with the junior high students, often staying after school to tutor them.

She began to feel less like "an English teacher" and more like "a counselor . . . or Dear Abby." Responsibility was taking its toll on Celia and she reflected sadly, "I love English . . . I love the content of what I'm teaching, but you lose sight of that and I would never have predicted [it], but I don't read novels anymore on my own except during the summer . . . I've kind of lost my connection to the whole reason I decided to teach."

Celia compared teaching English to

> conducting an orchestra of kazoo players and you keep trying to get them to play Chopin or Bach or something and it still ends up sounding like a circus.

This comparison reflected Celia's frustration with her situation and her sense of disconnection from the content she loved: Literature with a capital L (expressed here as Chopin and Bach). Regardless of the conductor's (teacher's) talent or enthusiasm, the music (literature) will never be properly played (appreciated) because the orchestra (students) is hopelessly ill equipped to do so.

"A Teaching Mom": Claire

Claire decided to teach middle school, because "my experiences particularly in middle school were so earth-shattering and cathartic . . . and teachers were such a huge influence on me at that time . . . I want to do that for someone else." She fondly remembered English teachers who were "empathetic, caring people who had the ability to get students very excited about themselves primarily, and the subject is secondary, which is what I believe should be the priorities."

Schools were "places where children learn how to communicate, how to be with other people." The study of literature helps serve this purpose because

> we can learn so much from others through literature and through working with each other. . . . It is such a wonderful thing to open a book, to go to a play, or to read a poem and [discuss the] feelings of the character, to get into other people's shoes for a while.

She saw the teacher as "a guide through the content material," and even though she believed that the subject was secondary to nurturing students, she believed a good teacher should "know the content inside and out." From the beginning, Claire consistently described her teaching style as "parenting."

After completing the TADMP, Claire found exactly the position she wanted: teaching reading and language arts at Gauley River Middle School, which served an urban/suburban school population. But Claire's first year was "very unpeaceful." She was assigned three different preparations, had a teaching load of 160 students, and had to juggle various required textbooks. The personal revelations seventh and eighth graders made in their language arts journals disturbed her deeply. Nevertheless, she knew by the end of her first year that teaching was what she was "supposed to do."

Over the next two years, Claire's situation improved. Her course load was cut in half. Her teaching assignment was reduced to two preparations—sixth-grade reading and language arts. Midway through her third year, she decided she had "quite a lot of freedom in curriculum development" within the district guidelines. She enjoyed her friendship and collaboration with another language arts teacher. By the end of her third year, she felt she had mastered "all the administrative things that just drove me crazy the first year."

As Claire entered her fourth year, she seemed content. In the classroom, she appeared serene and competent. She relied "less and less" on textbooks, weaving them judiciously into units she designed alone or collaboratively. Claire was pragmatic about the use of prepackaged materials: "There's no ceiling to how much you can do. . . . That's why they have textbooks for you to buy with all these materials that go with them. It's because you're backed into a corner and you don't have a choice." For example, she followed the district mandate to teach spelling and devoted time each week to the spelling workbook.

Claire still believed that "English is probably the most affective subject area . . . we should feel a responsibility to help the kids grow in that area." In her teaching, she focused on "writing and reading worthwhile materials, materials that help students explore who they are and what their relationships with other people are, how they fit into the world, and how far they can go." She read aloud to her students often and enjoyed seeing their listening skills grow. Her students had many opportunities to speak, because "the better a person can communicate verbally and in writing, the more power they have. And . . . one of the things that we're all trying to do is to empower these kids to grow and to succeed."

Parenting remained Claire's metaphor for teaching English: "I feel like a mom here, a teaching mom." In this role, she believed that one of her responsibilities was "helping them [students] know how to behave and solve their problems, and think through their conflicts." Claire drew on her own experience as a mother to decide what was best for her students and children and provided a structured classroom environment with opportunities for choices. But Claire discovered that the role of teacher/parent can be exhausting and emotionally draining. She learned to set limits on her time and emotional investment, and by her fourth year, she seemed to have attained a happy medium, aware of what she could and could not accomplish as a "teaching mom." Sixth graders, it seems, are ripe for both parenting and learning, and Claire had found her niche among them.

Discussion

This study found that each teacher's subject perspective was, for the most part, both coherent and consistent. That is, each teacher's beliefs and actions made sense in relationship to one another (coherence), and each teacher tended to act in ways that expressed those beliefs (consistency). Furthermore, each teacher appears to have entered teacher education with a perspective toward English teaching already in place (see also Clark & Peterson, 1986; Zeichner & Gore, 1990). Key features of participants' subject perspectives are summarized in Table 8.1.

The cases of Jack, Claire, and Celia also reveal inconsistencies between their beliefs and practices, as well as change, though subtle, over time. Finally, differences among the subject perspectives of Jack, Celia, and Claire suggest that, among these English teachers at least, there is at least as much diversity as similarity.

Inconsistencies in Subject Perspectives

When teachers' actions appear to be inconsistent with their expressed beliefs, it is worth looking at the contexts in which teachers are acting. For example, both Jack and Claire stated that direct instruction in grammar

TABLE 8.1 The Subject Perspectives of Selected Novice English Teachers

Subject Perspective	Jack	Celia	Claire
Purpose of Education	"Shape individuals . . . equip them to deal with life"	"Self-actualization"	"Learn how to communicate, how to be with other people"
Role of English	Effective communication; aesthetic purposes	Self-actualization and social change through literature study	Written and oral communication; learning about self and others through literature
Role of Teacher	"Expert" in subject and beyond	"Change agent"	"Guide through content"
Appropriate Content	Expository and creative writing; literature	Literature	"Writing and reading worthwhile materials" that help students explore self, relationships, and the world
Appropriate Pedagogy	Teacher-directed discussion and activity	Teacher-directed learning groups	Teacher-directed learning groups
Relationships with Students	Role model, respected authority	Role model, "Dear Abby"	Role model, "parent"
Metaphor for Teaching English	"Swallowing an elephant"	"Conducting an orchestra of kazoo players"	"A teaching mom"

was futile. Yet both engaged in this activity. Why? One reason is that they were required by their districts to do so. Jack, in his second year of teaching, felt more pressure to comply than Claire, who in her fourth year was finding ways to cope creatively with this mandate. Novice teachers, not yet assured of tenure, are especially vulnerable to such pressures.

In addition, novice teachers often face difficult teaching conditions that constrain them from implementing practices advocated in their teacher education programs. Claire's "unpeaceful" first year is illustrative. It seems ironic that support in the form of manageable class size, number of preparations, and membership in a departmental community is frequently unavailable to novice teachers, who most need such supports.

Change in Subject Perspectives

Of the three teachers portrayed here, only one—Celia—claimed to have changed. Celia's change might be described as a shift from a "subject-centered" approach to a "student-centered" approach—an approach often advocated in teacher education programs today. But if this change was for the good, why did Celia feel she had "lost" her "connection" to the "whole reason" she decided to teach?

Many features of Celia's teaching context clashed with her subject perspective. Eventually, Celia shifted her focus from literature to the well-being of the "whole child." She began pouring the energy that she had originally hoped to devote to literature study into a seemingly bottomless chasm of need. But in restructuring her teaching to meet her students' needs, her own needs for intellectual stimulation and innovation were not being met. Although her students appeared to be thriving in her classroom, Celia was not.

Comparison of Subject Perspectives

Jack, Claire, and Celia each emphasized a different, but legitimate, purpose of education. Jack, for example, noted "shaping individuals" and equipping individuals to succeed in society. Celia repeatedly stated that "self-actualization" for social change was the primary purpose of education. Claire talked about teaching "children" to communicate and "to get along." Each teacher's personal version of English teaching was consistent with his or her view of the purpose of education. Jack emphasized the utilitarian value of communication skills and, to a lesser degree, the aesthetic and educative value of literature. Celia believed that the study of literature would lead to personal growth and improvement of society. Claire's view of English combined oral and written communication for both utilitarian and social goals, and literature study for pleasure, learning, and personal growth.

Although Table 8.1 offers a capsule view of the subject perspectives of Jack, Celia, and Claire, it masks subtle differences among their beliefs and actions. For example, Table 8.1 suggests a great deal of similarity in beliefs about content (e.g., "literature") and pedagogy (e.g., "teacher-directed"). But literature and teacher-directed pedagogy looked quite different in each teacher's classroom. Jack, for example, presided over a sophisticated literary discussion of *The Crucible*. In contrast, Celia, hoping to encourage her students to connect with literature, was reading aloud *How the Grinch Stole Christmas*. Meanwhile, Claire's students worked collaboratively to construct collages representing "home," before beginning a unit on home-lessness.

For all three, being a role model was an important part of being an English teacher, but each interpreted the meaning of "role model" within the context of his or her subject perspective. Jack modeled being an "expert" in English and beyond. Celia and Claire were very concerned with modeling communication and social skills. Despite these differences, all three seemed comfortable in their relationships with students. Their students participated willingly, even eagerly, in activities, and some came early or stayed late to capture a few private minutes with Jack, Celia, or Claire.

Conclusions, Implications, and Questions

Although Jack, Celia, and Claire were not "typical" novice teachers, their cases raise several issues important to teacher educators. First, these teachers held diverse perspectives on the teaching of English. They entered teacher education with their perspectives in place and, for the most part, continued to hold them into their second, third, and fourth years of teaching. This finding suggests that teacher education programs need to accommodate the diverse perspectives aspiring teachers bring to them, and that teacher educators should be cautious about advocating "one best way" to teach. Do teacher educators prize diversity in perspectives or attempt to extinguish it? Are the reflective methods now popular in teacher education programs aimed at changing prospective teachers' perspectives or at helping them construct a practice that makes sense in the context of their beliefs?

As long as schools fill "slots" instead of employing "people," mis-matches between teachers and contexts are likely to occur. Successful and rewarded in her student teaching, Celia had no reason to suspect that teaching at Blackstone would be different. What would Celia's teaching have looked like and how would she have changed (or not changed) if she had been hired by the prosperous high school in which she completed her student teaching? Celia's case is probably not unique. Teacher educators should initiate discussions of differences in school contexts and of how beliefs and contexts can interact.

Teacher education programs and schools must work together to address the "disabling contradictions" between the knowledge prospective teachers acquire through their teacher education programs and the realities of school structure (Myers, 1991, p. 400). Jack, Celia, and Claire felt pressured to follow curriculum guides and textbooks that promoted practices long since discredited by research, for example, teaching grammar, spelling, and vocabulary in isolation from meaningful texts. The conditions common to novice teaching—numerous preparations, large classes, extracurricular assignments—can even induce beginning teachers to adopt such practices for survival. How many novice teachers, like Claire, can bridge the perceived gap between "theory" and "reality"? How can teacher education programs better prepare prospective teachers and support novice teachers during this difficult and often painful transition?

Finally, we should continue to build a base of description of English teaching and of other subjects as well. This seems particularly important as schools are seeking ways to integrate the traditional disciplines. Such description must be anchored in classroom teaching, include description of teaching contexts, and extend beyond student teaching or the first year of teaching, which can be anomalous periods in a teaching career. In education, we have often violated the principle that description must precede prescription. Perhaps this is one reason why so many prescriptions for educational reform have failed. Describing teaching in context, like teaching English, may be like "swallowing an elephant." But it can be done—one bite at a time.

Notes

1. Data on classroom ambiance and physical appearance were gathered but not reported here because of space limitations.

2. All names of individuals and schools in this chapter have been changed to protect the privacy of the participants. The program, TADMP, is referred to only by acronym for the same reason.

3. Complete case studies can be obtained from the author.

References

Applebee, A. N. (1974). *Tradition and reform in the teaching of English: A history.* Urbana, IL: National Council of Teachers of English.

Ball, S. J. (1985). English for the English since 1906. In I. Goodson (Ed.), *Social histories of the secondary curriculum: Subjects for study* (pp. 53-88). London: Falmer.

Ball, S. J., & Lacey, C. (1980). Subject disciplines as the opportunity for group action: A measured critique of subject sub-cultures. In P. Woods (Ed.), *Teacher strategies: Explorations in the sociology of the school* (pp. 149-177). London: Croon Helm.

Barnes, D., Barnes, D., & Clarke, S. (1984). *Versions of English.* London: Heinemann.

Bennett, C. (1991). The Teacher as Decision Maker Program: An alternative for career-change preservice teachers. *Journal of Teacher Education, 42*(2), 119-130.

Bennett, C., & Spalding, E. (1992). Teaching the social studies: Multiple approaches for multiple perspectives. *Theory and Research in Social Education, 20*(3), 263-292.

Bullough, R. V., Jr., Knowles, J. G., & Crow, N. A. (1991). *Emerging as a teacher.* London: Routledge.

Clark, C. M., & Peterson, P. (1986). Teachers' thought processes. In M. C. Wittrock (Ed.), *Handbook of research on teaching* (pp. 255-296). New York: Macmillan.

Clift, R. T. (1991). Learning to teach English—maybe: A study of knowledge development. *Journal of Teacher Education, 42*(5), 357-372.

Elbaz, F. (1983). *Teacher thinking: A study of practical knowledge.* London: Croon Helm.

Erickson, F. (1986). Qualitative methods in research on teaching. In M. C. Wittrock (Ed.), *Handbook of research on teaching* (pp. 119-161). New York: Macmillan.

Fox, D. L. (1995). From English major to English teacher: Two case studies. *English Journal, 84*(2), 17-25.

Grossman, P. L. (1990). *The making of a teacher: Teacher knowledge and teacher education.* New York: Teachers College Press.

Grossman, P. L., & Shulman, L. S. (1994). Knowing, believing, and the teaching of English. In T. Shanahan (Ed.), *Teachers thinking, teachers knowing: Reflections on literacy and language education* (pp. 3-22). Urbana, IL: National Council of Teachers of English.

Grossman, P. L., & Stodolsky, S. S. (1994). Considerations of content and the circumstances of secondary school teaching. *Review of Research in Education, 20,* 179-221.

Lacey, C. (1977). *The socialization of teachers.* London: Methuen.

Lincoln, Y. S., & Guba, E. G. (1985). *Naturalistic inquiry.* Beverly Hills, CA: Sage.

Merriam, S. B. (1988). *Case study research in education: A qualitative approach.* San Francisco: Jossey-Bass.

Morgan, D. L. (1988). *Focus groups as qualitative research.* Newbury Park, CA: Sage.

Myers, M. A. (1991). Issues in the restructuring of teacher education. In J. Flood, J. M. Jensen, D. Lapp, & J. R. Squire (Eds.), *Handbook of research on teaching the English Language Arts* (pp. 394-417). New York: Macmillan.

National Council of Teachers of English. (1982). *Essentials of English: A document for reflection and dialogue.* Urbana, IL: National Council of Teachers of English.

Sikes, P. J., Measor, L., & Woods, P. (1985). *Teacher careers: Crises and continuities.* London: Falmer.

Zancanella, D. (1991). Teachers reading/readers teaching: Five teachers' personal approaches to literature and their teaching of literature. *Research in the Teaching of English, 25*(1), 5-31.

Zeichner, K. M., & Gore, J. M. (1990). Teacher socialization. In W. R. Houston (Ed.), *Handbook of research in teacher education* (pp. 329-348). New York: Macmillan.

9 Multicultural Education and Monocultural Students

Curriculum Struggles in Teacher Education

Burga Jung

Burga Jung is Assistant Professor of Curriculum and Instruction at Texas Tech University. Her research interests are in solo and group curriculum decision making among school-based educators, preservice teachers, and teacher educators.

ABSTRACT

Prescriptive teacher education literature asks teacher educators to prepare preservice teachers who are sensitive to multicultural dimensions of society and who can enter and succeed in classrooms with multicultural populations of students. The commonplaces of teacher education programs are rarely considered in these curriculum prescriptions, however. This paper draws on Schon's epistemology of practice to describe curriculum commonplaces in one preservice course insofar as they point to ways in which monocultural preservice teachers journey to multicultural awareness. Data were collected through participant observation, interviews, and documents generated throughout a 15-week certification course for secondary preservice teachers. Data were analyzed using the constant comparative method. Findings highlight obstacles in the journey, specifically conflict within preservice teachers' tacit attitudes, beliefs, values, and knowledge claims as they journey from superficial accommodations of course requirements to subject matter, school, and student particularities not considered before.

The value of an education is to make a better person.
                            —Rita, preservice teacher

The Real World and Multicultural Education

In the 1990s, we are witnessing a renewed focus on multicultural[1] education. Educational movements for education *about* cultures other than one's own and *for* equitable educational opportunities of subordinated students have an honorably long history in American public schools in this century (Banks, 1993). Nonetheless, multicultural education is a phenomenon primarily of the second half of this century, and despite its prescriptive heyday in the 1960s and 1970s (Banks, 1993), it has had little effect on actual day-to-day teaching practices in public schools. Most renewed efforts have centered on the merely political and prescriptive and, in so doing, may have diverted energies away from classroom applications. In like manner, multicultural education has had little effect on the day-to-day teaching practices in teacher education programs over this same period of time, although exceptions such as the programs described by Reed (1993), Tellez and Hlebowitsh (1993), and Zeichner (1993) can be found. Little seems to have changed in preservice teachers' multicultural learnings. Although NCATE (1992) guidelines encourage multicultural education in the professional preparation of teachers, program requirements typically do not integrate multicultural education in thorough, persistent, and overt ways for adult learners (Grant, 1994), especially given adult learners' extensive store of tacit knowledge, beliefs, attitudes, and skills. By and large, teacher educators themselves are not all that comfortable with multicultural education. This is particularly so for those teacher educators whose areas of expertise lie outside of multicultural education and who are themselves monocultural.[2] In addition, the experiential (i.e., real) world of preservice teachers generally provides few multicultural educational experiences for them, according to all demographic indications (Graham, 1987; Haberman, 1989; Haberman & Post, 1994).

Why Study Preservice Teachers?

Teacher education programs share many of the same curriculum concerns as other programs at postsecondary institutions, that is, how best to educate adults (Civikly, 1986; Dunkin & Barnes, 1986; Eble, 1983; Tierney, 1990). In addition, teacher educators are asked to prepare preservice teachers who are sensitive to multicultural dimensions of society and who will be able to enter and succeed in classrooms with a multicultural population of students (Banks, 1993; Banks & Banks, 1993; Gonzalez, 1994; Grant & Secada, 1990; Holling, 1993; Ladson-Billings, 1994; Lynch, Modgil, & Modgil, 1992; Nieto, 1992; Reiff & Cannella, 1992; Sleeter, 1993). So reflective practices on multicultural components within teacher education programs should be studied carefully.

This tension between the demands of multicultural preservice education and the knowledge base, affective development, and life experiences that largely monocultural preservice students bring with them to teacher preparation programs is then at the core of teacher preparation programs in the 1990s (Ladson-Billings, 1994).

Secondary preservice teachers in my curriculum course are expected to become familiar with the language of curriculum planning, development, and evaluation so that they can more easily adjust to institutional exigencies of school systems. I consider the curriculum to be all that students have an opportunity to learn through the provisions made for this by the educational institution (McCutcheon, 1982). In addition, I draw on Schwab (1969, 1971, 1973, 1983) as I include the four commonplaces (student, teacher, subject, milieu) he asks us to consider in curriculum decision making; this helps me focus on the particularities of my own curriculum practices. In the practice-focused language of curriculum decision making for my preservice courses, curriculum decisions are active, ongoing, complicated, and messy; defy clean and linear depictions; and include ways of preparing for students' learning opportunities, reworking these learning opportunities as they are being enacted, and evaluating the results. In so doing, curriculum decision making focuses on resolving ongoing questions and concerns and necessitates reflective practice by me and by the preservice students. How do monocultural preservice teachers journey from prior knowledge, attitudes, values, and skills to multicultural awareness and pedagogical knowledge and skills that are essential to them in their teaching practices? I focused on preservice students' reflective practices along one part of this journey, namely that undertaken in their preservice curriculum development course that I teach.

A host of institutional factors certainly influenced our journey in ways that shape (through constraints as well as opportunities) what is possible in any given course. Among others, these factors include the length of time available to any single university-level course (10 to 15 weeks are certainly not enough to finish the journey—one barely begins); the availability of appropriate speakers from school communities during our class time; opportunities to interact informally with precollege students of differing ethnicities; the availability of appropriate videotapes that can provide vicarious experiences when "real" experiences are not accessible; the range of school-based experiences (clinical or otherwise) students may encounter during the course's 15 weeks; the amount of out-of-class time available to students to pursue multicultural readings on their own; and the scattered sources of multicultural readings (i.e., public libraries, campus libraries, community organizations, the popular press, commercial publishers).

So, in this chapter, I will focus on course-related reflective practices that maintained, increased, and obstructed preservice teachers' multicultural awareness and the development of related pedagogical skills and knowledge. Although preservice teachers' knowledge and expressions of that knowledge (as in completing course assignments, participating in school-based classroom activities, sharing small group and large group discussions, keeping reflection journals) are linked in ways that defy easy description and explanation (Lytle & Cochran-Smith, 1994), I believe an educative start must be made in that direction. This report is only one such effort.

Theoretical Framework

This study draws on Schon's (1983, 1987) epistemology of practice as it is grounded in premises useful to practitioners and practitioners-to-be in education. For example, reflective practice helps us better understand how curriculum decisions that consider Schwab's commonplaces are made, enacted, and evaluated. The following constructs in reflective practice are particularly useful: (a) knowing-in-action, (b) reflection-in-action, and (c) reflection on reflection-in-action. Knowing-in-action includes dynamic public and private displays of knowledge, values, attitudes, and skills. I take "tacit beliefs" to be those taken-for-granted and largely unexamined convictions derived mainly from personal experiences over time; these experiences can be direct but are often indirect and vicarious. I take "tacit attitudes" to be those taken-for-granted and largely unexamined dispositions toward people, objects, events, ideas (e.g., indifferent, for, against). I take "tacit knowledge" to be taken-for-granted facts and skills gained through schooling and other experiences. Reflection-in-action is a conscious and spontaneous questioning of the tacit assumptions supporting our knowing-in-action, and occurs when our knowing-in-action does not produce expected results, prompting on-the-spot testing of new actions. Reflection on reflection-in-practice is an inner dialogue over reflection-in-action that articulates a description of reflection-in-action.

These reflective practices resulted in a wide variety of student outcomes. I will limit the latter to some of the findings on the development of multicultural awareness, knowledge, and skills in preservice students as a result of their early experiences in actualizing reflective practices in preservice settings.

Research Methods and Data Sources

This case study is part of a larger ethnographic case study that combines participant observation with key informant conversations and the collection of student and instructor artifacts (Bernard, 1988; Erickson, 1986; Patton, 1990) during the length of a 15-week curriculum development course within a secondary education teacher certification program at a major southwestern university.

The preservice students enrolled in the case study's curriculum course can be described in terms that point to diversity rather than commonality in age, ethnicity, marital status, educational background, work experiences, teaching field, and life experiences with people of differing ethnicities. All names used in this paper are, of course, pseudonyms to protect the anonymity of the student participants.

A summary pointing to the ranges in each of these demographic categories might be helpful. Students' ages ranged from 21 to 55, and all students were European Americans.[3] Marital status included single, soon-to-be-married, married, and divorced. Educational background ranged from those who had just completed bachelor's degrees to holders of master's degrees. Work experience varied from limited experience outside of university-related work to extensive careers in the military, engineering, and business. Teaching fields included computer specialist, physical education, English, history, science, mathematics, music, art, and agriculture. The majority of these students had no substantive *informal* encounters with people of differing ethnicities; two students had considerable public school experiences in ethnically integrated communities, and one student spoke of his lengthy residence in foreign lands and many cross-cultural social experiences.

As instructor (European American), I participated in class activities in a number of ways: organizing, attending, and facilitating each class session; helping students as a resource person; scaffolding whenever possible (e.g., through in-class and out-of-class oral dialogue and written dialogue such as journals and reaction papers); engaging in daily conversations with students before, during, and after each class session; collecting and grading student reflection sheets, reaction papers, other assignments, and tests; initiating lengthy conversations with key course informants; and inviting guest speakers.

To include the larger world in our course discussions and assignments, I provided varied resources and constructed assignments designed to direct students' attention to multicultural concerns in Schwab's four curriculum commonplaces. These resources and assignments included novels, case studies, role model literature (e.g., Ladson-Billings, 1994), campus-based activities (e.g., cross-cultural simulations), school-based activities (e.g., tutoring), videos, speakers, readings from teaching field journals, readings from educational journals (e.g., *Kappan*), readings from popular magazines (e.g., *Time*) and the local newspaper, references on multicultural education, references on specific ethnic and cultural groups (such as Mexican Americans, African Americans, Native Americans), biographies, our course textbook (Pratt's 1994 *Curriculum Planning*), and an integrated team curriculum project that included multicultural objectives.

I made extensive field notes, kept a journal, and took advantage of many informal opportunities for asking questions on the meanings students held about class actions and discourse focusing on multicultural awareness. In addition, course sessions were tape recorded and particular sessions also videotaped.

The constant comparative method was used for data analysis (Bogdan & Biklen, 1992; Strauss, 1987). Both etic code and emic codes were used to generate analytic categories.

Monocultural and Multicultural
Meeting Places: Some Results

Findings in this study point to how monocultural European American preservice teachers journey to multicultural awareness and develop pedagogical knowledge and skills relevant to some multicultural goal. In various ways, students brought to the course the best of intentions. Early in the course, most students displayed altruistic beliefs about education, public school students, teaching, and multicultural education. One day, Rita listed nine worthy beliefs about the value of an education:

> Make a better person, get good jobs, learn social skills, learn specific knowledge, learn to be compassionate, acquire a sense of responsibility for one another's well-being, learn self-discipline, learn to be responsible, learn to work hard (effort pays off).

The class agreed with Rita wholeheartedly and so pointed to a shared attitude about education, public school students, and teaching. These components of knowing-in-action often conflicted, however, with other attitudes about education, public school students, and teaching that seemed to be embedded more solidly in students' knowing-in-action. Some of these conflicting attitudes, values, and claims to knowledge I discuss below as roadblocks.

Not all tacit knowledge, attitudes, and skills worked against multicultural goals. Brad's views on the place of multicultural education at the secondary level is representative of these preservice students' views: "I think it's important for students to know how different cultures affect us in our own culture." By this, Brad meant that the importance of multicultural education lay not only in meeting the educational needs of students whose ancestral contributions have been ignored historically in public school education. He also included those students whose ancestral contributions had been well represented in public school curricula but who were largely ignorant of the contributions of other cultural groups residing in the United States. In this way, Brad was pointing to an educational value of multicultural education for all public school students.

These preservice teachers also relied on their lived experiences as foundational to curriculum decisions they were asked to make in negotiating the multicultural content of the preservice curriculum course and in generating assigned multicultural curriculum documents. My decision to require cooperative learning groups helped monocultural preservice students extend their capacities to imagine ways of enriching secondary curricula with multicultural dimensions that took account of students' ethnicities. Students' knowledge-in-action in the form of their tacit beliefs, attitudes, and knowledge and learned canonical subject matter knowledge proved, however, to be a major obstacle to constructing professional knowledge grounded in multicultural education for secondary students.

These preservice teachers' autobiographies and tacit beliefs, attitudes, and knowledge influenced their construction of professional knowledge for teaching secondary students. This emerging professional knowledge will be illustrated through examples taken from the class.

Journeying Toward Multicultural Awareness and Pedagogy: Knowing-in-Action

During the first class session, the students and I spent time introducing ourselves, and I was able to develop an initial picture of each student based on precollege school experiences, career goals, and educational background. These initial pictures showed me how I might direct course objectives to better articulate with students' knowledge-in-action. For one, I hoped to widen the students' experiences by providing relevant and provocative readings on school experiences of African American and Mexican American precollege students as well as carefully selected video excerpts pointing to ways of including multicultural course content and instructional strategies in secondary teaching. The video excerpts were consistently well received and usually elicited a lively discussion afterward and many additional comments in the students' journals. The readings were drawn from relatively accessible journals and magazines targeting public school teachers. In addition, I provided references on multicultural education and specific ethnic and cultural groups. Although many (if not all) students found time to peruse these readings, none of the readings elicited the kind of collective response the speakers and video excerpts gave rise to. In part, this lack of collective response was the result of the structure of the assignment; the readings were one of several options from which students could choose, whereas the video excerpts were whole class experiences.

I asked the university's African American Director of the Multicultural Office and a recently retired African American principal of a local high school to speak to my preservice students on topics related to developing their multicultural awareness. I chose the director and the principal for these reasons: My previous encounters with them showed me they were knowledgeable about the difficulties encountered in schools because of teachers' and students' differing ethnicities; they each had a history of success in surmounting such difficulties; they were well respected in the local African American community; and they would be able to interact well with university students in discussing ramifications of teaching the 20% African American student population in local schools.

For somewhat similar reasons (e.g., the local school district had a 30% Mexican American student population), I asked two Mexican American doctoral students and a Mexican American teacher educator to engage my students in a simulation and role-playing exercise that included the learning of a new language and cultural mores, encounters with a new cultural group speaking an unfamiliar language, and a discussion of ethnic and racial stereotypes. In each case, my previous experiences with these speakers helped me judge the value of their potential contributions, and in each case I agreed with their respective positions.

A brief description of these five speakers' visits would have to include the students' rapt attention and eagerness to ask questions as well as to extend the visit into the "break" time built into each 3-hour class session. These five invited speakers were the first "credentialed" African Americans and Mexican Americans most students in this class had heard from in their university courses. These speaker opportunities extended themselves into open-ended discussion sessions, and my students told me they had never before asked African Americans and Mexican Americans about school situations. For many of the students, these discussions were the first times they had been in serious dialogue with any African American or Mexican American person. After the simulation exercise, Linda, who teaches computer literacy as an intern in a nearby rural junior high school, wrote in her course journal:

> I felt I learned more about the Mexican American culture through the exercise. It was fun as well to interact and get better acquainted with my fellow classmates. I have been brainstorming all week on how I might better relate [computer skills] to my Mexican American students.

This journal entry shows Linda reflecting on gaps in her knowledge of Mexican Americans: cultural beliefs, values, and actions as well as curriculum considerations of her Mexican American students' needs, interests, knowledge, and skills. She considers these gaps serious enough to take action to better educate her Mexican American students. I was not Linda's supervisor during her intern year, so I was not able to document ways in which she pursued her own quest for knowledge and ways in which she enacted multiculturally grounded curriculum decisions. But her journal entries continued to show progress in both directions. She also realized the importance of "fun" in learning that might not have been as clear to her before the simulation exercise.

For example, the very next class after the simulation exercise, she proudly told me in her journal that she'd located a new Macintosh-based math software (*Mathkeys*) that "toggles between English and Spanish at any time in the program." Plus, her own children tried it out and said that the math problem-solving strategies were "so much fun." Her increasing awareness that Mexican American students are often overlooked or categorized as deficient academically prompted her, by the end of the semester, to include the students in important and responsible ways, such as in software evaluation:

> I plan on having the students fill out an evaluation of [*The Cruncher*] as one of their assignments. I will then send these to Davidson's Education Department to aid their future development of new products. . . . The students' evaluations might possibly aid me in my future use of the program.

In these ways, Linda not only deepened her awareness of Mexican American culture (although she never disclosed pursuing any further readings or social encounters) but also began to search for ways of increasing the relevance of her teaching field to her Mexican American students through culturally specific curriculum decisions (e.g., *Mathkeys* with Spanish) and proactively inclusive teaching (e.g., including students in software evaluation). On the other hand, although she was enthusiastic about locating "fun" software for her students, including the English and Spanish *Mathkeys*, she never questioned her own lack of Spanish as a possible lack in language knowledge and skills that could be worked on.

I presented a part of Linda's story here to show knowing-in-action applied to curriculum decisions in secondary classrooms. Preservice students who had the opportunity of working with African American and Mexican American students as volunteers, substitute teachers, and interns were able to increase their multicultural awareness through personal experiences and to reflect on these experiences. The rest of the students were able to share in these experiences vicariously through first-person stories.

So far I've pointed to evidence illustrating interplay between knowing-in-action and reflection-in-action resulting in preservice teachers' productive changes in knowledge, attitudes, values, and skills. Evidence illustrating obstacles in this multicultural journey is taken up next.

Roadblocks to Multicultural Awareness: Knowing-in-Action

Many of the students' tacit beliefs, attitudes, and knowledge claims proved to be major obstacles to constructing professional knowledge grounded in multicultural education for secondary students. These roadblocks included psychologizing student failure, acceptance of facile generalizations and dichotomies as answers to problems, the lack of personal time for including experiential learning, the pandemic ease of labeling students, rules of proper school behavior, temptations of the status quo, and the stranglehold of the melting pot metaphor. Of these, perhaps the first two will illustrate obstacles to multicultural awareness.

Student Failure

My students were able to display appropriate attitudinal rhetoric in reciting their altruistic beliefs about education, public school students, and teaching. Nonetheless, most of the class understood student failure as solely a student's (and by extension, parent's) problem. School-as-social-institution was typically not seen as leading to individual student failure. Neither was the teacher seen as possibly contributing to student failure. David, for example, was convinced that every child already has opportunities to learn and "it's the child's fault if learning doesn't happen." David returned periodically to this theme, especially when discussing the desirability of students taking full responsibility for their failures. David pointed to *The Bell Curve* to support his position. Although David had not read the book, he was convinced that existing group differences in IQ tests and academic scores on college admissions tests (highlighting the lower group scores of students of color) resulted from students' failure to take personal responsibility for their achievement. Although the psychologizing of student failure is in the foreground here, my students' ready and reflective acceptance of pejorative beliefs about students as members of subcultural groups was equally forceful.

Educational Slogans, Generalities, and Dichotomies

Tension between inspirational slogans (such as "all students can learn") and pejorative tacit beliefs (such as "African American and Mexican American homes are unsupportive and even disruptive of school learning") vie for dominance in these preservice teachers' thinking. For example, these tacit beliefs easily surface when secondary students' homework is missing or their behavior is judged "inappropriate" in other ways.

My students rejected the "image of WASPs as present-day oppressors" (as one student phrased it) as the only alternative to what many favored as "cultural transmission." Their everyday thinking patterns also encouraged dichotomies that support the status quo. For example, Christine, a math TA, wrote the following in her course journal:

> I suppose I could be labeled a "cultural transmissionist" [referring to a term in our course textbook, Pratt, 1994] or traditionalist. I definitely believe that there are certain bodies of knowledge that should be handed down from one generation to the next. There are topics in math, science, history, and English that every "educated" person should be familiar with, beyond the survival skills of reading, writing and arithmetic.

Christine's generalities about "what every 'educated' person should be familiar with" tend to encourage the habit of dichotomizing problems (in this case, change in the "traditional curriculum" will necessarily undermine its "integrity"). Christine's voiced concern here is an example of this habit as well as a disclosure of tacit beliefs, attitudes, and knowledge about public schools' curriculum obligations to students and their families, the nature of "bodies of knowledge," American culture, and national identity.

Steve writes the following as a direct result of his experiences listening to his classmates talk about themselves during class sessions early in the semester:

This exercise also individualized everyone in my mind, which made me realize the importance of being your own individual and seeing others as individuals.

School-based experiences, however, pushed him to write about students as if they had only a group identity ("all," "they"). The school-based teacher paired with Steve told him about two female high school students "molested by relatives." Although the concerns he expresses are in at least one sense laudatory, they also point to the loss of a sense of "seeing others as individuals" which he claimed to value at the beginning of the semester:

I was talking with Mrs. _____ and we were wondering how can we expect students to do all their work, be interested, and learn etc. when they have all sorts of problems at home. They do not care about school when they have this type of home life.

Steve and Mrs. _____ have framed the problem in ways that preclude *teacher* solutions. More fundamentally, however, Steve (and Mrs._____) believe that such students cannot be expected to "learn" or "care about school." Of course, Steve also believes Mrs. _____ , as school practitioner in a junior high school with a 100% African American and Mexican American student body, really knows these students better than outsiders like university faculty. So whereas course discussions on Steve's school experiences can reinforce the value of interacting with students as individuals, his school experiences are framed by an esteemed teaching field practitioner in very different ways.

Concluding Comments

What do preservice students see as the real world for themselves, their future students, and their future colleagues? Preservice teachers' actions show a reluctance to work at deepening their multicultural awareness through personal experiences (with persons of differing cultures) and vicarious ones (such as readings, documentaries). On the other hand, no single course or program of courses can fill the knowledge and experiential gaps that monocultural preservice teachers have as they prepare to teach in secondary schools. Self-knowledge through a reflective exploration of otherwise tacit beliefs, attitudes, and knowledge holds some promise for personal multicultural education and thereby a place to start.

Although this chapter does not describe my discourse and actions as instructor, I believe it helpful to think of my curriculum decisions as ways in which these preservice teachers and I met to discuss, share, and learn from each other. So, at one level, our meeting places were largely decided by me in choosing course content, instructional strategies, and assessment. At another level, however, the curriculum decisions were largely in the hands of the students as they decided what to share from their prior and current autobiographies, what to choose to read out of the wide array of journal readings, references, and other resources made available. Last, the students chose which problems, examples, successes, and other experiences they wanted the class to "visit" through presentations and discussions and that they wanted me to read in their journals, reflection sheets, and other assignments.

So, in these ways, these preservice students and I found meeting places during which we focused on multicultural education for ourselves and future students: not an easy journey for any of us. Most of my students demonstrated they were starting on their personal journeys, but few were able to show much progress by the end of our time together.

So Where Are We?

Although I would like to pretend that my students share my valuing of multiculturalism and that they have learned and experienced enough before enrolling in preservice courses to include multicultural content and instructional strategies in their everyday teaching, I know this is by and large not the case. Where do we start if we support any reasons for teachers integrating multiculturalism into precollege curricula? I believe carefully organized clinical experiences are necessary but not sufficient to move preservice teachers beyond their knowing-in-action status quo or Nieto's (1992) awareness level of personal multicultural education (the lowest of four levels she describes). Readings geared as much as possible to the individual preservice teacher's educational and experiential background plus teaching field are critical as are chances to meet people of color who are school and community leaders, opportunities for reflection, personalized student-teacher dialogue, and course assignments structured to provoke thoughtful answers. Can all of these changes for the better be accomplished in a teacher education program? Is any of these strategies a magic bullet? We must not fool ourselves in this any more than we would want to claim that adult beliefs, values, and actions can be *expected* to change dramatically based on a course or even a series of courses. This, however, does not mean we must not do all that is possible to educate ourselves and preservice teachers into the real world of precollege schooling peopled as it is with students who will not (and should not) leave their cultural heritages at the school door.

Notes

1. For the purposes of this chapter, Nieto (1992) is the source for the term *multicultural*, which she considers to be the type of "learning that builds on previous knowledge and experiences in the first culture . . . and develops more extensive knowledge and awareness of other cultures" (p. 307).

2. The term *monocultural* is being used here as Nieto (1992) describes it: "reflective of only one [culture] reality and biased toward the dominant group" (p. 212).

3. Nieto (1992) discusses the complexities in labeling Americans as belonging to particular ethnic groups (even the term *American* is problematic and she differentiates ethnic from racial groups). She concludes that European American is the most satisfactory descriptor of those Americans whose ancestry is European (or mainly so) and whose "habits, values and mores are grounded in European mores and values . . . adapted and modified to create [an American culture]" (p. 16). Although I am not altogether satisfied with the term *European American*, I use it in this paper for lack of an equivalent term.

Nieto argues for the use of the term *African American* as a more accurate term than *Black* because the former announces a cultural base rather than primarily a focus on a superficial characteristic such as skin pigmentation and also highlights cultural contributions to this society.

In like manner, Nieto argues that the term *Mexican American* is more descriptive culturally and less political than terms such as *Chicano, Chicana,* and *Latino, Latina* and should be used when the ancestral country of origin is known. The federal term *Hispanic,* although widespread and well known, seems to rest on particularly shaky cultural grounds as its links are only with language. Even though language is an important cultural vehicle, it is not the only cultural demarcation commonly acknowledged. For much the same reason, *Anglo* as a term to indicate mother tongue English speakers has little *cultural* meaning.

Last, *Native American* is used interchangeably by Nieto with *Indian* and *American Indian*. Her reasons derive from tribal usage and preferences expressed by her Indian students.

References

Banks, J. A. (1993). Multicultural education: Historical development, dimensions, and practice. *Review of Research in Education, 63,* 3-49.

Banks, J. A., & Banks, C. A. M. (1993). *Multicultural education: Issues and perspectives.* Boston: Allyn & Bacon.

Bernard, H. R. (1988). *Research methods in cultural anthropology.* Newbury Park, CA: Sage.

Bogdan, R. C., & Biklen, S. K. (1992). *Qualitative research for education: An introduction to theory and methods.* Boston: Allyn & Bacon.

Civikly, J. (Ed.). (1986). *Communicating in college classroom.* San Francisco: Jossey-Bass.

Dunkin, M., & Barnes, J. (1986). Research on teaching in higher education. In M. Wittrock (Ed.), *Handbook of research on teaching* (pp. 754-777). New York: Macmillan.

Eble, K. (1983). *The aims of college teaching.* San Francisco: Jossey-Bass.

Erickson, F. (1986). Qualitative methods in research on teaching. In M. Wittrock (Ed.), *Handbook of research on teaching* (pp. 119-161). New York: Macmillan.

Gonzalez, V. (1994, April). *Taking the risk to change schools from within: Educators' cognitive growth through multicultural education.* Paper presented at the annual meeting of the American Educational Research Association, New Orleans, LA.

Graham, P. A. (1987). Black teachers: A drastically scarce resource. *Phi Delta Kappan, 68*(8), 598-605.

Grant, C. (1994). Best practices in teacher preparation for urban schools: Lessons from the multicultural teacher education literature. *Action in Teacher Education, 16*(3), 1-18.

Grant, C., & Secada, W. G. (1990). Preparing teachers for diversity. In W. R. Houston (Ed.), *Handbook of Research on Teacher Education* (pp. 403-422). New York: Macmillan.

Haberman, M. (1989). More minority teachers. *Phi Delta Kappan, 70*(10), 771-776.

Haberman, M., & Post, L. (1994). Multicultural schooling: Developing a curriculum for the real world. *Peabody Journal of Education, 69*(3), 101-115.

Holling, E. R. (1993). Assessing teacher competence for diverse populations. *Theory Into Practice, 32*(2), 93-99.

Ladson-Billings, G. (1994). *The dreamkeepers: Successful teachers of African American children.* San Francisco: Jossey-Bass.

Lynch, J., Modgil, C., & Modgil, S. (Eds.). (1992). *Cultural diversity and the schools: Vol. 1. Education for cultural diversity convergence and divergence*. Washington, DC: Falmer.

Lytle, S., & Cochran-Smith, M. (1994). Inquiry, knowledge, and practice. In S. Hollingsworth & H. Sockett (Eds.), *Teacher research and educational reform* (Part I, pp. 22-51). Chicago: NSSE

McCutcheon, G. (Ed.). (1982). Curriculum theory [Special theme issue]. *Theory Into Practice, 21*(1).

National Council for the Accreditation of Teacher Education. (1992). *Standards, procedures and policies for the accreditation of professional education units*. Washington, DC: Author.

Nieto, S. (1992). *Affirming diversity*. New York: Longman.

Patton, M. Q. (1990). *Qualitative evaluation and research methods*. Newbury Park, CA: Sage.

Pratt, D. (1994). *Curriculum planning: A handbook for professionals*. Fort Worth, TX: Harcourt Brace.

Reed, D. F. (1993). Multicultural education for preservice students. *Action in Teacher Education, 15*(3), 27-34.

Reiff, J. C., & Cannella, G. S. (1992, February). *Preparing teachers for cultural diversity: Rhetoric or reality*. Paper presented at the annual meeting of the Association of Teacher Educators, Orlando, FL.

Schon, D. A. (1983). *The reflective practitioner: How professionals think in action*. New York: Basic Books.

Schon, D. A. (1987). *Educating the reflective practitioner: Toward a new design for teaching and learning in the professions*. San Francisco: Jossey-Bass.

Schwab, J. J. (1969). The practical: A language for curriculum. *School Review, 78*, 1-23.

Schwab, J. J. (1971). The practical 2: Arts of eclectic. *School Review, 78*, 493-542.

Schwab, J. J. (1973). The practical 3: Translation into curriculum. *School Review, 81*, 501-522.

Schwab, J. J. (1983). The practical 4: Something for curriculum professors to do. *Curriculum Inquiry, 13*(3), 239-265.

Sleeter, C. (1993, April). *This curriculum is multicultural . . . isn't it?* Paper presented at the annual meeting of the Educational Research Association, Atlanta, GA.

Strauss, A. L. (1987). *Qualitative analysis for social scientists*. Cambridge: Cambridge University Press.

Tellez, K., & Hlebowitsh, P. S. (1993). Being there: Social service and teacher education at the University of Houston. *Innovative Higher Education, 18*(1), 87-94.

Tierney, W. G. (1990). Cultural politics and the curriculum in postsecondary education. In C. F. Conrad & J. G. Haworth (Eds.), *Curriculum in transition: Perspectives on the undergraduate experience* (pp. 39-54). Needham Heights, MA: Ginn.

Zeichner, K. M. (1993). *Educating teachers for cultural diversity.* East Lansing: Michigan State University, National Center for Research for Teacher Learning.

CURRICULUM:
REFLECTIONS AND IMPLICATIONS

Sandra J. Odell

In the introduction to Division III, I described curriculum development as a complex process and identified elements of curriculum building that, considered with other commonplaces of education, illustrate that complexity. Specifically, I provided the rationale for building a conceptual framework as a first step in teacher education program development. I described subject matter knowledge as one commonplace of education and explained its relationship to curricular knowledge and pedagogical knowledge domains. Furthermore, the influence of beliefs and dispositions on learning to teach was discussed, with particular emphasis on the difficulty of changing the long-lived beliefs and dispositions of preservice students. Last, I discussed the role of context on the teaching and learning process. With this framework in mind, I next examine the three chapters in the division.

Developing a Constructivist
Teacher Education Program

In Chapter 7, Guyton, Rainer, and Wright described their participation in the development of a master's degree program in early childhood education using strategies of observation, interviewing, survey administration, and document analysis for data collection. The chapter is basically a description of the process of program development and a summary of their findings over three and a half years rather than a detailed presentation and analysis of the data. The authors present an excellent example of developing a conceptual framework for a teacher education program to which importance was given in the overview section of Division III.

Guyton, Rainer, and Wright described how faculty attended policy development meetings and retreats over the course of three months where the faculty studied the literature on a constructivist approach to learning and developed shared understandings about constructivism, including its history, philosophical foundations, and applications. The following two academic years were spent in a program development phase defining constructivism-in-action by trying it out in the university culture. Guyton, Rainer, and Wright further described how the faculty discovered that the constructivist strategies were working. Although progress was described as nonlinear during these two years, overall movement forward in the program development phase occurred. Finally during a yearlong program design phase, faculty designed course content and staffing procedures, recruited and admitted students, and determined faculty teaching loads and grading procedures.

Consistent with the established theme of curriculum complexity, Guyton, Rainer, and Wright affirm that "program development in teacher education is a complex process" (p. 150, this volume) based on their experience as participant observers. Particular elements that contributed to the complexity for faculty who participated in building the program included the time-consuming nature of the effort, the ambiguity that existed as part of the process, and the attempt to stay true to constructivism despite the tug to remain traditional in their approach. Developing the underlying conceptual framework and building the program took three and a half years, a considerable amount of time for any faculty to commit. A constructivist approach, by its very nature, relies on contextual factors, participant involvement and interaction, and higher-order thinking events that are nonlinear and often unpredictable. This requires, as a result, a higher tolerance for ambiguity than many faculty easily accept. Because old habits are difficult to break, the tug toward past and comfortable thinking and practices had to be overcome.

The influence of context is another factor of complexity identified by Guyton, Rainer, and Wright. In particular, they described the university context as one where program development was encouraged and where leadership was strong. The faculty group was described as being generally open-minded, trusting, and collaborative and were provided resources and time for program development. Faculty felt ownership for the program and openly collaborated with school-based teachers. These contextual conditions clearly seemed to support change.

Subject Perspectives of
Novice English Teachers

Spalding's Chapter 8 focused on the subject of English as a "whole" and was an investigation of the interaction of teacher beliefs, context, and teaching actions. In particular, Spalding studied three middle school teachers, all of whom were graduates of the same alternative certification program, and described their beliefs and the interaction of their school contexts as a result of observations, interviews, and immersion in the field settings.

Spalding's interpretive study explored how three teachers thought about the subject of English and how they acted on their beliefs about teaching English in the contexts of their individual schools. In the first case, Jack—who was a thoughtful, scholarly, dedicated teacher with high standards and expectations for students—felt overwhelmed by the complexity of teaching English. Although the context for teaching was a positive and supportive one from his point of view, responsibilities for teaching the subject matter were so extensive that he used the metaphor of "swallowing an elephant" for the teaching of English. Putting subject matter content knowledge and pedagogical content knowledge (Shulman, 1986) to work was overwhelming for Jack. Moreover, as described in the overview section, pedagogical content knowledge requires understanding the structure of the subject and how to demonstrate and explain the content so that others can understand it (Shulman, 1986). This blend of understanding and practice is complex for experts, let alone for beginning teachers who have limited teaching experience on which to draw.

Celia was described as very energetic and excited about the subject of English and about teaching. The context in which she worked was in a blue-collar neighborhood, which she saw as rather provincial, and she attributed students' struggles to poor teaching in the schools. Initially she found herself playing by the rules and exclusively teaching the subject matter of English, which she enjoyed. In her third year of teaching, however, she developed a comprehensive, "whole-child focus" and relinquished her earlier focus on subject matter. Spalding saw this refocusing as a compromise in Celia's prior belief about the centrality of subject matter. Consistent with earlier references regarding the importance of context, Spalding credited context variables for the adjustment in Celia's perceptions about the relative importance of subject matter in her teaching.

Finally, the third case was a study of Claire, who saw English subject matter as secondary to nurturing students and viewed teaching as a gentle guide through content. The context was a difficult one for her during her first year of teaching, however. Claire found being a "teaching mom" required spending an enormous amount of time and energy. Like other references to the sink-or-swim nature of induction to teaching (Huling-Austin, 1990; Odell, 1990), Claire faced three different preparations, had a teaching load of 160 students, and struggled trying to use the district-required texts on top of the "reality shock" that occurs during the first year of teaching (Veenman, 1984). Claire's subsequent three years of teaching were more manageable as a result of having set limits on the time and emotional investment in teaching.

In all three cases, Spalding found the perspectives of the subjects to be coherent and consistent across time. Moreover, all three individuals seemed to enter teacher education with their subject matter perspectives in place. There were some discrepancies between expressed beliefs and teaching practices, however. Discrepancies occurred when the context of teaching did not support particular practices. Moreover, Spalding found that difficulties in teaching conditions can constrain teachers from implementing instructional practices suggested to them in teacher education programs.

A key finding in Spalding's chapter is the interaction between beliefs about teaching and context. Spalding's study generally supports the notion that beliefs about teaching are difficult to change. Contextual variables in Celia's case, however, seemed to contribute significantly to a change of perspective about teaching. Rather than focusing exclusively on subject matter, Celia changed her perspective to one of focusing on the whole child.

Multicultural Education
Curriculum Struggles in Teacher Education

As emphasized in the overview section to Division III, the context of America's schools has changed considerably during the past 15 years in that poor students, children of color, and children with minority language backgrounds are found in increasing numbers in our schools. Burga Jung argues in Chapter 9 that multicultural education has had little effect on teaching practice in schools and on teacher education curricula and practice in universities.

Using participant observation, conversation, and artifacts for data, Jung described how monocultural preservice students attempted to develop multicultural awareness, knowledge, and skills. Jung exposed students to ideas by using interventions such as readings, speakers, and provocative videotapes. Although Jung did not specifically present data from the research, she did present summary information from the study. Consistent with the literature presented on the difficulty of changing beliefs and dispositions of preservice students, Jung found students' prior beliefs to be obstacles to developing understandings of multicultural education. Jung described the enthusiasm with which students responded to the various interventions she provided but concluded, again consistent with the literature, that long-held beliefs are not likely to change as a result of experiences in one course or even a series of courses (McDiarmid, 1992; McDiarmid & Price, 1993). Given Richardson's (1996) review of the role of attitudes and beliefs in learning to teach and Haberman's (1993, 1995) efforts to identify differential selection factors, resources may be better spent in the recruitment and selection of candidates for teaching who already hold particular beliefs rather than trying to change beliefs that are inconsistent with those needed to teach productively in diverse contexts.

Implications for
Teacher Education

The interactions of curricular elements are complex, as argued in the overview section of this Division and as evidenced by the findings presented in the three chapters. Although this complexity suggests that there are no magic bullets or easy solutions for understanding the interactions of curricular commonplaces or for implementing foolproof teacher education programs, the following guidelines seem to be implied by the foregoing:

- Well-researched, well-articulated conceptual frameworks should be developed in teacher education programs.

- Teacher education programs should incorporate strong subject matter emphases.

- The development of pedagogical content knowledge and curricular content knowledge should become a more central teacher-education program focus.

- Experiences for students in teacher education programs should include opportunities to make overt and analyze personal beliefs and dispositions about teaching, learning, and schooling.

- Consideration should be given to examining the beliefs and dispositions of teacher education candidates and admitting those students who match best the characteristics of teachers that programs are intending to prepare.

- Teacher education programs should include the study of contextual variables that influence teaching and learning.

- Opportunities should be created for teacher education candidates to experience and analyze firsthand the interactions of content, learner, teacher, and social milieu.

References

Haberman, M. (1993). Contexts: Implications and reflections. In M. J. O'Hair & S. J. Odell (Eds.), *Diversity and teaching* (pp. 84-89). Fort Worth, TX: Harcourt Brace Jovanovich.

Haberman, M. (1995). *STAR teachers of children in poverty.* West Lafayette, IN: Kappa Delta Pi.

Huling-Austin, L. (1990). Teacher induction programs and internships. In W. R. Houston, M. Haberman, & J. Sikula (Eds.), *Handbook of research on teacher education* (pp. 535-548). New York: Macmillan

McDiarmid, G. W. (1992). What to do about differences? A study of multicultural education for teacher trainees in the Los Angeles Unified School District. *Journal of Teacher Education, 43*(2), 83-93.

McDiarmid, G. W., & Price, J. (1993). Preparing teachers for diversity: A study of student teachers in a multicultural program. In M. J. O'Hair & S. J. Odell (Eds.), *Diversity and teaching* (pp. 31-57). Fort Worth, TX: Harcourt Brace Jovanovich.

Odell, S. J. (1990). *Mentor teacher programs.* Washington, DC: National Education Association.

Richardson, V. (1996). The role of attitudes and beliefs in learning to teach. In J. Sikula, T. J. Buttery, & E. Guyton (Eds.), *Handbook of research on teacher education* (pp. 102-119). New York: Macmillan.

Shulman, L. (1986). Those who understand: Knowledge growth in teaching. *Educational Researcher, 15*(2), 4-14.

Veenman, S. (1984). Perceived problems of beginning teachers. *Review of Educational Research, 54*(2), 143-178.

DIVISION IV

Examining Differences in the Education of Our Nation's Teachers

COMMUNICATION: OVERVIEW AND FRAMEWORK

Robert E. Floden

Robert E. Floden is Co-Director of the National Center for Research on Teacher Learning and Professor of Teacher Education and Educational Psychology at Michigan State University. Active in the design and conduct of teacher education programs, he has written extensively on teaching and teacher education. He is currently studying connections between professional development and education reform.

Teaching is a social activity, yet typically teachers are prepared to teach by themselves. Teacher education does attend to the social interactions between teacher and student, through course work and experiences about classroom management and pedagogy. Recently, this part of teacher preparation has been extended to address cooperative learning.

Working with students is not, however, the only way teaching is social. Teachers also encounter many adults connected to schooling—parents, other teachers, teacher educators. Teacher preparation seldom helps teachers learn how to work productively with these groups.

Neglect of this social dimension reflects a tradition that casts teaching as an isolated activity. Working in individual classrooms in egg-carton buildings, teachers have been expected to shut their doors and make sure that their students did nothing to bother other classes. Talk in the teachers' lounge studiously avoided any mention of teaching. Teachers kept parents at a distance, reporting on student progress and making requests for assistance with homework or with extracurricular activities but never leaving an opening for parental involvement that would intrude on teachers' autonomy. Teacher educators were criticized for their distance from practice and encountered only in mandated staff development activities used for salary increments.

Times have changed. Accumulated research has demonstrated the important roles that families play in education. Moreover, sustained educational improvement is clearly tied to informed community support. Citing studies showing the benefits of workplace collaboration in several industries, educators have begun exploring collegial joint work. School-based decision making, team teaching, and professional community are promoted for their promise to enhance student learning. Closer connections between K-12 teachers and their counterparts in higher education offer potential benefits to all involved, helping teachers continue to learn, enabling school reform, and revitalizing schools of education.

Teachers must work, not only with their young charges but also with adults. Some adult collaborators are also educators; some support education in other ways. Teachers and teachers-to-be must learn how to collaborate, something for which their own years as students offer little guidance. Teacher educators, recognizing that they must add course work addressed to this need, have begun to allot curricular space, either as topics within existing courses or as separate courses. What should be offered in this space is, however, a matter deserving careful deliberation. Research on teacher-parent relations usually documents difficulties, rather than offering solutions. Research on professional community has more to say about how those who have it benefit than about how it can be created. The literature on school-university collaboration describes a few efforts that are off to a good start but also discusses many reasons to expect eventual failure.

The three chapters in this section add to our understanding of the relationships between teachers and other adults. The authors suggest that these relationships can be improved by helping teachers and their collaborators better understand each other. The authors also reveal—sometimes explicitly, sometimes indirectly—that important issues of purpose must be engaged to decide what should be done to prepare teachers for the several collaborative arenas.

In their studies of Asian American teachers, Goodwin, Genishi, Asher, and Woo found that non-Asian parents often held stereotyped views of Asian Americans, assuming, for example, that they would not be good teachers of English. If teachers learned how to educate parents about the varieties of Asian American culture, perhaps the degree of stereotyping would decrease. Alternative changes in teacher preparation might, however, also be defended. Because stereotyping seems prevalent and immutable, for example, we might rather train teachers in the political skills needed to thrive despite parental stereotyping. Or perhaps preparation should give more attention to working with parents from different minority groups, where there appears to be some pan-minority identification but where parent activism can be important in securing adequate resources for the students. Goodwin and her colleagues highlight areas of teacher-parent interaction that are particularly salient for Asian American teachers. Deliberation is needed to develop promising approaches to addressing the problems they have uncovered. (Note that relations with parents is only one of several issues Goodwin and her colleagues address.)

In an analysis connecting instructional planning and thinking patterns, Manning and her students compare collaborative planning with individual planning. To their surprise, they find more off-task and unhelpful thinking occurring in the collaborative setting. Moreover, they find that the expected association between level of thinking and quality of planning is present for individual planning but not for collaborative planning. Something about having to collaborate with other teacher candidates produces unwanted patterns of thought and disconnects the quality of individual thought from the quality of the group's plan. What does this suggest for teacher education? Manning, Glasner, and Aeby indicate that the unfamiliarity of having to work together yields unhelpful thinking. If so, perhaps more practice in working together, with attention to the level of individual thought, is indicated. Another possibility is that the ostensibly undesirable levels of thought play some productive role in the collaborative process, either in allowing for more widely divergent (hence, apparently "off-task") thought or in developing group capacities for criticism. Manning et al.'s investigation draws attention to the unexpected consequences of having teacher candidates practice collaboration. The response for teacher education requires deliberation on what thinking processes are indeed most desirable and how those processes might be fostered.

In her account of four school-university collaborations, Sandholtz describes factors that promote success and challenges that impede it. Although her chapter often addresses institutional, rather than individual, issues, many of her points give clues about aspects of teacher knowledge that would support institutional collaboration. One challenge to collaboration, for example, is that participants did not get rewards from collaboration that were sufficient to sustain extended engagement. On the one side, this may signal the need for a change in the reward structure. On the other side, it may arise because teachers see their primary rewards in short-term success of their current pupils, rather than in long-term improvements in their instruction. Just as corporate executives are taken to task for seeking to maximize short-term profits, teachers might be criticized for attaching too little value to long-term improvements in their schools. Consideration of this issue might begin in teacher preparation, though it is likely to become more salient once teachers experience their own reactions to their occupation. Sandholtz identifies the problem; as with the other aspects of collaboration, careful deliberation will be needed to develop changes in teacher preparation with some promise for addressing the issue.

By getting below the surface of teacher education, these chapters reveal problematic situations that our current teacher education practices do not address, or at least do not address successfully. Our curricula do not speak to the specific experience of Asian American teachers and the difficulties these teachers perceive. Although lesson planning is treated in our programs, our current approaches may fail to consider differences in how teachers think through a plan or differences between individual and collaborative planning. The success of school-university joint teacher education endeavors remains variable, hampered by structural and institutional factors.

The chapters offer those of us working to enhance teachers' learning much to consider. They cannot give us solutions to our perennial problems and dilemmas, but these chapters can help us move our discussions from exchanges of opinions and hunches to arguments supported by evidence about what our students are actually experiencing and learning.

10 Voices From the Margins

Asian American Teachers' Experiences in the Profession

A. Lin Goodwin

Celia Genishi

Nina Asher

Kimberley A. Woo

A. Lin Goodwin is Associate Professor of Education and Codirector of the Preservice Program in Childhood Education in the Department of Curriculum and Teaching, Teachers College, Columbia University. Her research and writing focus on multicultural teacher education, educational equity, transformative teaching, teacher beliefs, and the educational experiences of Asian Americans. Recent publications include "Teaching and Teacher Education" in the first *Asian American Almanac*, "Making the Transition from Self to Other: What Do Preservice Teachers Really Think About Multicultural Education?" in the *Journal of Teacher Education*, and "Racial Identity and Education" in AERA's *Review of Research in Education*. She is currently editing a book titled *Assessment for Equity and Inclusion: Embracing All Our Children* for release in 1997. Dr. Goodwin also serves as a consultant and staff developer to a wide variety of organizations, including school districts, philanthropic foundations, higher education institutions and professional educational organizations around issues of diversity, educational equity, and multicultural curriculum development.

Celia Genishi is Professor of Education in the Program in Early Childhood Education and Chairperson of the Department of Curriculum and Teaching at Teachers College, Columbia University. She is a former secondary Spanish and preschool teacher and teaches courses related to early childhood education and qualitative research methods. Previously she was on the faculty at the University of Texas at Austin and Ohio State University. She is coauthor (with Anne Haas Dyson) of *Language Assessment in the Early Years*; coauthor (with Millie Almy) of *Ways of Studying Children*; editor of *Ways of Assessing Children and Curriculum*; and coeditor (with Anne Haas Dyson) of *The Need for Story: Cultural Diversity in Classroom and Community*. She is also the author of many articles about children's language, observation, and assessment. Her research interests include collaborative research on alternative assessment, childhood bilingualism, and language use in classrooms.

Nina Asher is a doctoral student in the Department of Curriculum and Teaching, Teachers College, Columbia University. She is currently working on her dissertation, "School-Related Issues Confronting South Asian American High School Students in New York City High Schools," which focuses on the students' academic and career goals and the evolution of their identities as they attempt to find a balance between the worlds of home and school. Her research and writing interests include issues of representation and identity among minority populations in curriculum and education, multiculturalism, and diversity and the education of Asian Americans. Her writings include *Making Multiculturalism Meaningful: South Asian American High School Students—A Case in Point* (paper presented at the Cultural Studies Symposium, Kansas State University) and a chapter-in-progress on South Asian identities and the hybrid music of the South Asian diaspora.

Kimberley A. Woo is a doctoral student in social studies in the Department of Languages, Literature, and Social Studies at Teachers College, Columbia University. She also serves as a program assistant, university supervisor, and instructor in the

Teaching of Social Studies Program within the department and works closely with preservice high school teachers. Her research interests include Asian American and ethnic studies, teacher education, and the relationship between theory and practice. In addition to her research on Asian American teachers, she and a colleague recently received a Teacher College Dean's Grant to help support an investigation of social studies methods—Bridges: Reflections on the Social Studies Classroom.

ABSTRACT

This chapter presents the findings of a two-part investigation of preservice and inservice Asian American teachers. The study examined and analyzed the perspectives of Asian American educators regarding the following:

- Their motives for entering the profession
- Their assessment of teacher education curricula
- Their interactions with other preservice teachers, school colleagues, parents, and children

The study broadens current conversations around minority teacher shortages to include Asian Americans who are often excluded from recruitment and retention efforts. Asian American teachers are visibly absent from the nation's classrooms and there need and deserve the attention of teacher education programs, schools, and policymakers, particularly given dramatic increases in the Asian school-age population.

Changing demographics are evident at all grade levels in the nation's schools as American society grows increasingly multiracial (American Council on Education and the Education Commission of the States, 1988). A familiar estimation is that by the year 2020, 40% of schoolchildren will be non-White (Pallas, Natriello, & McDill, 1989). This contrasts with a predominantly White population of teachers, teacher educators, and administrators (American Association of Colleges for Teacher Education [AACTE], 1990a; Dilworth, 1990; Goodwin, 1991; Research About Teacher Education Project, 1990). In fact, teachers of color constitute only about 10% of the teaching force. Clearly, the increasing diversity of today's classrooms has brought the issue of minority teacher recruitment and retention to the foreground of teacher preparation policy and practice.

Despite the worrisome dearth of teachers of color, conversations about attracting "minorities" to teaching often bypass Asian Americans, ignoring demographic trends among this group. Asians have been the fastest-growing racial group in the United States during the last decade (O'Hare & Felt, 1991). Between 1980 and 1990, the Asian population in the United States doubled to constitute 3% of the total population (U.S. Bureau of Census, 1993). Estimates indicate that by 2010, the Asian community will increase 150% and constitute 6% of the country's population (Edmonston & Passel, 1992). This growing population has generated a rapidly rising school-age cohort even while the number of Asian American and Pacific Islander elementary and secondary public teachers hovers at around 1% of the teaching force (AACTE, 1994; see also Goodwin, 1995).

Although the educational achievements of the Asian population are often emphasized, there is great diversity within this population. For instance, the immigration of large numbers of Southeast Asians is challenging stereotypical conceptions of Asian populations as public school systems struggle to accommodate to their needs. The nature of their difficulties includes undereducation, poverty, linguistic isolation, illiteracy, and nonschool completion (Rong & Grant, 1992; Waggoner, 1991). Clearly, the absence of initiatives designed to draw Asian Americans into the field of education is shortsighted and troubling, given this current context.

This chapter presents the findings of an investigation of Asian American teachers, both those entering the field and those who are currently teaching. The study aimed to unearth and analyze the perspectives of Asian American educators regarding

- Their motives for entering the profession
- Their assessment of teacher education curricula
- Their interactions with other preservice teachers, school colleagues, parents, and children

The significance of the study lies in its broadened perspective vis-à-vis the minority teacher shortage. We know very little about why people of color choose to teach and how they experience the profession. The little that we do know is likely to focus on African American and Latino participants. Asian Americans should be seen as a viable candidate pool and deserve the attention of teacher educators and schools for hiring and recruitment.

Ignoring this potentially rich resource, given dramatic increases in the Asian school-age population, is unwise in a pluralistic society.

The Study: Phase 1

The first phase of this qualitative study, completed in 1994, involved a group of 21[1] Asian Americans and is summarized briefly here (see Goodwin & Genishi, 1994). Everyone in the group was a citizen or permanent resident; thus, all the participants perceived themselves as Americans and were intending to participate in American education. Ethnically, the sample represented five groups—nine Chinese, six Koreans, three Filipina, two Japanese, and one South Asian (East Indian). Except for two Chinese American males, the sample was female and consisted of 12 newly certified teachers (less than 2 years experience), one experienced teacher (more than 5 years experience) and eight preservice teacher education students. Their age range was from 22 to 33, with a mean age of 24.9 years. Nearly all sound "American," that is, their speech does not reflect a "foreign accent."

Data for Phase 1 of the study were collected through a combination structured and open-ended questionnaire (see Appendix A). The data were tallied and categorized in an effort to learn about (a) primary motivators for entering teaching, (b) perceptions of the minority teacher shortage, (c) how respondents were perceived in and experienced their teacher education programs, and (d) recommendations for teacher education programs in a diverse society. Findings are presented according to those four general topics, with the first two, motivations and the teacher shortage, combined.

Motivations for Teaching and the Teacher Shortage

Respondents[2] were presented with seven reasons indicated by the literature as related to decisions to enter teaching (Goodwin, 1988; Lortie, 1975) and asked to rank order as many of the seven as they chose. The following were ranked highest: making a difference or engaging in meaningful work—82%; love for children/interactions with young people—56%. The study also sought to ascertain the barriers that can keep Asian Americans away from teaching. Given six choices, the following were selected as the most problematic: perception of teaching as not intellectual/challenging—64%; teachers' salaries and teaching as low status work—50%.

Regarding the minority teacher shortage, 19 (90%) of the respondents agreed that "there is a growing number of minority students and not enough minority teachers." Only one student spoke directly to the Asian American teacher shortage, however. "There is definitely a shortage of Asian teachers who are 'advocates' for Asian children." The rest of the respondents spoke more generally of the need for more diversity in the profession.

When respondents were asked if the publicity or programs surrounding the minority teacher shortage included them, only 3 students responded affirmatively, 12 subjects said no, 2 were ambivalent, and 4 left the question blank. Half the students who felt that the minority teacher shortage did not apply to them believed recruitment efforts focused on other racial groups, for example, African American or Latino.

Finally, 16 of 21 students offered a wide range of suggestions for recruiting Asian American teachers. The most frequently mentioned recommendation had to do with financial support through better salaries, tuition benefits and scholarships, teaching fellowships or internships, and forgivable loans. Interestingly, students seemed most interested in financial assistance *before* service. Students also emphasized gaining information about the teaching profession. Moreover, students highlighted the need for emotional support, again especially in the *preservice* phase, through the use of mentors, support groups for Asian American teachers, Asian American role models (e.g., faculty), and a buddy system with other minority students.

School and Curricula: Perceptions and Experiences

Four questions related to the respondents' school or classroom experiences, either in the public schools or in their university preservice program. The respondents said that faculty in their teacher education program perceived them the most favorably of the five groups with whom they interacted. Twelve of the respondents said the faculty perceived them favorably or like everyone else, that is, they didn't feel the perception was discriminatory. Two said there were negative perceptions, three said they were perceived as "quiet," and two said they were perceived as "Asian." Peers appeared to view them like everyone else, with a few exceptions. The perceptions of the college supervisor, cooperating teacher, and children were more mixed, with most perceptions being positive or the same as everyone else.

Another question addressed whether being Asian resulted in any significant experiences with parents, administrators, fellow teachers, student teachers, and children. Eleven of the respondents said the influence of their ethnicity was positive; however, 8 of the 11 specified that these positive experiences were related to other Asians in the school or community. For example, Asian children or parents seemed more comfortable with them or other Asian teachers sought them out. Nine of the respondents felt that being Asian American resulted in negative experiences, particularly with parents or administrators who "question the cultural influence [an Asian] could bring into the classroom." Four felt their race seemed irrelevant.

Respondents were next asked to assess their preservice curriculum and its relevance to their own experiences and needs. There was no striking pattern of response, although almost half (10) indicated the curriculum was "fine" and "did try to address a variety of backgrounds and experiences." One cited the benefit of having Asian American professors in the program, and another mentioned the relevance of a children's literature course that included books about Asian American experiences. The overall sentiment, however, was that the curriculum was general and, thus, did not address the Asian American experience directly.

The tenth question related to the curriculum of the school in which the respondents teach: Is the curriculum of the school where you teach relevant and responsive to Asian American children? Eleven said that the curriculum was not, stating in two cases that there were no Asian American children in their classes. Nine said that the curriculum was relevant and responsive; most of these nine were in schools with a notable Asian population or referred to curricula they themselves developed about their own heritage. Two had no response.

Recommendations for Change

A final question focused on recommendations for change, "If you were to recommend changes that would result in teacher preparation programs being more relevant and responsive to Asians and Asian Americans, what would these be?" Responses were prospective and overlapped with earlier statements regarding curriculum and support. Nine respondents specified the need for a greater Asian or Asian American focus. Of these nine, six cited Asian and Asian American content in teacher preparation courses;

three recommended incorporating Asian American teachers into the College faculty and in the field. Four respondents suggested support groups, primarily for Asian American preservice teachers but not always excluding others. Five responses were more general, recommending courses about *multicultural* issues, including the history, language, and learning styles of many groups of learners.

Methodology: Phase 2

The second phase of the study consisted of follow-up interviews (see Appendix B) that were conducted with a subsample of 12 respondents: 11 women and 1 man (four Chinese, three Korean, two Filipina, one East Indian, one Japanese, and one biracial: Japanese/Irish). The interviews were conducted primarily on the phone (7 of 12) and ranged in length from one to two hours. Six respondents were teaching in the New York City area, four in California, one in Connecticut, and one in Virginia. At the time of the interviews, all 12 were teaching (6 in their first year, 5 in their second, and 1 in her third). Two were teaching prekindergarten, nine were teaching elementary, and one was teaching middle school. Eight were in public schools; four were in private schools. Eight schools were in urban settings; four were suburban.

Recurring themes and patterns emerging from analysis of Phase 1 data became the conceptual foundation for the follow-up interview questions and for the analysis of Phase 2 responses as well. Data were analyzed to address the following research questions in greater depth than was possible in Phase 1:

1. How would Asian American teachers characterize their experiences as new teachers or as teachers-to-be?
2. In what ways do the respondents feel they were perceived by faculty in the teacher education program, other preservice students, cooperating and supervising teachers, and children in the field-placement classrooms?
3. What recommendations would Asian Americans make for teacher education programs in a racially and culturally diverse society?

Teachers' responses to these three questions are organized according to themes. We identify a topic such as *Happy to Be Teaching* as a theme when at least three teachers mentioned it. We also present quotations from some of the teachers to show the uniqueness of each one's perspective on teaching and the range of those perspectives.

Speaking Out:
Experiencing Teaching

We identified clusters of themes that could be described as negative or positive in teachers' interview responses. For example, *Thinking of an Alternative to Teaching* and *Overwhelmed or Burned Out* were themes that occurred in the same teachers' responses. Similarly, *Feels Competence Doubted*, *Experiences or Observes Racism*, *Feels Alone or Isolated*, and *Feels Invisible or Voiceless* showed some overlap among respondents (i.e., if a respondent felt her competence was doubted, she may also have felt alone or isolated).

Of these two clusters, the second (*Feels Competence Doubted*, etc.) appeared to be more closely related to the teachers' Asian American identity. Thus, although Magdalena[3] was in a small private school where she felt engaged with her second graders, she thought her competence was doubted initially. In her words,

> Biases are very subtle. Especially when you are working with a population that is open-minded but not used to having an Asian American teach their kids. Once they see that I am qualified and can do the job, they get used to me and their cold initial reaction—"let's wait and see" attitude—leaves. I don't know if I got this response because I am new and young? Because of cultural differences? Could be many things going on at once.

Betty also sensed the doubting of her abilities, but she viewed them within the context of teaching English as a second language to sixth graders in inner-city Los Angeles. Her perception was that if you were Asian or Asian American, you were not typically allowed to teach English because you were assumed not to know the language well enough. This respondent also heard a racist comment from a colleague who stated emphatically that if a situation like World War II arose, the bomb should definitely be dropped again on Hiroshima. Betty was as concerned with the speaker's insensitivity as she was with the effect of statements like this on children at the school. She went on to say that the facts of Asian

American history tend to be invisible in many curricula, thus adding to the potential for racism and ignorance.

Like many teachers, new or experienced, a number in our study commented on how they felt isolated and unsupported in a variety of ways. As Asian Americans, several wished there were support networks of teachers of color, people who might have experiences and issues similar to their own. A longing for contact with people of like interests was also expressed as invisibility. Shoba put it this way:

> I have not made many contacts [with people], but maybe I have just gotten used to being invisible . . . maybe subconsciously I am searching for people I can connect with and because I don't see them I just kind of give up.

Others spoke not of invisibility but of being voiceless. As Seung said, "It [the Asian American voice] doesn't make a difference." According to Kate, "I think teachers need to be more vocal and involved. They tend to be quiet in their voices, like they're observing and don't want to bump the scale."

On the other hand, teachers did describe positive feelings and experiences. Several were *Happy to Be Teaching* (as opposed to "not unhappy"), believed that they had the power to *Initiate Curriculum Changes*, *Affected Students Positively*, and were *Treated the Same* as everyone else (not discriminated against). Those who were happy to be teaching were not necessarily *perfectly* happy. For example, Wanda said she would prefer a public school setting to day care but that she still loved working with children. Heather seemed unable to think of anything she would prefer to teaching: "I think [I chose] teaching over anything else because it's knocking a lot of stereotypes that I hate." Teaching gave her a powerful voice, an opportunity to speak out on behalf of the need for many voices, an opportunity to be a role model, and an opportunity to change the status quo.

Changes they could make in the curriculum itself were closely connected with being Asian American. A number of teachers created a link between their backgrounds and the curriculum. Kate said,

> I always do this big unit on China. I can pull on a lot of resources and bring those ideas into my class. Like I can bring in the experiences of what my father and mother do.

Shoba, after a trip to her native country, brought many materials related to India to her class. Thus, the teachers themselves were the primary sources for multicultural themes in their curricula.

Being a *Role Model* was another positive theme for many of the teachers. According to Seung,

> In multiethnic communities, it is critical that students have role models. Also, Asians—students and parents—find it easier to relate to me. So, role models are important. They can realize that they too can pursue teaching. When I was in elementary school, I never thought of myself as a teacher. So, my being a teacher provides a seed. Perhaps the seed can grow into a flower.

Perceptions of Asian American Teachers: The Act of Silencing

We found some overlap between Asian American teachers' experiences in the profession and the ways in which they feel they are implicitly perceived. Teachers reported that they seem to be categorized in four ways: *incapable, approachable,* as *other,* and as *universal oriental.*

The Asian American teachers in our sample spoke often of experiencing parents' (and others') lack of confidence in their capabilities as teachers, which resulted in their feeling the need to "prove themselves." About half the sample indicated that they felt as though parents questioned whether or not they were good enough. Interestingly, respondents did not seem to feel that children exhibited this perception. These perceptions seemed to come almost solely from White parents, particularly those from middle- to upper-middle-class families. One teacher spoke of an administrator's perceptions, and another spoke of comments made by another teacher about another Asian American teacher at her school. These perceptions were sometimes linked to language—Asian Americans are perceived as not speaking English well enough to teach.

> One teacher said to me, "The first-grade (bilingual) teacher is not that good. She doesn't speak English that well. I don't know why she was hired."

Even though this remark was not directed at her, Betty felt silenced; "I don't know how to deal with such remarks or how I feel about them." Seung states,

It is White parents, upper-middle-class community. But it frustrates me. Why do we have to prove ourselves? . . . Parents think, "She's Asian American, and so she's not good enough to teach our kids."

Nan has "the parents of my kids telling me what to do in my classroom."

Although it is hard to say whether this lack of confidence by parents stems from these teachers being Asian American or being new teachers, what is quite clear is that respondents feel this perception quite deeply. Indeed, teachers across the sample expressed this perception, regardless of whether they were in their first or, in the case of Seung, in her third year of successful teaching.

On the other hand, parents of color, particularly Asian American parents, seem to perceive these Asian American teachers as more capable and certainly approachable. The majority of the sample spoke of how their presence as Asian American teachers enabled parents of color to feel more connected to schools. Again, language as well as race was a critical factor. According to Susie, "My parents who are Spanish-speaking love the fact that I can speak Spanish." On the other hand, as an Asian American teacher, she finds too that "Asian American parents are very receptive . . . there is this cultural bond . . . they get this look on their face that—this is great."

Asian parents seemed to express a greater comfort with the Asian American teachers in this sample *regardless* of language (i.e., whether the teacher spoke the same dialect or spoke the same language at all), whereas Latino parents relate to these Asian American teachers *through* language. Susie, however, feels torn between two groups, Filipino and Mexican:

One student . . . was excited that I was Filipino and that I spoke Tagalog because he could speak with me . . . but I think he was upset because I spoke more Spanish than I spoke Tagalog, mostly because my Spanish speakers needed much more help than he did. Although I have one student who hates the fact that I speak Spanish . . . she just doesn't think that anyone else other than Mexicans should speak Spanish.

Interestingly, 6 of the 12 interviewees speak Spanish (some were bilingual only in Spanish and English) and one is learning to speak Spanish. Perhaps their membership in minority groups has sensitized them to the role of language as a barrier to entering mainstream society and as a key to unlocking children's potential. Says Wanda,

> To be a whole teacher, you need to be able to communicate with parents; to work with a child as a whole, it helps to be able to communicate fully with them.

The theme of *otherness* traversed the interviews. Otherness was expressed through a variety of perceptions and actions that seemed to heighten respondents' feelings of invisibility, a theme that also characterized the data from Phase 1. Otherness was expressed in name-calling and racist comments, such as the comment shared earlier about the dropping of the bomb on Hiroshima made by a teacher in Betty's presence. Seung remembers when she was

> . . . student teaching, I would come home in tears. The kids would make comments . . . "She's a chink" and things like that.

Hattie had to deal with "a lot of . . . racial name-calling" and a child "pulling his eyes and stuff like that," and Betty found that "kids mimic Asian languages by making weird sounds. I have always found that offensive." Otherness was also embedded in respondents' lack of connection with other student teachers and teachers. Seung reflected on her teacher preparation and said,

> All the White people were together and all the Asian people were together and so on. It wasn't intentional; it just ended up being that way. It was an identity issue. [I needed] someone who understood my past experiences. Others who were there did not seem to value/validate/accept my Korean heritage . . . not just validate it but value it.

Shoba echoes this feeling of isolation and difference:

> There are other teachers and they are interesting people, but they don't have the same issues (as Asian Americans) that they came to teaching with.

Otherness was apparent in the caricatures and exotic images of Asian Americans that were held up to respondents by their students and their colleagues. Betty was angered by the limited knowledge of Asian Americans her students seemed to have: "Their knowledge is limited to what's on TV—for instance, China for them might mean kung fu or Connie Chung."

Finally, Otherness is contained in stereotypical images of Asian Americans that characterize Asian Americans as quiet, non-English speaking, and science oriented. These teachers are frustrated by these images and some actively rebuff them. Kate is "mean and loud" and works at standing on principle so that even though she'd "rather sit back like everyone else . . . I realize that sometimes you have to do things for the good of the whole, not just yourself." Magdalena "feels good being the only Asian teacher in the school because I am in a position that is a nonstereotypical role." Similarly, Heather chose "teaching over anything else because it's knocking a lot of stereotypes that I hate."

A last theme that seemed to define the ways in which these teachers feel they are perceived is that of *universal oriental*. This term was chosen to connote the ways in which Asians have been defined by others and named by others and are often seen as interchangeable units, members of a single, monolithic, and, therefore, faceless group. For some of the respondents, this meant that their Asian identity was brushed aside as extraneous by non-Asians around them; people did not "see" them as Asian. Other respondents spoke of the many occasions when non-Asians spoke of the different Asian ethnicities as interchangeable and assumed respondents belonged to a group they did not. Kate recounted an incident:

> The secretary of our school is Vietnamese with an accent. One lady came up to me, tapped me on the shoulder and said, "Oh, you must be the one I'm always talking to."

Betty spoke of students who "don't know the difference between Japanese American, Chinese American, Korean American . . . " and Maki could not persuade a substitute teacher who suggested that she teach in Chinatown that it was inappropriate because she is Japanese. Last, respondents became the Universal Oriental when they were tapped as the Asian expert on traditions, culture, and language. Sometimes this was not negative if the questions were within the cultural knowledge boundaries of the respondent. Thus, both Wanda and Winston felt that they were used positively as resources; however, Kate is "one of the few Asian teachers in my school and people always come up to me and ask me how to do things and how to say things," to which she often has to say, "I don't know."

Speaking Out: Recommendations for Teacher Educators

The teachers had a full range of ideas for both recruitment and retention of Asian Americans. First, they thought Asian American youth seldom had teaching presented to them as a possible profession. Thus, they suggested providing experiences in high school that would encourage students to think about what teachers *do,* as well as opportunities to work as assistants to see what the profession actually entails before enrolling in teacher education programs.

To recruit Asian Americans to the profession, Susie noted, "Money always works." Maki, on the other hand, worried about whether providing scholarships for particular ethnic groups was appropriate. Nevertheless, several of her colleagues mentioned the need for more scholarships, as well as publicity at job fairs and through businesses and community-based organizations. Alumni networks should assist as well.

Kate mentioned the need for networks that make more rational placements. She thought working in a part of the country that had a larger Chinese population than the suburbs of Washington, D.C. (to which she was recruited) would be a better match with her background and abilities. This was also an issue for Betty, who knew Chinese but was teaching Spanish speakers instead.

Almost all teachers mentioned the need for support groups, either within their schools or within a geographic area. The particular interests of teachers of color, who are strongly motivated to make curricula multicultural and who may have experiences different from teachers of European descent, need to be emphasized. These groups would not be limited to Asian Americans but, rather, should include them. Also related to support, a number of teachers cited the importance of role models in teacher education programs, noting that an Asian American professor's participation in the preservice program they had attended was invaluable in that regard.

Finally, Susie had this poignant wish: "If I had a way of making teaching really a profession and not a labor union kind of thing . . . it doesn't make sense that teaching should be like if you're working at a mill or a plant or a steel factory."

Discussion

In both phases of this study, a number of overlapping issues and themes recurred. Two were especially notable: Invisibility and marginality were dual interwoven themes that characterized our findings. Respondents' descriptions made clear that Asian Americans are largely absent from recruitment efforts to build a more diverse teaching pool and from discussions about minority teacher shortages and communities of color. These Asian American teachers did not see themselves reflected in such discussions or, more concretely, in the curricula of their schools and teacher preparation programs.

Despite this apparent invisibility, an important understanding derived from this study is that Asian Americans *are* joining the discussions. They are choosing to teach for many of the same reasons that other groups do: looking for meaningful work that will allow them to make a difference in society. Although low salaries and status can be barriers to Asian Americans considering teaching, the perception that teaching is not an intellectually demanding endeavor was identified as the most significant barrier. This finding opposes a common perception that Asian Americans' vocational aspirations are guided primarily by financial remuneration and prestige.

Being invisible or at the margins must send mixed messages to the Asian American community. Is there is a need for teachers of color but *not* for Asian teachers? Is there a push for multicultural curricula but *not* for Asian cultural curricula? With these questions in the air, Asians may eschew teaching and yet, this study is proof that there *are* Asians who desire to teach. Obviously, they are a resource that has been ignored.

These Asian American teachers also did not see themselves reflected in the curricula of their schools or their teacher preparation programs. Their marginality and invisibility seemed further intensified by three factors:

1. A common perception of them as "foreigners" and therefore as "other"

2. Frequent incorrect categorizations of them by their country of "origin" (i.e., ethnicity)

3. An implicit equation of African American or Latino with "minority" or people of color, which excluded them

Although the data, at first glance, appear to indicate that respondents were just as likely to characterize school and teacher preparation curricula as relevant to the needs and experiences of Asian Americans, a more critical examination of the findings reveals this curricular relevance to be contingent on an Asian American presence. Thus, in schools where Asian American children were in the majority, curricula were relevant. In schools with a minimal Asian American presence, curricula acknowledged the Asian American experience only if respondents initiated these curricula themselves. Similarly, in assessing their teacher education program, respondents who spoke positively identified a *multi*cultural curriculum that focused on other racial groups, not on Asian Americans.

The observation that positive experiences for Asian Americans seem to be contingent on the presence of other Asian Americans was apparent again when respondents talked about their experiences as teachers or student teachers. Clearly, Asian American teachers were more likely to feel that their ethnicity was an advantage in interactions with Asian American students, parents, and colleagues. Being Asian resulted in cultural comfort and ease of communication and did not depend solely on sharing a language or a particular background.

Thus, there seemed to be a rising, but not yet articulated or uniform, Asian American consciousness among many of these teachers. We speculate on a reason for this lack of articulation: When one is a member of a "model minority," one is not expected to dwell on cultural distinctiveness. What makes a minority a model is a willingness to blend in at the margins, to become culturally invisible—in other words, to be acculturated and take on the views and practices of the dominant culture. The current emphasis on multiculturalism in society at large perhaps gives permission to formerly invisible, model persons to focus on their distinctiveness, to argue that their cultural stories are unlike mainstream stories. Therefore, these stories need to be told unofficially to members of the many other cultures around them—as well as officially in curricula for children in schools and for those who will teach them.

Appendix A

Asian American Teacher Questionnaire

Please answer the following questions as completely as you can. Feel free to use the backsides of the questionnaire if you need additional space.

Male_____   Female_____
Ethnicity _____
Age_____
Place of birth_____
U.S. citizen? Yes_____   No_____
If no, are you a U.S. permanent resident? Yes_____   No_____
Undergraduate institution _____
Undergraduate major _____
Graduate institution _____

(If you attended graduate school for the purpose of attaining teacher certification)
Grade levels/subjects certified to teach_____
Number of years of teaching experience_____
Where do you now teach (school/city/grade)?_____
How long have you been in this position? _____

   1. According to research, individuals usually choose to teach for the reasons listed below. Please indicate those that apply to you. Mark off your choices in descending numerical order of priority (1 = 1st priority, 2 = 2nd priority, etc.)

   I love children/interacting with young people_____
   I love learning and being in schools_____
   I enjoy my subject area & want to share it with others_____
   I want to give something back to my community/to contribute to society_____
   I want to make a difference/engage in meaningful work_____
   I like the hours/teaching schedule_____
   Teachers have a lot of autonomy in the classroom_____

If there were other reasons that motivated you to enter the teaching profession, please describe them below.

2. According to research, decisions to enter teaching are sometimes impeded by certain obstacles that are listed below. Please indicate those that you struggled with. Mark off your choices in descending numerical order of priority (1 = the most difficult obstacle to overcome).

Teachers' salaries_____

Teaching is seen as low status work_____

Teaching is seen as women's work_____

Teaching is seen as not intellectual/challenging_____

Parents/friends/significant others were unsupportive_____

Negative publicity about the state of schools/education_____

If there were other obstacles that you had to deal with before you entered the teaching profession, please describe them below.

3. What are your perceptions of the minority teacher shortage?

4. Do you feel that the publicity, dialogue, and programs surrounding the minority teacher shortage include/apply to you? Why or why not?

5. What strategies, programs, or other special recruitment efforts appealed to you and helped you make the decision to enter teaching? If none did, what recruitment strategies would you recommend?

6. As an Asian/Asian American, how do you feel you were/are perceived by the following?

Faculty in your teacher preparation program

Classmates in your teacher preparation program

Your student teaching supervisors

Your cooperating teachers

The children in your student teaching placements

7. If you think about your teaching experience thus far, has being Asian resulted in any significant experiences with parents, administrators, fellow teachers, student teachers, children, etc.? Please describe below.

8. When you think back to your teacher preparation, how would you assess the courses, curricula, field experience of your program in relation to your experiences as an Asian American (issues, content, history, background, etc.)?

9. If you were to recommend changes that would result in teacher preparation programs being more relevant and responsive to Asians and Asian Americans, what would these be?

10. Is the curriculum of the school where you teach relevant and responsive to Asian American children? If yes, please explain. If no, what would you recommend?

Thank you so much for participating. If you are willing to be contacted for a follow-up interview, please indicate your name and phone number below. Please remember that you will speak to us in the strictest confidence. Thanks again.

SOURCE: Goodwin, A. L., Genishi, C. S., Asher, N., & Woo, K. A. (1994, April). *Voices from the margins: Asian American teachers' experiences in the profession.* Paper presented at the annual meeting of the American Educational Research Association, New Orleans, Louisiana.

Appendix B

Asian American Teacher Interview Guide

1a. What were some of the reasons that you chose teaching as your profession? Is there any one overriding reason that motivated you?

1b. In what ways is teaching personally satisfying for you? Can you cite an example/illustrative episode?

2. How, if at all, has your own Asian Americaness been a factor in your opting for teaching as your profession?

3. What, if any, are the personal struggles that you underwent as you decided to pursue teaching as a profession?

4. What, if any, are the new issues/struggles that have emerged in your work as a teacher?

5. In general, why do you think there is a shortage of minority teachers?

6a. In your opinion, what are some of the specific reasons why people from a minority background may not opt for teaching/are deterred from choosing teaching as their profession?

6b. What might be the one major deterrent? Can you discuss that further?

7. Why do you think it is important to increase the number of minority teachers in our schools?

8. How can the recruitment of minority teachers be made more effective?

9. What are some of the perceptions of/attitudes and behaviors toward minority teachers by their students, the parents of the students, peers, fellow student teachers, teacher education faculty, their own ethnic/racial community?

10. Generally, what needs to change to make it possible to have increased numbers of minority teachers and to make their voices better heard?

11. How, specifically, can these minority teacher issues be addressed? What forms of support are needed? What mechanisms, if any, need to be institutionalized?

SOURCE: Goodwin, A. L., Genishi, C. S., Asher, N., & Woo, K. A. (1995, April). *Asian American voices: Speaking out on the teaching profession.* Paper presented at the annual meeting of the American Educational Research Association, San Francisco.

Notes

1. Although a sample size of 21 may appear small, it is important to note that a recent national study of teacher education (AACTE, 1990b) included only 18 Asian Americans.

2. For this segment of the study, $N = 22$ respondents; one subject completed only this section of the study.

3. The names used in this chapter are pseudonyms; however, pseudonyms in the spirit of the respondents' real names were chosen to preserve authenticity. Thus, for respondents with Western names, another

Western name was substituted; if respondents had "culturally specific" names, then, similarly, names in the same vein were used.

References

American Association of Colleges for Teacher Education. (1990a). *Teacher education pipeline II: Schools, colleges, and departments of education enrollments by race and ethnicity.* Washington, DC: Author.

American Association of Colleges for Teacher Education. (1990b). *Metropolitan Life survey of teacher education students.* Washington, DC: Author.

American Association of Colleges for Teacher Education. (1994). *Teacher education pipeline III: Schools, colleges, and departments of education enrollments by race and ethnicity.* Washington, DC: Author.

American Council on Education and the Education Commission of the States. (1988). *One-third of a nation: A report of the commission on minority participation in education and American life.* Washington, DC: AACTE.

Dilworth, M. E. (1990). *Reading between the lines: Teachers and their racial/ethnic cultures.* (Teacher Education Monograph: No. 11). Washington, DC: ERIC Clearinghouse on Teacher Education and American Association of Colleges for Teacher Education.

Edmonston, B., & Passel, J. S. (1992). *Immigration and immigrant generations in population projections.* Washington, DC: Urban Institute.

Goodwin, A. L. (1988). *Teaching images: Unlocking preservice student teaching beliefs and connecting teaching beliefs to teaching behavior.* Unpublished doctoral dissertation, Teachers College, Columbia University, New York.

Goodwin, A. L. (1990). *Fostering diversity in the teaching profession through multicultural field experiences.* National Symposium on Diversity. Tampa, FL: AACTE.

Goodwin, A. L. (1991). Problems, process, and promise: Reflections on a collaborative approach to the solution of the minority teacher shortage. *Journal of Teacher Education, 42*(1), 28-36.

Goodwin, A. L. (1995, February). Asian Americans and Pacific Islanders in teaching. In *ERIC Digest* (No. 104). New York: ERIC Clearinghouse on Urban Education.

Goodwin, A. L., & Genishi, C. S. (1994, April). *Voices from the margins: Asian American teachers' experiences in the profession.* Paper presented at the annual meeting of the American Educational Research Association, New Orleans.

Lortie, D. C. (1975). *Schoolteacher.* Chicago: University of Chicago.

O'Hare, W., & Felt, J. (1991). Asian Americans: America's fastest growing minority. *Population Trends and Public Policy* (No. 19). Washington, DC: Population Reference Bureau.

Pallas, A., Natriello, G., & McDill, E. (1989). The changing nature of the disadvantaged population. *Educational Researcher, 18*(5), 16-22.

Research About Teacher Education Project. (1990). *RATE IV; Teaching teachers: Facts and figures.* Washington, DC: AACTE.

Rong, X. L., & Grant, L. (1992). Ethnicity, generation, and school attainment of Asians, Hispanics, and non-Hispanic Whites. *Sociological Quarterly, 33*(4), 625-636.

U.S. Bureau of the Census. (1993). *1990 census of population and housing.* Washington, DC: Government Printing Office.

Waggoner, D. (1991). *Undereducation in America.* New York: Auburn House.

11 Content Analysis of Prospective Teachers' Self-Guiding Speech During Solitary and Collaborative Planning

Brenda H. Manning

Sandra E. Glasner

Victor G. Aeby

Brenda H. Manning is Professor and Head, Department of Elementary Education, School of Teacher Education, The University of Georgia. Dr. Manning is coeditor of *Action in Teacher Education*. Her research interests include teachers' cognitive and metacognitive thinking strategies, especially mental coping strategies for difficult or tedious tasks. She has published in numerous prestigious journals, including the *Journal of Teacher Education, Teaching and Teacher Education*, and the *American Educational Research Journal*.

Sandra E. Glasner is a doctoral student in the School of Teacher Education at the University of Georgia and former classroom teacher of 17 years. Her research interests include preservice teachers' metacognition and creativity during instructional planning and decision making.

Victor G. Aeby is a doctoral student in the School of Teacher Education at The University of Georgia and current teacher in

AUTHORS' NOTE: A version of this chapter was presented at the annual meeting of the American Educational Research Association, San Francisco, April 1995.

an alternative school for chronic behavior disruptive children. His research interests include family involvement in alternative schooling and this connection to teacher education.

ABSTRACT

This study was developed to investigate preservice teachers' mental self-guidance and problem solving during solitary and group instructional planning contexts. Twenty-five preservice teachers wrote collaborative and individual lesson plans during 2-hour sessions. Accompanying self-talk, recorded by the preservice teachers every 20 minutes for a duration of 10 minutes, was later coded by two independent coders, yielding acceptable interrater reliabilities. Findings indicated significant correlations between self-guiding speech-to-self and lesson planning performance for the solitary but not the collaborative planning context. Implications for teacher education include (a) promoting a greater awareness of preservice teachers' mental problem solving during the learning of a novel and complex skill such as instructional planning and (b) carefully structuring collaborative groups, with the inclusion of a more knowledgeable and informed peer or instructor to model, scaffold, coach, fade assistance, and teach transfer when new skills are introduced. By so doing, perhaps the negative impressions often associated with instructional planning will be eliminated, or at least reduced.

This study was developed to investigate self-guiding speech during two planning contexts, solitary and collaborative, in relation to instructional planning. Preservice teachers are introduced to the concept of planning at the collegiate level, during both formal course work and field experiences. Learning to plan effectively is a source of painful frustration and difficulty for many preservice teachers. The teacher education literature in planning is characterized mainly by descriptions of preservice teachers' thinking and actions. For example, John (1991) found that the planning strategies of preservice teachers generally reflect less sophistication and awareness of contextual factors affecting individual pupil needs. Borko, Livingston, McCaleb, and Mauro (1988) studied how student teachers think about instruction: Their planning and reflection about classroom lessons indicated that preservice teachers reflect first on their teaching, followed by thoughts about pupils and their behavior, then by the students' participation and comprehension of material.

These and other studies have promoted a greater understanding of novice teacher planning. In the current study, an effort was made to push beyond descriptions of preservice teachers' planning to identify cognitive and metacognitive thinking profiles that relate to higher levels of lesson planning performance. If these profiles can be consistently established with research replication, then perhaps we, in teacher education, can plan instruction that will foster this kind of thinking. First, however, we must know the nature and characteristics of verbal self-guidance of teachers during planning. Another aspect of such consideration is to determine the influence of context or environment on teacher cognition and metacognition during a planning experience. In the current study, the contexts of solitary planning and collaborative planning, with accompanying self-reported inner dialogue for each context, were analyzed.

There is limited research evidence in which to ground such a teacher education study. A thorough review of preservice teachers' planning revealed very few studies, and none that were directly related. The specific research questions framing this study were as follows.

Research Questions

1. How many self-talk utterances are made in each planning context (solitary versus collaborative) by linguistic categories and levels? What percentage of the total utterances is each self-talk category and level by planning context?

2. Is there a significant correlation between self-guiding linguistic category Level 1 (off-task or unhelpful speech-to-self) and lesson planning performance in the solitary and in the collaborative contexts?

3. Is there a significant correlation between self-guiding linguistic category Level 2 (focusing, describing, questioning, or directing) and lesson planning performance in the solitary and in the collaborative contexts?

4. Is there a significant correlation between self-guiding linguistic category Level 3 (correcting, coping, reinforcing, and solving) and

lesson planning performance in the solitary and in the collaborative contexts?

5. Is there a significant difference in the amount of self-guiding speech for each of the 10 linguistic categories (off-task, unhelpful, focusing, describing, questioning, directing, correcting, coping, reinforcing, or solving) by planning context (solitary and collaborative)?

6. Is there a significant difference in the amount of self-guiding speech for the three major linguistic levels (nonfacilitative, cognitive, or metacognitive) by planning context (solitary and collaborative)?

Method

Participants

Twenty-five preservice teachers participated in the study. All were female, European American students between the ages of 22 and 38 with a mean age of 23.8. They were all majoring in Early Childhood Education in a teacher education program at a southeastern U.S. university. All were enrolled in a general methods course focusing on planning, teaching strategies, and classroom management.

Procedure

Collaborative Planning Context

Participants were assigned to task groups at the beginning of the quarter. These groups interacted on a weekly basis for seven weeks before they were asked to develop collectively one group lesson plan related to a group-selected theme. During the 2-hour collaborative planning session, the instructor of the class timed 10-minute breaks, every 20 minutes, so that each participant could record her self-guiding speech. Participants were given the following directions orally and in writing:

> When I ask you to stop working as a group, I would like you to stop immediately, write what you are presently saying to yourself or any other thoughts you have had during the last 20 minutes

that you wish to record. You will have 10 minutes to write your self-talk. At the end of class, I would like you to give me your self-talk log; therefore, please record on a separate sheet. Any questions?

These participants had been keeping self-talk logs all quarter for another assignment; therefore, they were very familiar with recording their inner speech. There were no questions from participants about what it meant to record self-talk or how this was done. Participants appeared to understand the expectation for the collaborative planning context, with accompanying self-talk logs.

Solitary Planning Context

From the collaborative unit, individual lesson plan topics were then selected by each participant of the group. These individual plans had to relate to the theme established earlier in the collaborative group. A 2-hour class session was provided for individual planning time. The instructor was present during this time and called for 10-minute breaks every 20 minutes for the purpose of recording self-talk. Participants were given the following directions orally and in writing:

> As you work on your individual plan today, please do not talk to others around you. This plan is supposed to be your original work. After you have written your plan for 20 minutes, I will ask you to stop and record what you are presently saying to yourself or any other thoughts you have had during the last 20 minutes that you wish to record. You will have 10 minutes to write your self-talk.
>
> At the end of class, I would like you to give me your self-talk log; therefore, please record on a separate sheet. Any questions?

Coding Scheme

The coding scheme used to categorize self-talk utterances from both planning contexts was developed by Manning (1991) and was applied in classroom research with young children (Manning, White, & Daugherty, 1994). Minor modifications were made to adjust for adult participants. Table 11.1 illustrates the Manning Coding Scheme and example utterances drawn from the raw data.

TABLE 11.1 Manning Coding Scheme for Teachers' Self-Guiding
Speech Utterances

Self-Guiding Linguistic Categories		*Examples of Teacher Self-Talk During Planning*
Off-Task	Level 1 Nonfacilitative	I'm craving chocolate. It will take me forever to
Unhelpful		think of activities.
Focusing		OK, time to think about this plan.
Describing	Level 2 Cognitive	I am on the last part of my lesson plan.
Questioning		What am I interested in teaching?
Directing		I will teach the students the order of planets from the sun.
Correcting		My objective is missing something.
Coping	Level 3 Metacognitive	What am I so worried about? I can do this—just stay calm.
Reinforcing		I'm off. This is really a good plan.
Solving		Oh, this is it! The evaluation was missing.

A brief explanation of the 10 self-guiding linguistic categories and the three levels follow:

1. *Off-task* self-talk utterances are those that are not related to the task at hand; a break in cognitive or metacognitive thinking about a particular task.

2. *Unhelpful* self-talk utterances are related to the task, but because of their negative, pessimistic, or depressing nature, they do not facilitate appropriate action toward accomplishing the task at hand.

These two categories (1 and 2) compose *Level 1* or what is termed the *nonfacilitative* level because at face value they seem to impede task accomplishment.

3. *Focusing* self-talk utterances bring one's attention to bear on the task at hand.

4. *Describing* self-talk utterances simply characterize one's behavior in relation to the task or describes the task itself.

5. *Questioning* self-talk utterances are those that ask a question related to the task at hand.

6. *Directing* self-talk utterances guide, command, or prompt one's action toward accomplishing some aspect of the task.

Categories 3 to 6 compose *Level 2* or what is termed the *cognitive* level and indicate the flow of thinking about task focusing, persistence, completion, and mastery.

7. *Correcting* self-talk utterances indicate the awareness of an error or strategies for checking and changing responses related to progress toward task accomplishment.

8. *Coping* self-talk utterances aid the emotional or physical reaction to task tedium and frustration to motivate and progress toward task achievement even in the face of barriers and difficulties.

9. *Reinforcing* self-talk utterances are praise turned inward, characterized by encouragement, compliments, and self-appreciation for performing well any aspect of the task at hand.

10. *Solving* self-talk utterances indicate an awareness of resolution, knowing that a problem has been solved, or an answer(s) has been identified, or a task has been completed efficiently.

Categories 7 to 10 compose Level 3 or what is termed the *metacognitive* level and indicate the mental interruption of cognitive functioning to bring about metacognitive awareness or regulation of one's own thinking; the mental overseeing of cognitive processing consists of self-correction, self-coping, self-reinforcing, and self-solving.

Coding of Self-Talk Utterances

A doctoral student and former classroom teacher was instructed in the Manning Coding Scheme (Manning, 1991). She practiced coding example utterances with appropriate monitoring and coaching from an educational researcher, familiar with coding self-talk utterances. The doctoral student and the educational researcher independently coded both sets of self-talk utterances from the solitary and collaborative planning contexts. The overall intercoder reliability for solitary and collaborative self-talk was .92 and .90 correspondingly.

Analyses

Descriptive data, including a frequency chart and percentages, were used to report response to Question 1. Questions 2, 3, and 4 were addressed using the Pearson product-moment correlation statistic, and Questions 5 and 6 were answered with the application of an independent means t test. The alpha level was set a priori at .05.

Results

Table 11.2 shows the data related to Question 1. Amounts and percentages of each self-talk level and category divided by the number of total self-talk utterances according to planning contexts indicate that mental deliberations, reflected in self-reports of speech-to-self, are very different in solitary versus collaborative planning. During solitary planning, compared with collaborative planning, self-talk of preservice teachers is less off-task and unhelpful; more descriptive, questioning, and directing; less coping and reinforcing, and more correcting and solution finding. On the other hand, collaborative planning self-talk is characterized by more off-task and unhelpful self-talk; less focusing, questioning, directing; more coping and reinforcing self-talk; and less correcting and solving self-talk.

In Table 11.3, the correlational matrix relates to research Questions 2-4. As shown by these data, there was a statistically significant moderate, negative correlation ($r= -.446$; $p < .03$) found between Level 1 self-talk utterances of preservice teachers during solitary planning and their lesson planning performance. When off-task, unhelpful self-talk utterances increased, lesson planning scores diminished. On the other hand, when cognitive or metacognitive self-talk increased, lesson plan scores improved as illustrated by the stable, moderate, positive correlations shown in Table 11.2. No significant relationships resulted from the correlational calculations in the collaborative planning context. It appears that internal deliberations via speech-to-self play a more critical role in individual planning. Perhaps, the collective thinking of the group supersedes the

TABLE 11.2 Preservice Teachers' Self-Guiding Speech During Two
Lesson Planning Contexts

Self-Guiding Linguistic Categories and Levels	Solitary		Collaborative	
	Number	Percentage	Number	Percentage
1. Off-task	27	5	51	10
2. Unhelpful	55	9	76	16
Level 1 (nonfacilitative)	82	14	127	26
3. Focusing	23	4	20	4
4. Describing	140	24	89	18
5. Questioning	96	16	73	15
6. Directing	75	13	26	5
Level 2 (cognitive)	334	56	208	43
7. Correcting	36	6	17	3
8. Coping	33	6	37	8
9. Reinforcing	45	8	60	12
10. Solving	64	11	39	8
Level 3 (metacognitive)	178	30	153	31
Totals	594	100	488	100

individual mental self-guidance, needed during solitary planning. During collaborative planning, the social construction of knowledge may substitute for individual verbal self-guidance.

In Table 11.4, the independent t-test results provide insight into Questions 5 and 6. Significant differences were noted for each self-talk category, with the exception of "describing," and for all three levels of self-talk. These findings indicated that mental deliberations vary greatly by planning contexts. It is interesting to note, however, that in both contexts describing accounted for the largest percentage of the total self-talk behavior during lesson planning. In studies conducted with young children performing novel and challenging tasks, describing self-talk also accounts for the largest percentage of self-talk (Manning et al., 1994). Obviously,

TABLE 11.3 Correlational Data: Relationships between Self-Guiding Linguistic Categories (Levels 1-3) and Lesson Planning Performance in Solitary and Collaborative Planning Contexts

	Lesson Planning Scores (n = 25)	
Self-Guiding Speech Levels	*Solitary*	*Collaborative*
Level 1/nonfacilitative (off-task, unhelpful)	$r = -.446$ $p < .03$	NS
Level 2/cognitive (focusing, describing, questioning, directing)	$r = .546$ $p < .01$	NS
Level 3/metacognitive (correcting, coping, reinforcing, solving)	$r = .543$ $p < .01$	NS

these preservice teachers are adult learners, not children; however, the lesson planning task was novel and challenging for them. These and other findings indicate that verbal self-guidance may be less age dependent and more task dependent. Other interesting patterns are found within these self-guiding verbal profiles by planning contexts. These patterns are outlined in Table 11.2 by planning context.

Discussion

Off-Task/Unhelpful Self-Guiding Speech

Solitary Planning

The findings from the current study emphasize the importance of linguistic self-guidance during preservice teachers' solitary planning. Off-task and unhelpful self-talk was associated with lower performance on

TABLE 11.4 Differences Between Self-Guiding Speech Categories and Levels Based on Planning Contexts: Solitary or Collaborative

Self-Guiding Linguistic Categories and Levels	Mean Differences	SD	t-test Value	p Value	Effect Size on Levels
1. Off-task	12.56	18.82	3.34	< .01	
2. Unhelpful	14.28	21.22	3.36	< .01	
Level 1	26.84	31.48	4.26	< .001	.853
3. Focusing	21.48	26.63	4.03	< .001	
4. Describing	2.48	11.39	1.09	NS	
5. Questioning	23.80	25.74	4.62	< .001	
6. Directing	22.20	25.19	4.41	< .001	
Level 2	69.96	53.62	6.52	< .001	.999
7. Correcting	8.96	10.82	4.14	< .001	
8. Coping	5.52	7.50	3.68	< .01	
9. Reinforcing	9.00	19.09	2.36	< .05	
10. Solving	21.48	22.66	4.47	< .001	
Level 3	44.96	46.33	4.85	< .001	.960

lesson planning, so an effort to divert such inner speech to cognitive or metacognitive levels seems desirable. Preservice teachers need awareness about the potential impact of their own mental problem solving. Such awareness is the first step to reducing counterproductive self-talk.

Collaborative Planning

Even though there was no association between self-talk and planning performance during collaborative planning, the amount of off-task, unhelpful self-talk during collaborative planning was almost double the percentage (26% of total), when compared with the amount during solitary planning (14% of total). The preservice teachers in groups spent approximately one fourth of their total self-talk using off-task, irrelevant, or unhelpful speech-to-self. Quality of the final group plan was not negatively associated with such talk, however. Perhaps a combination of factors explain this. First, everyone in a group received the same grade when their collective plan was assessed, although individual performance contributing to the quality of the plan was not equal. Because a number of students received the same score, this repetition of "like scores" may have statistically altered the correlational calculation.

Second, it is possible that group work, learning a new skill such as lesson planning, without an experienced and more knowledgeable peer caused this large amount of nonfacilitative self-talk. The literature supports this explanation (e.g., Bickel & Hattrup, 1995; Castle & Giblin, 1992). Collaboration requires much work and effort, a sufficient degree of self-concept, a willingness to relinquish power, and patience in allowing others adequate time for reflection. Castle and Giblin (1992), while working with 23 preservice teachers, found that reflection occasionally produced tension in some novices as a result of personal dilemmas.

Drawing on the theoretical framework of Vygotsky (1978) and the applied work of Rogoff (Radziszewska & Rogoff, 1988; Rogoff, 1990), collaboration with a more skilled or knowledgeable individual provides the opportunity to practice skills that are in advance of independent skill development. Although this literature targets children's thinking and development, when adult learners are introduced to an unfamiliar, complex, and novel task such as instructional planning, it is very likely that they, too, would profit from an experienced, knowledgeable other, scaffolding the learning process. The data in the current study document the frustration, via off-task, pessimistic, discouraging, and panicking verbal self-guidance. Teacher educators should consider these data and the potential damage of collaboration during new skill development, without appropriate scaffolding by an informed member of the group. This damage manifests as pervasive negative attitudes toward planning that can be difficult to overcome, even when preservice teachers become proficient at planning.

Third, "group complaining" with accompanying "unhelpful" self-talk may not be unhelpful at all. Instead, this initial "off-task, pessimistic, discouraging, and panicking" self-talk may serve as an emotional release when approaching a novel task, especially in a group setting. All three explanations can be combined to explain the large amount of "nonfacilitative" self-talk and the role such speech-to-self may play in group process.

Cognitive Self-Guiding Speech

Solitary Planning

More than half the total number of self-talk utterances were cognitive in nature. This type of self-guidance in preservice teachers was associated with higher levels of performance on lesson planning. Within this linguistic category Level 2, participants spent the least amount of time focusing their attention, perhaps because they were already focused and did not have to make an effort to prompt themselves verbally. A large chunk of self-talk in this area was describing self-talk. As mentioned earlier, an interesting parallel is that young children, when performing a challenging new task, such as a tangram exercise, also use a large percentage of describing. Self-questioning and directing oneself verbally were also used quite frequently during solitary planning.

Collaborative Planning

Even in the collaborative setting, describing self-talk was quite prevalent (18% of the total); however, there was much less "directing" self-talk (only 5% of total) than in the solitary setting (13% of total). It is likely that various self-selected group members assumed uninformed leadership and took over the direction of the group's thinking, diminishing the need for individual mental direction. This may be a positive occurrence; however, one does question what will happen later to certain preservice teachers who did not experience sufficient practice directing the process of planning for their own pupils. When collaboration is characterized by the absence of a more knowledgeable or experienced individual and, thus, omits the modeling, scaffolding, coaching, and fading, then preservice teachers may not spontaneously "construct" sufficient skills and mental problem solving to support effective instructional planning.

Metacognitive Self-Guiding Speech

Solitary Planning

This was initial learning of instructional planning, so it is not surprising that cognitive self-guidance was more prevalent than metacognitive self-guidance. Flavell (1987) posited that metacognition occurs more frequently for tasks somewhere optimally between familiar and unfamiliar. Learning instructional planning for the first time is very "unfamiliar" and, therefore, does not meet this criterion for *metacognitive* thought. However, 30% of the total utterances were categorized as metacognitive. Solitary planning self-talk was characterized by equal amounts of self-correcting and self-coping (6% of the total), 8% self-reinforcing, and 11% self-solving. When comparing solitary with collaborative self-talk, however, solitary contexts evoked more self-correction and awareness of problem resolution.

Collaborative Planning

The cognitive self-guidance was more prevalent than the metacognitive self-guidance during group brainstorming and planning sessions. Individuals reported only 3% of the total for self-correcting self-talk. With group members present, self-checking or correcting was not as probable, because of the distraction of others' thinking or the assumption that other group members would take responsibility for "catching errors." Participants engaged in equal amounts of self-coping (8% of the total) and self-solving (8% of the total). Interestingly, self-reinforcing self-talk was more prevalent (12% of the total) during the collaborative group planning session than during solitary planning (8% of the total). This may be due to group support of ideas, which prompted self-support or self-reinforcement. Preservice teachers often praise each other's ideas, and this praise may have been internalized and used during verbal self-guidance.

Implications for Teacher Education

The findings from this study offer insights into preservice teachers' mental self-guidance and problem solving during solitary and group planning. With the national trend toward shared governance, teacher decision making, and collaborative group process, teachers often work collectively, rather than individually. The characteristics of such practice include diligent work, exemplary practice, an awareness of new ideas, and a willingness to help other members of the "community" succeed, as well as the community itself (Sergiovanni, 1992). Loyalty to the school and shared values, "respect for and connectedness to the professional expertness of one's colleagues and the shared commitment to the goals and values of the profession and a true concern for real teaching are key components to successful collegiality/collaboration" (Sergiovanni, 1992, p. 213). Because of this emphasis, teacher education would be remiss not to include quality experiences of collaboration for prospective and inservice teachers. The key words are "quality experiences," however.

When prospective teachers are introduced to new skills, tasks, and abilities related to classroom functioning (such as learning how to plan), then the collaborative process should include a knowledgeable, more experienced peer or instructor to model, scaffold, coach, monitor, fade assistance, and teach transfer for preservice teachers. Data from this study indicate that without such informed assistance, preservice teachers engage in off-task, pessimistic, discouraging, and panicking self-guidance that can have a lasting negative influence on instructional planning. Therefore, the careful development of collaborative group process is critical to preservice teacher development.

References

Bickel, W. E., & Hattrup, R. A. (1995). Teachers and researchers in collaboration: Reflections on the process. *American Educational Research Journal, 32*(1), 35-62.

Borko, H., Livingston, C., McCaleb, J., & Mauro, L. (1988). Student teachers' planning and post-lesson reflections: Patterns and implications for teacher preparation. In J. Calderhead (Ed.), *Teachers' professional learning* (pp. 86-95). London: Falmer.

Castle, J., & Giblin, A. (1992, February). *A collaborative venture in preservice education: Participant practices and learnings.* Paper presented at the annual meeting of the American Association of Colleges for Teacher Education, Atlanta, GA.

Flavell, J. H. (1987). Speculations about the nature and development of metacognition. In F. E. Weinert & R. H. Kluwe (Eds.), *Metacognition, motivation, and understanding.* Hillsdale, NJ: Lawrence Erlbaum.

John, P. D. (1991). Course, curricular, and classroom influences on the development of student teachers' lesson planning perspectives. *Teaching and Teacher Education: An International Journal of Research and Studies, 7*(4), 359-372.

Manning, B. H. (1991). *Cognitive self-instruction for classroom processes.* Albany: State University of New York Press.

Manning, B. H., White, C. S., & Daugherty, M. (1994). Young children's private speech as a precursor to metacognitive strategy use for task execution. *Discourse Processes: A Multidisciplinary Journal, 17*(2), 191-211.

Radziszewska, B., & Rogoff, B. (1988). Influence of adult and peer collaborators on children's learning skills. *Developmental Psychology, 24*, 840-848.

Rogoff, B. (1990). *Apprenticeship in thinking.* New York: Oxford University Press.

Sergiovanni, T. J. (1992). Moral authority and the regeneration of supervision. In C. D. Glickman (Ed.), *Supervision in transition* (pp. 203-214). Alexandria, VA: Association of Supervision and Curriculum Development.

Vygotsky, L. S. (1978). *Mind in society: The development of higher psychological processes.* Cambridge, MA: Harvard University Press.

12 A Model, Not a Mold

A Comparison of Four School-University Partnerships

Judith Haymore Sandholtz

Judith Haymore Sandholtz is Director of the Comprehensive Teacher Education Institute at the University of California, Riverside. Her research interests are in the areas of collaborative teacher education, professional development schools, and technology. She is the coauthor of a book on teachers' experiences in technology-rich classrooms.

ABSTRACT

This research examines and compares the experiences of four institutions involved in a state initiative to improve teacher preparation through collaboration and innovation. The paper describes the state's mission and goals, provides an overview of the four programs, and discusses the factors that both fostered and constrained reform. The study uses comparative case methodology and covers a 5-year period during which the institutes received funding for planning, implementation, and institutionalization of collaborative teacher preparation programs.

AUTHOR'S NOTE: This research was supported by the California Department of Education. Findings, conclusions, and recommendations are those of the author and do not necessarily reflect the views of the California Department of Education. A version of this paper was presented at the 1995 meeting of the American Educational Research Association, San Francisco.

Operating in different contexts, the four institutes developed diverse approaches to their overall mission of improving and revitalizing teacher preparation. Although the programs varied, six elements appeared to enhance the progress and achievements at each site. Each institute also faced six main challenges to progress and change. This study provides practical information for those interested or involved in setting up collaborative programs.

Although you may know your subject like a close friend, nowhere as an undergraduate did they ever tell you how to teach it!

Mike Martinez made an important discovery: Knowing a subject is different from teaching a subject. Fifth-year teacher credential programs promote the subject matter mastery and educational breadth of prospective teachers. These programs, however, obscure connections among the main elements of preservice teacher education: subject matter preparation, professional preparation, and field experience. Prospective teachers frequently explore subject matter in academic departments as undergraduates, study pedagogy in the education department during their fifth year, and complete field experiences in schools during only a portion of the fifth year.

In addressing this issue and calls for reform, the California Department of Education and the California State University System established Comprehensive Teacher Education Institutes (CTEI) based on three-way partnerships. The stated purpose of the institutes is to strengthen teacher preparation programs through collaboration among local school educators, approved teacher education programs, and undergraduate academic departments. The state delineated four common goals: collaborative decision making; articulation of undergraduate, graduate, and student teaching components; integrated curricula and instruction; and assessment of candidates' knowledge and skills.

This chapter examines the experiences of four institutes in the second 5-year funding cycle, highlighting common elements that enhanced success and challenges that hindered progress. Although addressing collective goals, the institutes operated in different contexts and developed diverse approaches to their overall mission of improving teacher preparation. California State University—Northridge designed a collaborative program to prepare teachers to work in multicultural, multilingual environments. The program includes a 3-year field experience followed by a 2-year outreach component. San Francisco State University developed an innovative program to prepare candidates specifically for middle school positions. The University of California—Riverside created a professional development school program to prepare prospective teachers as well as provide professional development and research opportunities for experienced teachers. California State University—Fresno developed a collaborative governance structure to initiate reform and link initiatives with mainstream activities.

The Task of Linking Institutions

Many reforms in teacher education focus on collaboration where school districts and universities form partnerships (Carnegie Forum, 1986; Holmes Group, 1986; Kennedy, 1992; Levine, 1992). Although some collaborative ventures are primarily symbolic, many are based on the premise of equal partners working together in a mutually beneficial relationship (Sirotnik & Goodlad, 1988). Creating such partnerships is complicated because it involves combining institutions with distinctive and possibly conflicting missions, organizational structures, and cultures. These distinctions lead to numerous challenges such as developing a common mission (McIntyre, 1994), establishing interinstitutional authority and fiscal responsibility (Neufeld, 1992), resolving conflicting fundamental interests (Snyder, 1994), competing with other reform efforts (Grossman, 1994), and defining roles and responsibilities (Miller & Silvernail, 1994). In essence, institutional differences arise in nearly every aspect of collaborative ventures.

Those involved in establishing partnerships inevitably report unanticipated conflicts in linking institutions in collaborative work. The most commonly identified logistical issues are time, rewards, and funding. Other issues are less obvious. For example, some find universities, more than schools, to be tradition-bound "with a culture based on individual entrepreneurship, deep seeded conservatism, and an avoidance of risk and change" (Miller, 1993, p. 5). Others encounter a gulf between teachers' and professors' views that results in people frequently working at cross-purposes (Winitzky, Stoddart, & O'Keefe, 1992). In resolving conflicts, the critical aspects appear to be sensitivity to differences and a problem-solving spirit within the partnership (Bickel & Hattrup, 1995). The difficulty in creating institutional alliances is superseded by the challenge of making them permanent. Both schools and universities are masterful at creating programs that operate outside the core activities of the organization, thus leading to superficial rather than institutional change (Lieberman, 1992). This "ad-hocracy" fosters innovation, avoids bureaucratic restrictions, and enables the creation of collaborative programs, but it also can relegate them to the periphery of institutions (Grossman, 1994).

Despite numerous challenges, collaborative ventures hold considerable promise and potential. School-university collaboration enhances prospects for individual and institutional renewal by infusing the workplace with expertise and knowledge from inside and outside the setting (Goodlad, 1988). In teacher education, many school-university collaborations are successfully "restructuring teaching knowledge, the form and content of teacher education, and the nature and governance of teaching" (Darling-Hammond, 1994, p. 3). Individual partnerships report transforming teacher education programs while restructuring schools to become "a true 'center of inquiry' for teachers and students" (Miller & O'Shea, 1994, p. 17). Individual teachers identify benefits, including "expertise in mentoring student teachers, increased knowledge and efficacy in teaching techniques, enhanced collegial interaction, and more positive attitudes and feelings about themselves as teachers" (Sandholtz & Merseth, 1992, p. 312). Student teachers describe coming to view teaching as continual learning, problem solving with colleagues, and shifting their concerns from survival to student learning (Snyder, 1994).

In collaborative research, studies proceed in directions more attuned to practice and in ways that yield greater external validity (Porter, 1987). The group interaction and the content of what is learned narrow the gap between "doing research" and "implementing research findings" (Lieberman, 1986). Involving teachers as researchers generates knowledge useful for teachers and for the larger school and university communities (Lytle & Cochran-Smith, 1992). Moreover, educational materials and instructional strategies are improved through sustained collaboration between researchers and teachers (Bickel & Hattrup, 1995).

Given potential challenges and benefits in creating partnerships, the critical issue becomes the balance between the two. The work for the future must focus on addressing the pattern of obstacles and fostering the forces that result in benefits for individuals and institutions (Harris & Harris, 1994). Ultimately, the value of school-university partnerships depends not on individuals' self-interests or attempts to reform one institution but, rather, on the extent to which "all parties seek to use them for the simultaneous reform and renewal of both schools and universities" (Clark, 1988, p. 62).

Methodology

This research used comparative case methodology to investigate the change process across the four institutes. The study covers a 5-year period during which the institutes received funding for planning, implementation, and institutionalization of collaborative teacher preparation programs. The investigation drew from three sources: documents, interviews, and participant-observations. Relevant documents included case studies and evaluation reports by an outside evaluator, correspondence and written requests from the state, and program descriptions and manuscripts from the institutes. Open-ended interviews with key participants were conducted to corroborate themes, verify explanations, and augment case studies. As director of one of the institutes, I observed, participated in, and took notes at directors' meetings, conferences, and retreats during the 5-year period. Data analysis used case study analytic techniques, including pattern matching and explanation building (Yin, 1984), and focused on identifying factors that both fostered and constrained reform.

Enhancing the Success of Collaborative Programs

Although the programs varied, six factors appeared to enhance progress and achievements: broad goals, involvement at all levels, shared decision making, parallel organizations and pilot programs, incremental changes, and effective collaboration.

Broad Goals

Broad goals set by the California Department of Education gave general direction for reform yet allowed sites to build on local needs and strengths. Differences in the programs confirm differences in local needs. The pressing need for teachers in the Los Angeles Unified School District allowed the collaborative program with CSU—Northridge to offer paid part-time teacher aide positions for candidates beginning in the junior year, leading into full-time positions on completion of the credential program. An existing relationship between UC—Riverside and Jurupa Unified School District supported creating a professional development school. At San Francisco State University, a professor's long-term interest led to a program emphasizing middle school. The variety of reform activities at CSU—Fresno compelled them to link their CTEI project with mainstream reform initiatives. Broad goals provided a critical foundation and direction for reform efforts, but freedom to work on specific issues most meaningful to sites increased the amount of significant change.

By setting broad goals, the state also reinforced the collaborative decision-making process. In true collaboration, precise goals and outcomes cannot be mandated; all partners must be integrally involved in establishing objectives and developing specific activities to meet those objectives.

Involvement at All Levels

The most successful partnerships garnered the commitment of individuals at all levels. Making changes in teacher preparation demanded negotiating not only the maze of bureaucratic requirements at the university but also conditions in individual classrooms where student teachers are placed. When higher-level administrators were involved, partnerships had a broader impact on structures and programs. Changes typically needed to be carried out by individual professors or classroom teachers, however, thereby necessitating their commitment as well.

Involving individuals across levels also promoted the notion of change as an institutional endeavor rather than the project of one or two people. One director noted that their progressive, visionary dean not only provided direction and the recognition that CTEI was for everyone but also facilitated communication with "top decision makers."

Partnerships found that not everyone needed to be involved to the same degree or in the same way. One institute formed a broader committee for policy decisions and a smaller group for operational decisions. Another institute developed a variety of activities and roles that allowed people to become involved in ways that most closely fit their interests, talents, and schedules.

Shared Decision Making

A genuinely shared decision-making process was critical in establishing meaningful partnerships. When partners had a bona fide role in formulating policy and saw their ideas implemented, commitment and ownership were fostered. Teachers, in particular, have a history of token involvement in decision making outside of classrooms. As one teacher commented, "The only decisions you make at school concern things within your own classroom. Curriculum is even given to you. . . . In CTEI, we have been able to decide and develop." Previously, although numerous people were involved in teacher preparation, there were few opportunities to make decisions together.

Partnerships also benefited from the various perspectives that individuals contributed to decisions. As one director described, "With shared decision making, the program is richer. In addition, growth is assured because the program can move ahead and be institutionalized more easily when more people are involved." Although some institutes had a stable group of decision makers, others varied the group depending on the decision to be made and on people's interest or stake in what was happening.

Parallel Organizations and Pilot Programs

A viable yet risky method for dealing with resistance to change was creating parallel organizations or pilot programs. Each institute essentially functioned as a parallel system that offered a place, time, and resources for innovation and collaboration.

University and school faculty are familiar with pilot programs, but both benefits and risks accompany that familiarity. Pilot programs, particularly those funded by outside grants, frequently never become institutionalized. When the money dries up, the program often disappears. Consequently, individuals may be hesitant to devote time and energy to pilot programs that they believe will disappear in several years. Moreover, the programs may be viewed as separate and irrelevant. Because they are viewed as experimental (and probably short-term), however, there may be less opposition to pilot programs than full-scale restructuring. As a "separate" program or organization, there is time for innovation and experimentation, which can lead to incremental changes in mainstream programs and, eventually, larger scale reform.

After a planning year, UC—Riverside piloted the professional development school program for four years at one school. During this period, participants developed strong collaborative relationships, designed specific program features, experimented with and evaluated various approaches, built a reputable program, and drew interest from other schools. Over the years, the pilot program increased its credibility with the university and school communities, leading to the restructuring of the secondary teaching credential program.

CSU—Northridge also implemented its program gradually, beginning with one cohort of students. Knowing that making changes in the mainstream program could take years, planners reasoned that a pilot program involving numerous people was "a better way to begin to make some inroads." By beginning with one cohort, they also could experiment and make changes as necessary—such as admitting both juniors and seniors into their second cohort.

Over time, parallel organizations present a challenge in balancing dual goals of institutionalization and experimentation. To institutionalize programs and exert a broader influence, institutes cannot remain totally separate and distinct; however, without retaining some separate identity, they lose the ability to experiment. One CTEI determined that the separation was resulting in less efficient use of resources and decided to link the CTEI initiatives with their mainstream reform activities. Others began to look for additional outside funding to maintain and expand their innovative focus while working to institutionalize their programs.

Incremental Changes

Although aiming toward larger goals, the sites found that change occurred through a series of smaller accomplishments. The experiences of the institutes highlight three main lessons related to incremental change. First, they had to find the appropriate balance between aims and activities that were so small as to be insignificant and so large as to be overwhelming. In some cases, partnerships were trying to do too many things at once. One CTEI initially attempted to implement three main programs: teacher preparation, inservice professional development, and teacher research. After failed attempts, the management team recognized that a more reasonable, and ultimately more successful, approach involved staged implementation. Another CTEI originally aimed to improve teaching strategies of professors in entire departments across campus. They soon realized that this goal was unrealistic; changes in individuals directly associated with the program did not quickly or easily transfer to changes across entire departments.

Second, their experiences reinforced the fact that change is not linear or systematic. As Michael Fullan (1994) described, "No matter how well we plan it . . . it will not unfold in a linear way; there'll be surprises, there'll be detours, there'll be unpredictable things that happen for better and for worse." More important than the surprises themselves was the ability to learn from them and make appropriate adjustments. One university, when faced with budget constraints, began assigning two students to each elementary classroom to streamline university supervision. Unexpected benefits, such as camaraderie and collaboration among student teachers, resulted. Another institute, after spending months unsuccessfully attempting to house their program within a particular department in the School of Education, finally approached another department. In retrospect, they realized that they could have progressed more quickly by initially exploring collaboration with several different departments.

Third, a long-term view underscored the value of incremental changes. Although full-scale restructuring in three to four years was unrealistic, the foundation for systemic reform could be established. For example, the CTEIs established ongoing collaborative structures and steering committees, improved the relationships between universities and schools, focused on field sites with multicultural settings, created new courses that became permanent, improved clinical settings and supervision for student teachers, and established a basis for experimentation. At some sites, successful pilot projects led to the expansion of programs. In creating solid groundwork for systemic reform, the most critical incremental change was establishing effective, ongoing collaboration.

Effective Collaboration

Over the years, CTEI directors viewed ongoing collaboration as the most important goal delineated by the state. A primary benefit of effective collaboration was a better understanding of partner institutions, including contexts, constraints, and roles of various stakeholders. For example, professors from academic departments discovered that "it is not that easy to teach out in the public schools," and teachers recognized the complexity of the university system. At one site, a professor originally scheduled meetings at a time that precluded teachers' attendance; "now, he wouldn't think of having a meeting without including those who would be most affected—the public school people." Another site adjusted the student teaching experience and university supervisors' schedules to conform to the public school calendar rather than the university calendar.

Collaboration also promoted change across institutions. At one university, student teachers in the new program encountered scheduling conflicts between university courses and their school responsibilities. The associate dean organized a session with faculty to program all teacher education courses for the coming year, placing greater emphasis on needs at the partner schools than professors' preferences. As another example, the Language Arts Department at one partner school considered shifting from tracked to heterogeneous classes and requested input from university faculty. As one teacher described, "Many teachers were resistant to the change and the incorporation of university faculty increased their confidence about handling a heterogeneous group." After discussions with several professors, the department decided to experiment with heterogeneous grouping at one grade level for one year. Subsequently, they moved to heterogeneous classes for all grade levels.

Collaboration also led to pooling of resources. Ideas and talents of additional people were obvious resources, but others were less apparent. One director pointed out the value of "just getting somebody's else's mailing list." Not only did they secure the mailing list, but their new collaborators also agreed to do the mailings. Established collaboration also put institutes in a strong position to compete for other grants requiring school-university partnerships. One administrator stated that his school received more funds through collaborative grants with CTEI than any of the school's individual efforts.

Another benefit involved establishing collaborative working relationships that extended beyond teacher preparation. For example, while developing a new university course, two teachers from different high schools talked casually about course offerings. Intrigued by foreign language courses for native speakers, one teacher independently arranged for the other to visit her department and discuss how they developed these courses. At another site, people who made contact through CTEI activities initiated a program where 120 high school sophomores attend school at the university everyday, taking their core courses from high school teachers but going to academic departments for physical education and drama.

By establishing ongoing collaboration, the CTEIs also promoted their long-term abilities to bring about reform. They recognized that they couldn't focus on collaboration as an end in itself, however. The most successful projects focused on concrete activities using a collaborative process.

Challenges to Teacher Preparation Reform

The experiences of the institutes illuminate six main challenges to progress and change: acting as a change agent, time demands, differing rewards, long-term participation, bureaucratic constraints, and economic conditions.

Acting as a Change Agent

Institute directors had little, if any, training as change agents. Yet they were being asked to initiate reform and institutionalize changes across organizations—an incredibly complex task. Feeling they were learning by trial and error, directors appreciated retreats where they could share strategies, successes, and challenges. Many of them proposed that the state provide formal training on strategies for bringing about change. Because of budget constraints, however, the formal training never took place and directors' retreats were canceled.

Directors typically were not in organizational positions that allowed them to change pertinent components such as reward systems or workloads. One approach to dealing with this limitation ties back to involving individuals at all levels. Although the institutes must have people who are involved in and knowledgeable about teacher education, they also need committed participants in positions to induce institutional change. As one director experienced, however, these issues "were not the top priority or the pressing needs of the people in those positions—even if they were involved."

Time Demands

True collaboration takes a great deal of time. Collaborative ventures never proceed as smoothly and quickly as those undertaken by one or two individuals. It takes time to build trust and working relationships, particularly when forming partnerships among institutions with different missions and cultures. There are inevitable differences, disagreements, and conflicts that must be resolved. The length of funding and the expected outcomes must recognize and support this complex process.

Involving people from separate institutions meant that groups couldn't work together as frequently as desired. University professors, school teachers, and district administrators, for example, all have different obligations and schedules. The simple task of setting times and places for meetings often became complex. One CTEI scheduled meetings after 4:00 P.M. or sometimes at 6:30 A.M. Another institute held monthly full-day meetings for its management team, using grant funds for teachers' substitutes. They found a longer period of time more productive and easier to schedule than shorter, more frequent sessions.

Another challenge related to time arose from directors' workloads. Because of differences across universities and positions, directors had varying amounts of time to devote to CTEI activities. For example, one person received half-time release time whereas another had a quarter release time, which meant teaching three courses a semester in addition to committee and research responsibilities. Another university structured the position to allow the director to focus primarily on the institute.

Differing Rewards

Participants in the partnerships had varying stakes in teacher preparation and required different rewards. For academic professors and classroom teachers, collaboration in teacher education means little in the formal promotion and tenure process. Even for education professors, publishable research typically outweighs involvement in the schools. Although everyone recognizes long-term benefits of well-prepared teachers, this alone doesn't compensate for demands of collaborative programs.

Although the need for rewards is obvious, providing them is more difficult, particularly when faced with such varied participants. In providing compensation, institutes had to find rewards that were adequate, genuine, and valued by individual participants. Some programs offered research opportunities for junior faculty or provided release time or pay for academic faculty to engage in intellectually engaging seminars. One site found that travel funds appealed to faculty more than direct pay because "so much is taken out by the time you get it." Another director wrote letters for junior faculty that recognized their efforts and provided documentation for promotion files.

Most partnerships compensated for teachers' time, usually with substitute coverage or stipends; however, time and effort often exceeded the direct compensation. Programs also provided opportunities such as attending state and national conferences, designing and coteaching university courses, and participating in research; these activities resulted in benefits such as increased knowledge, efficacy, and collegiality.

Another strategy for accommodating individual differences was to include multiple activities and roles in the collaborative project. Multiple activities offered greater opportunities to engage diverse individuals with varying interests and values and allowed people to select forms of engagement depending on personal circumstances and preferences.

Long-Term Participation

After initially attracting participants and forming partnerships, the institutes confronted the issue of long-term participation. Requirements and expectations fluctuated as participants became accustomed to assignments or as institutes added new components. Similarly, benefits that attracted involvement were not always those that sustained ongoing participation.

Although many people relished their new roles and sought long-term involvement, others limited their participation. Some people, initially attracted to an innovative project, lost interest as the novelty wore off. Others, when faced with limited time, simply began to question the long-term trade-off. This situation posed a particular challenge for institutes because teacher education is not the primary mission of many participants. For instance, at one site, the original district office contacts left their jobs, and their replacements had little interest in or commitment to the project.

The institutes' long-term success largely depends on providing ongoing extrinsic and intrinsic rewards that meet individuals' self-interest. Although the grants help significantly in attracting involvement and providing release time or stipends, these supports are difficult to sustain over the long term, primarily because of the cost. Depending on economic conditions, the institutes may be unable to shift university and district resources to support ongoing participation.

The eventual solution may be in collaboration and slowly changing views about school-university relationships. One director, whose university president has "clearly signaled that involvement and service with K-12 schools is important," suggested that collaboration ultimately should be part of the job rather than an addition to it. Moreover, district and school administrators increasingly may recognize that staff development of practicing teachers can take many forms other than traditional inservice activities.

Bureaucratic Constraints

Institutes encountered a host of bureaucratic restrictions and con-straints to change. At one university, making course changes required consideration and approval by five separate committees. In addition to university procedures, the institutes had to work within the California Commission on Teacher Credentialing standards, state legislation, and school district policies. The collaboration among institutions compounded the number of restrictions.

To some extent, the regulated environment contradicted the notion of innovation. Project directors often questioned how to instigate change and promote innovation while adhering to numerous bureaucratic require-ments. One person noted that she didn't realize various activities required committee approval at the university—until she was questioned about not going through proper channels. Regulations also increased the time re-quired to implement new approaches. For example, getting approval from one committee might take several months depending on how frequently the committee meets, how much additional information is requested, and how much committee members disagree.

One strategy CTEIs had for making their way through restrictions was to determine whether they were battling tradition or a true regulation. For example, one university required students to take a specific course that resulted in a huge enrollment. Wanting to implement a more individual-ized approach, a professor investigated the "requirement" and arranged for some students to enroll instead in a graduate-level course with a smaller enrollment. Another approach involved finding creative ways to operate within existing structures. One institute piloted a "new" methods course by unofficially dividing an existing course into two sections with different instructors. Officially, all students registered for one course with one instructor.

A third method was to include key individuals, who were knowledge-able about specific policies, on central planning teams. For instance, one site always involved a teachers' union representative. A fourth possibility was to apply for official experimental status through the California Com-mission on Teacher Credentialing. This approach, although lifting restric-tions, posed concerns. Some people felt the application and evaluation process for experimental status (being used at that time) simply replaced one set of requirements with another. In addition, they worried that the official label as an experimental program might impede, rather than enhance, their ability to make changes in mainstream programs.

Economic Conditions

Miserable statewide economic conditions during this funding cycle hampered progress. Some years, the grants were significantly reduced, and funds didn't reach the universities until 6 months late. These reductions and delays created problems in program continuity, project activities, personnel, and interest in innovation. At some universities, an official grant notification was sufficient to allow spending; others had to wait until the actual funds arrived. Consequently, a 6-month delay greatly impeded the continuity of projects at some sites; delays over consecutive years became increasingly problematic.

Budget reductions led to adjustments in program activities and personnel. Poor economic conditions caused universities to reduce support staff, impose hiring freezes for faculty positions, institute across-the-board salary cuts, and increase faculty and staff responsibilities. These university-level actions had ramifications for the CTEIs. Increased responsibilities diminished people's time for project activities, and reduced grant funds compounded the problem. Without funds to reduce teaching loads, some sites essentially had to reduce the number of people involved and limit program expansion. As one director described, "When you buy only a *piece* of people, you don't get much sustained effort."

The overall economic climate also affected people's attitudes. Budget reductions and salary cuts raised people's concerns about survival, thus stifling interest in innovation and risk taking. For instance, at one university, professors recognized the caliber of the middle school emphasis program but considered it a duplication of efforts because "both elementary and secondary programs can credential for middle school." As one director described, the dampened attitudes resulted in the omission of potential activities—missed opportunities to make changes.

Implications

Examining the experiences of these four partnerships and the literature on school-university collaboration leads to three overarching conclusions. First, collaboration in teacher education is essential. In viewing the process of learning to teach as a continuum, it makes little sense to relegate preservice teacher preparation to universities and inservice teacher education to schools and districts. All educational institutions have a stake in the lifelong professional education of teachers, and it is counterproductive to divide the process into discrete parts. For too long, university course work has been isolated from the realities of practice, and the status of professors has been inversely related to the amount of sustained work with teachers and schools. The inherent difficulties in establishing and maintaining viable school-university partnerships are significant, but they don't outweigh the long-term potential of collaboration. Teacher education requires strong roots in reflective practice and strong bonds to the public schools—a partnership among peers (Holmes Group, 1990).

Second, the context is important. The most successful partnerships are not mandated but, rather, emerge from a context that is ready for and supportive of collaboration. The trust and mutual respect that are critical in a true collaboration in large part stem from the existing context. In addition, the context forms the basis for determining specific goals and activities of the partnerships. Significant change is more likely to occur when partnerships have freedom to build on local needs and strengths while following general direction for reform. The context also influences the severity of challenges faced and the ability to overcome and learn from them. Although common problems exist across sites, the level of difficulties encountered and the capability to solve them productively varies across contexts. What becomes an insurmountable obstacle in one context is a relatively minor problem in another.

Third, school-university partnerships need valid opportunities and time to experiment. Without chances for trial and risk taking, the entire notion of collaborative reform is undermined. Collaborative partners must have opportunities to "revisit plans, incorporate new understandings and ideas, and change priorities as experiences dictate" (Robinson & Darling-Hammond, 1994). Creating and implementing new ideas requires flexibility and uncertainty—and the opportunity to fail. Yet in schools and universities, failure is seen as a weakness rather than a strength. As a new organizational enterprise, school-university partnerships must incorporate broader definitions of both success and failure. In our efforts to improve teaching and learning, we "must work for the changes that we believe to be right, rather than those we know can succeed" (Holmes Group, 1986, p. 3).

References

Bickel, W. E., & Hattrup, R. A. (1995). Teachers and researchers in collaboration: Reflections on the process. *American Educational Research Journal, 32*(1), 35-62.

Carnegie Forum on Education and the Economy. (1986). *A nation prepared: Teachers for the 21st century.* The Report of the Task Force on Teaching as a Profession. New York: Carnegie Corporation.

Clark, R. (1988). School-university relationships: An interpretive review. In K. Sirotnik & J. Goodlad (Eds.), *School-university partnerships in action: Concepts, cases, and concerns* (pp. 32-65). New York: Teachers College Press.

Darling-Hammond, L. (1994). Developing professional development schools: Early lessons, challenge and promise. In L. Darling-Hammond (Ed.), *Professional development schools: Schools for developing a profession.* New York: Teachers College Press.

Fullan, M. (March, 1994). [Keynote address.] Annual Conference of the Association for Supervision and Curriculum Development, Chicago.

Goodlad, J. (1988). School-university partnerships for educational renewal: Rationale and concepts. In K. Sirotnik & J. Goodlad (Eds.), *School-university partnerships in action: Concepts, cases, and concerns* (pp. 3-31). New York: Teachers College Press.

Grossman, P. (1994). In pursuit of a dual agenda: Creating a middle level professional development school. In L. Darling-Hammond (Ed.), *Professional development schools: Schools for developing a profession* (pp. 50-73). New York: Teachers College Press.

Harris, R. C., & Harris, M. F. (1994). University/school partnerships: Exploring tangible and intangible costs and benefits. In M. J. O'Hair & S. Odell (Eds.), *Partnerships in education* (pp. 45-68). Fort Worth, TX: Harcourt Brace.

Holmes Group. (1986). *Tomorrow's teachers: A report of the Holmes Group.* East Lansing, MI: Author.

Holmes Group. (1990). *Tomorrow's schools: Principles for the design of professional development schools.* East Lansing, MI: Author.

Kennedy, M. (1992). Establishing professional schools for teachers. In M. Levine (Ed.), *Professional practice schools: Linking teacher education and school reform* (pp. 63-80). New York: Teachers College Press.

Levine, M. (1992). A conceptual framework for professional practice schools. In M. Levine (Ed.), *Professional practice schools: Linking teacher education and school reform* (pp. 8-24). New York: Teachers College Press.

Lieberman, A. (1986). Collaborative research: Working with, not working on. *Educational Leadership, 43*, 28-32.

Lieberman, A. (1992). School/university collaboration: A view from the inside. *Phi Delta Kappan, 74*(2), 147-155.

Lytle, S. L., & Cochran-Smith, M. (1992). Communities for teacher researcher: Fringe or forefront? *American Journal of Education, 100*(3), 298-324.

McIntyre, D. J. (1994). Contexts: Overview and framework. In M. J. O'Hair & S. Odell (Eds.), *Partnerships in education* (pp. 1-10). Fort Worth, TX: Harcourt Brace.

Miller, L. (1993, June). Spotlight on sites: University of Southern Maine. *Center Correspondent.* Seattle: Center for Educational Renewal.

Miller, L., & O'Shea, C. (1994). *Partnership: Getting broader, getting deeper.* New York: National Center for Restructuring Education, Schools, and Teaching.

Miller, L., & Silvernail, D. (1994). Wells Junior High School: Evolution of a professional development school. In L. Darling-Hammond (Ed.), *Professional development schools: Schools for developing a profession* (pp. 28-49). New York: Teachers College Press.

Neufeld, B. (1992). Professional practice schools in context: New mixtures of institutional authority. In M. Levine (Ed.), *Professional practice schools: Linking teacher education and school reform* (pp. 133-168). New York: Teachers College Press.

Porter, A. C. (1987). Teacher collaboration: New partnerships to attack old problems. *Phi Delta Kappan, 69*(2), 147-152.

Robinson, S., & Darling-Hammond, L. (1994). Change for collaboration and collaboration for change: Transforming teaching through school-university partnerships. In L. Darling-Hammond (Ed.), *Professional development schools: Schools for developing a profession* (pp. 203-209). New York: Teachers College Press.

Sandholtz, J. H., & Merseth, K. K. (1992). Collaborating teachers in a professional development school: Inducements and contributions. *Journal of Teacher Education, 43*(4), 308-317.

Sirotnik, K. A., & Goodlad, J. I. (Eds.). (1988). *School-university partnerships in action: Concepts, cases, and concerns.* New York: Teachers College Press.

Snyder, J. (1994). Perils and potentials: A tale of two professional development schools. In L. Darling-Hammond (Ed.), *Professional development schools: Schools for developing a profession* (pp. 98-125). New York: Teachers College Press.

Winitzky, N., Stoddart, T., & O'Keefe, P. (1992). Great expectations: Emergent professional development schools. *Journal of Teacher Education, 43*(1), 3-18.

Yin, R. K. (1984). *Case study research.* Beverly Hills, CA: Sage.

COMMUNICATION:
REFLECTIONS AND IMPLICATIONS

Robert E. Floden

Educational reform is too often thought of as a search for the one best approach. If a single magic bullet were available, it would indeed be a boon. In human affairs, however, the "best" approach typically varies by geographical location, group demographics, and variation among individuals within a classroom.

As teacher educators, we need to be reminded periodically about these prevalent differences, lest we succumb to some educational prophet's persuasive prose. Cooperative learning groups, for example, may have important consequences for student learning, but they are as unlikely to be *the* solution as were the prior solutions offered by behavioral objectives or Piagetian stage theory. Each chapter in this section described how differences encountered in teacher education affect the likely results of our work and revealed central educational issues as they play out in action. Goodwin and her colleagues reminded us that conceiving of "minority group teachers" as a homogeneous set ignores salient intergroup differences, as well as differences within a group such as "Asian American." Manning and her students highlighted both differences in teachers' thinking patterns and differences created when teachers work in groups, rather than as individuals. Sandholtz used the differences among four school-university partnerships to illuminate why some partnerships are more successful than others. Before considering the broad teacher education issues raised by this set of studies, I consider key insights and concerns generated by each chapter.

Commentators too often gloss over distinctive situations by referring generally to "minority" children or teachers. Such loose usage may be a convenient shorthand, provided that the audience understands it as such. Unfortunately, many of those who hear the term come away believing that a single characterization fits all minority group members, at least to a first approximation. Not so. Differences in life chances, for example, are often more related to concentration of poverty than to race or ethnicity. Minority groups do not all face the same challenges or enjoy the same legal protections. Moreover, the actual and perceived circumstances for a particular minority group can change over time.

In teacher education, concern about recruitment and preparation of minority teachers has usually focused on African Americans. Goodwin and her colleagues argued that Asian American teachers are also needed and that attention should be given to their special needs. Their surveys and interviews reveal the stereotyping and prejudice these teachers face and show how their needs vary according to the communities in which they work. Although the sample is fairly small, the perspectives reported may be common in the national population of entering teachers from this group. Questions for teacher educators include these: What changes should be made in recruitment? How should the curriculum of teacher education be adjusted?

The reasons for entering teaching and the barriers faced seem especially important. Money and status are mentioned but are not the most important factors. The main reason reported for entering teaching is wanting to make a difference. The main barrier is that teaching isn't intellectually challenging. These responses suggest an approach to recruitment that concentrates on the critical role teachers play in helping students understand the subjects they study and the opportunities for future success linked to such understanding. Perhaps more important, these reasons suggest the need to alter the work of teaching, to create continuing opportunities for engagement in learning and in professional improvement. If teaching becomes an activity that is more intellectually engaging and socially effective, it should be more attractive to Asian Americans.

How does the Asian American profile of career attractions compare with the profile for other beginning teachers? In *Schoolteacher*, Lortie (1975) mentioned wanting to work with children (for elementary teachers) and enjoyment of the subject matter (for secondary teachers) as two main reasons for entering teaching. Lortie's book, however, is based on interviews from the mid-1960s, when college students seemed to worry less about salary and job security than they do now. To interpret the responses of Goodwin's Asian American sample, it would be helpful to have some contemporary, national basis for comparison.

At the conceptual level, recent affirmative action debates have revived questions about proportionality. In teacher education, Goodwin and her associates point to rapid growth in the number of U.S. Asian Americans as a reason to increase emphasis on recruitment of teachers from the corresponding group. The implicit argument is that the proportion of Asian Americans in the teaching force should roughly match the proportion in the school-age population. Various reasons might be given to support this argument: Asian American students need role models; they need someone in their school who can help other teachers understand cultural differences; they need teachers in the system who will act as advocates; having Asian American teachers in the school will increase parental trust in the school system. These reasons, and others that might be given, need to be weighed carefully. Given a fixed number of teaching positions in any given year, if more Asian Americans enter teaching, fewer members of other groups will enter. What are the costs of that trade-off? Goodwin stressed that Asian American should be recognized as a distinct minority group. Scholars such as John Ogbu argue that intergroup differences are important but concludes that those deserving most favorable treatment are the groups—especially African Americans—with a history of subjugation in this country. Asian Americans' generally strong performance on standardized tests also sets them apart from Hispanics and African Americans. How should these differences shape the conclusions drawn about the small proportion of Asian American teachers? Goodwin is right to draw our attention to the special case of Asian Americans. Teacher education should not "bypass" this group. The deliberations about practice and policy should include proportionality as one of several substantive considerations.

Although Goodwin examines teachers' perceptions of their work, Manning focuses on teachers' thought processes. The research she and her students conducted has its roots in studies of teacher planning from the 1970s (e.g., Yinger, 1980; Zahorik, 1975). Reports from those earlier studies confronted teacher educators with the disparity between recommendations in teacher preparation courses and the practices of competent teachers. Teacher educators were recommending that planning begin with goals for student learning; experienced teachers were starting with engaging activities. Recognition of this mismatch played a part in renewed discussions about the curriculum of lesson planning. The attention Manning and her colleagues bring to cognitive processes brings the new surprise that having teachers plan collaboratively throws them back into unproductive thought processes. Like the earlier planning studies, Manning has opened a window into how teachers actually think; once again it is different from what we imagined.

As with earlier research on teacher thinking, teacher educators' best response to this new information is not evident. One initial reaction to discovering that teachers did not start with learning goals was to strengthen efforts to convince teachers to start with learning goals. A quite different reaction was to alter the teacher education recommendations to fit competent practice, with the thought that the competent teachers were probably on to something. Still a third reaction was to see learning goals as the appropriate starting place for novices but to endorse a move toward activities once teaching routines had been mastered (see Floden & Feiman, 1981). Analogous reactions can be expected to Manning's work. Which mixes of approaches are well suited to a teacher preparation program should be determined in light of each program's orientation and its students' characteristics, then revised in light of investigations of the students' later learning, in the program and on the job.

Where research on teacher planning contrasts what we tell teachers to do and what they actually do, Sandholtz's study of school-university collaboration contrasts lofty rhetoric about new advances in cooperation with the reality of trying to link complex organizations with divergent agendas and cultures. Collaboration is always to be desired, and often promised. Delivering on it, especially for any length of time, is harder, although not impossible.

Sandholtz's conclusions about the helps and challenges for collaboration highlighted the political components of institutional change. Institutional structures and cultures function in education, as in most institutions, to promote stability and continuity. The drawback of these virtues is that they operate to inhibit change. As Cuban (1984) and others (e.g., Cohen, 1988; Sarason, 1990; Tyack & Cuban, 1995) have shown, educational practices and arrangements are particularly stable. Thus, it is no surprise, although a sobering, necessary reminder, that changes are likely to be small and short-lived.

The political analogy is instructive for understanding why change does occasionally occur. Coalition building is a critical feature. In legislative work, support is built by using language that is broad enough to allow disparate groups to interpret a bill as consistent with their goals. In promoting collaboration, success is achieved when goals are established with wide participation and kept broad enough to allow local accommodation. Lawmakers who might shy away from a sharp change in direction may be willing to approve a gradual shift, beginning with a trial period. Likewise, Sandholtz found that a move toward collaboration has a better chance of success if it is made incrementally, starting with pilot or parallel programs, which can gradually achieve permanent status.

Each of the chapters in this section elaborated on differences among those engaged in teaching and teacher education. People differ in their race, ethnicity, language, and gender. They differ in the positions they occupy, in the rewards they get from their work, in their long-term commitment to innovations. They differ in how self-reflectively they engage in professional tasks such as planning. And people themselves differ according to context, whether they are working individually or in groups, whether they are working with people like themselves or different from themselves, whether they are expected to learn, to teach, to lead, to collaborate.

Differences such as these must be considered as we revise, refine, or restructure the ways we educate teachers. These chapters move us forward by reminding us of difference, of the reactions it provokes and of its consequences. We must be careful, however, that we do not mistakenly believe that attention to difference can occur in isolation from other educational goals. One important example is the attention that must be given to helping teachers learn to teach subject matter, whether it be mathematics, art, or economics.

Education reform often concentrates on subject matter or on diversity. The post-Sputnik curriculum movements stressed increased mastery of mathematics and science. Equality of educational opportunity has been a recurrent theme for the past 40 years. The rhetoric of current reforms stresses both subject matter excellence and equality of opportunity, insisting that all children meet more challenging content standards.

Teacher educators typically stress one or the other of these two goals, rather than unifying them. Some teacher educators teach courses on educational foundations or multicultural education; others teach methods of teaching science or mathematics for elementary teachers. Teacher education students are asked to combine these goals in their instruction. Are we, as teacher educators, helping them learn how to combine these goals in practice? Or are we leaving the difficult synthetic task for them to work out independently?

Research on teaching and teacher education—like the corresponding practice—also usually addresses only one of these paired goals. These chapters are no exception, giving insights into differences but leaving the subject matter of instruction out of the picture or including it only as part of an undifferentiated background.

One way to bring these two goals together is to describe and discuss concrete examples of instruction that try to attend to both. In a series of recent symposia (Anderson et al., 1995; Ball et al., 1995), for example, Chazan described how he reconceptualized algebra to fit the experiences and understanding of his working-class high school students, and Featherstone depicted how an experienced elementary school teacher tried to connect her personal difficulties in learning mathematics to the way she taught a diverse group of elementary school students. In these same symposia, however, Melnick highlighted the tensions inherent in choosing approaches to teaching history to Native Alaskans: Tying in-struction to traditional cultures may increase student engagement, but it may also limit their horizons. Bringing subject matter and diversity together may require rethinking particular topics in light of the particular students being taught. Such fine-grained, inventive curriculum work, however, requires a depth of understanding few teachers have the oppor-tunity to attain.

These chapters show once again that research can inform, but not dictate, our choices about the goals, processes, and structure of teacher education. Each study works from a provisional understanding and en-riches that understanding by systematic investigation. We can use the richer understanding in our continuing deliberation.

Sometimes our deliberations leave us with the sense that we are on the right track. At other times, they lead us to conclude that our under-standing was a misunderstanding, or that redirection is needed. If we are to improve the education of teachers, our deliberations must allow for both possibilities.

The growth of understanding, in teacher education as in other fields, can be thought of as an evolutionary process. As with the evolution of species, understanding grows through the joint operation of processes for generating variations and for the winnowing of those new possibilities. In biological evolution, variation is created by genetic recombination and mutation; winnowing occurs as some variants are less suited to survive in a particular ecological niche. In the growth of understanding about teacher education, variation occurs when people—scholars, practitioners, politi-cians, parents, citizens—put forward new ideas or try out new policies and practices. Among the novel thoughts and activities generated, some will be better suited to contemporary contexts and purposes than others. Progress toward current goals can take place if the best variants are supported and the weaker ones abandoned.

Neither part of this process is easy to maintain in education. It is comfortable to maintain existing habits, rather than embracing the risks and efforts inherent in change. If new approaches are attempted, they are hard to discard; it is easier to maintain that every innovation was a success, to be continued if possible. Moreover, it is especially difficult to sustain an environment in which educators continue to innovate, knowing that not all innovations will survive. When Sandholtz said that "creating and implementing new ideas requires flexibility and uncertainty— and the opportunity to fail" she reinforced that point that improving teacher education depends on teacher educators being willing to try out new approaches, knowing that their innovation may fail but also being confident that a discarded approach does not mean exclusion from the next attempt. Indeed, although we should not support failure per se, we should support those who are willing to risk failure to test a promising idea.

As these chapters show, teacher educators face daunting problems. Mismatches between the backgrounds of teachers and those of the communities in which they teach create dissatisfaction. Established methods of teacher education may not prepare teachers for collaborative work. Attempts to connect elementary, secondary, and higher education founder on clashes of culture and stubborn bureaucracies. Moreover, tensions among educational purposes are revealed as we attempt to reach practical accommodations. It is helpful to see these difficulties clearly. We need, however, to build on these insights, pushing beyond merely saying that our work is hard. We need to investigate particular promising approaches, and to pursue analyses that show *why* things are hard, in the hopes of gradual, but significant, improvement.

References

Anderson, L., Ball, D. L., Chazan, D., Featherstone, H., Floden, R. E., McDiarmid, G. W., Melnick, S., Secada, W., & Young, L. (1995, April). *Learning to teach and change practice in the key of reform: An NCRTL examination of the harmony and counterpoint.* Symposium presentation at the annual meeting of the American Educational Research Association, San Francisco.

Ball, D. L., Chazan, D., Floden, R. E., McDiarmid, G. W., Melnick, S., & Young, L. (1995, February). *Learning to connect diverse students and subject matter: Problems, puzzles, and promise in an age of reform.* Featured panel presentation at the annual meeting of the Association of Teacher Educators, Detroit, MI.

Cohen, D. K. (1988). Teaching practice: Plus ça change. In P. Jackson (Ed.), *Contributing to educational practice: Perspectives on research and practice* (pp. 27-84). Berkeley, CA: McCutchan.

Cuban, L. (1984). *How teachers taught: Constancy and change in American classrooms, 1890-1980.* New York: Longman.

Floden, R. E., & Feiman, S. (1981). Should teachers be taught to be rational? *Journal of Education for Teaching, 7,* 274-283.

Lortie, D. C. (1975). *Schoolteacher.* Chicago: University of Chicago Press.

Sarason, S. B. (1990). *The predictable failure of educational reform.* San Francisco: Jossey-Bass.

Tyack, D., & Cuban, L. (1995). *Tinkering toward Utopia: A century of public school reform.* Cambridge, MA: Harvard University Press.

Yinger, R. J. (1980). A study of teacher planning. *Elementary School Journal, 80,* 107-127.

Zahorik, J. A. (1975). Teachers' planning models. *Educational Leadership, 33,* 134-139.

Index

**CORWIN
PRESS**

The Corwin Press logo—a raven striding across an open book—represents the happy union of courage and learning. We are a professional-level publisher of books and journals for K-12 educators, and we are committed to creating and providing resources that embody these qualities. Corwin's motto is "Success for All Learners."